Frederic Baraga's

SHORT HISTORY OF THE
NORTH AMERICAN INDIANS

Frederic Baraga's

SHORT HISTORY OF THE NORTH AMERICAN INDIANS

*Translated from the French
and edited with an Introduction by*

Graham A. MacDonald

UNIVERSITY OF
CALGARY
PRESS

© 2004 Graham A. MacDonald
University of Calgary Press
2500 University Drive NW
Calgary, Alberta
Canada T2N 1N4
www.uofcpress.com

Baraga, Frederic, trans. MacDonald, Graham A.
A Short History of the North American Indians

A translation of *Abrégé le l'histoire des indiens de l'Amérique septentrionale*.
Paris: A La Société des Bons Livres. E. J. Bailly, 1837.

We acknowledge the financial support of the Government of Canada through the Book
Publishing Industry Development Program (BPIDP) for our publishing activities.

National Library of Canada Cataloguing in Publication Data
Library and Archives Canada Cataloguing in Publication

Baraga, Frederic, 1797-1868.
Frederic Baraga's Short history of the North American
Indians / translated from the French and edited with an introduction
by Graham A. MacDonald.

Translation of: Abrégé de l'histoire des
indiens de l'Amérique septentrionale.
Includes bibliographical references and index.
ISBN 1-55238-102-1 (University of Calgary Press)
ISBN 0-87013-735-2 (Michigan State University Press)

1. Indians of North America--Great Lakes Region-History.
2. Indians of North America--Great Lakes Region--Social life and
customs--19th century. I. MacDonald, Graham A. (Graham Alexander),
1944- II. Title. III. Title: Short history of the North American Indians.

E77.B3413 2004   977.004'97
                                                       C2004-906582-3

Printed and bound in Canada by Transcontinental Printing Inc.
This book is printed on acid-free paper.

Cover design by Mieka West.
Book design and typesetting by Elizabeth Gusnoski.

Contents

List of Maps		vi
List of Illustrations		vii
Preface		ix
Acknowledgments		xiii
A Note on the Translation		xv
Editor's Introduction:		
Piety, Perception, and Justice:		
Frederic Baraga in the New World		1
	Introduction	47
1	Manners and Customs	
	of the North American Indians	71
2	Dress of the Indians	77
3	Habitations and Food	
	of the North American Indians	85
4	Arts of the North American Indians	97
5	Hunting Practices	
	of the North American Indians	103
6	Hunting Practices (Sequel)	109
7	Fisheries of the North American Indians	119
8	Marriage and Education of the Young	
	among the North American Indians	125
9	Religion of the North American Indians	133
10	On Religion (Sequel)	145
11	Warfare of the North American Indians	153
12	Forms of Government	
	among the North American Indians	167
13	Diseases and Cures	
	of the North American Indians	177
14	Mortuary Customs	
	of the North American Indians	185
	Notes	193
	Bibliography	211
	Index	225

Maps

Map 1 Distribution of tribes
around the Great Lakes,
later eighteenth century. 2

Map 2 Treaty of Greenville Line: 1795. 3

Map 3 Main mission stations
associated with Baraga during
his time in North America. 16

Map 4 Contemporary Slovenia and
Baraga's birthplace, Dobrnic 43

Illustrations

1	Emperor Joseph II (1741–1790)	12
2	Prince Wenzel Anton von Kaunitz (1711–1794)	13
3	Trader Louis Campau and his wife, Sophie De Marsac	18
4	Lewis Cass (1782–1866)	19
5	Chief Andrew J. Blackbird (ca. 1815–1909)	20
6	Cover page of an early Baraga publication in the Ottawa vernacular	21
7	La Pointe in the 1850s.	22
8	Pierre Crebassa and his wife, Nancy (Roussain) Crebassa	23
9	Mining community in Northern Michigan, 1840s	25
10	Church of the Most Blessed Virgin Mary, Goulais Mission, Ontario. 1974.	25
11	John Bouche, guide to Bishop Baraga at Sault Ste. Marie.	26
12	Fr. Albert Lacombe (1827–1916)	27
13	Fr. George A. Belcourt (1803–1874)	27
14	Chief Shingwaukonse (1773–1854) and his fourth wife, Ogahbagehequa (b. 1798)	28
15	Henry Rowe Schoolcraft (1796–1860)	29
16	Frontispiece of the original German edition of Baraga's *History*	31
17	Trader Ramsey Crooks (1787–1859)	33
18	William Whipple Warren (1825–1853)	33
19	The Reverend John Heckewelder (1743–1823)	34
20	Alexander Henry the Elder (1739–1824)	35
21	Johann Georg Kohl (1808–1878)	37
22	Marquette, Michigan, about 1840	39
23	Benjamin Armstrong (1820–1900)	40
24	Chief Buffalo (ca. 1760–1855)	41

Colour Images

Cover *After Their Sitting at Meat* by John White (1590). Hand-colored Engraving by Theodor de Bry. This engraving depicts Secotan people of Virginia eating a meal.

Plate 1 The young Frederic Baraga: a self-portrait, ca. 1826.

Plate 2 Jean-Baptiste Assiginack (ca. 1768–1866)

Plate 3 Mala Vas, the birthplace of Frederic Baraga

Plate 4 The Landscape around Metlika, Slovenia

Plate 5 Birch bark vessel decorated with dyed porcupine quills

Plate 6 Tobacco Pouch: woven wool and strings of white beads

Plate 7 Bishop Baraga's residence in Marquette (1998)

Plate 8 Memorial to Baraga in Dobrnic Church (2001)

Preface

The origins of this project go back to the early 1970s when the editor worked as an historian for the Ontario Parks Branch and spent some years in the Lake Superior area. A visit to an old frame Church along the east coast at Goulais Mission, some forty kilometres north of Sault Ste. Marie, provoked curiosity about the personality of its founder, Bishop Frederic Baraga, the author of a well-regarded Ojibwa dictionary published in 1853. A cursory study of Baraga's biography eventually turned me towards pursuit of his little-known study of the North American Indians published in 1837 in Europe in German, French and

Slovenian editions. The following translation from the French edition is the belated result.

There is still much to be gained from reading first-hand accounts by North American missionaries concerning their experiences with Native peoples in earlier times. It is valid to ask not just what were these people about, but also, what did *they* think they were about? Reports home by missionaries were awaited by members of domestic and foreign sponsoring organizations living at considerable remove from the field, many eager to hear about the "goings on" in "heathen" lands. Today, such reports are frequently regarded as ethnocentric, over-weighted with "the white man's burden," patronizing, lacking in objectivity with respect to the diversity of the human condition, and sometimes just plain offensive. Such complaints, however, merely identify longstanding difficulties associated with first-hand historical accounts of any kind, especially those created in so-called "cross-cultural" situations. The "barbarians" on the fringes of the Roman Empire presumably did not know they *were* "barbarians" until Caesar told them so, influenced as he was by an earlier student of life in Gaul, that elusive and observant Greek, Posidonius. The latter did not doubt that the Mediterranean peoples were superior to those of Gaul, and yet he was moved by curiosity to ask: how was such a rich human diversity to be explained intelligently? His refreshing, pioneering ethnological answer was that these societies were not fixed creations of the gods, but mainly the products of their own environments and ways of life. In quieter moments, Posidonius and Caesar might reflect on the interesting and odd ways displayed before them, but in the greater business of empire it would be necessary for these people to adjust their ways for Rome's greater good, and, incidentally, for their own good as well, for Rome was not ungenerous. The more intelligent and prudent would seek out, and sometimes be granted, the greatest thing the world could then bestow: Roman citizenship. What the Gauls thought of the Romans, of course, is a matter of unknown record.

Empires come and go, but attempts to forge the chains of persuasive international law remain frustrating. Lawgivers of the day, past and present, have trouble moving out of the sun in which they bask. It does not come as a surprise, then, that lesser agents of imperial enterprise often display this same weakness. As it was in Caesar's time, so it was on the early nineteenth-century American frontier: everyone had an opinion, but few had knowledge. Such caveats attend all historical enquiries. First-hand reports on Native life and circumstances for the upper Great Lakes area in these years are few enough. Flawed as they might seem from certain contemporary perspectives, they still represent primary documents and expressed points of view capable of shedding light on the observer, the observed, and the conditions of the day.

The project of the European "civilizing mission" in the Americas has come in for minute historical review and criticism in recent decades. Appreciation of the "heroic" carrying-out of the apparently self-evident need for Christians to be "outward bound" on behalf of the lost, pagan souls of the world has steadily been replaced, in academic circles at least, by reflection upon the conduct of competing empires, their associated land and resource hunger, and the shifting fashions of the intellectual history of Europe and North America. In the often gloomy passages in these pages of imperial history, there remains room, nevertheless, to make distinctions.

Columbus, who characteristically provides the jumping off point for Baraga's *Short History*, has in recent years been allowed to become caricatured and to take the ideological rap for the historical advent of European invasions of the New World, a process which had, in fact, been going on for several centuries, and would have continued with or without the Columbian landings in the Caribbean. His arrival had great symbolic significance, however, and detailing the complexities and consequences, pro and con, of Euro-American interactions has engaged writers ever since. Recent students of this clash, such as Anthony Pagden and James Axtell, have shown just how rich and complex were these resulting literary reflections.

In the work in hand, it is clear that Baraga was often making his own critique of imperial power, as had many mission workers and theologians before him. Inevitably, these were often partial or confused critiques, reflecting diverse personal or institutional agendas. Baraga's interest in and gift for languages placed him in a somewhat more specialized context. He shared with certain others the belief that Native vernaculars were important to preserve and use, rather than displace. It is for his singular contribution to the recording of Ottawa and Ojibwa (Chippewa) dialects, grammar, and language that he is mainly remembered today. His youthful success as a pastor in his native Slovenia, marked by his promotion of the holy word by means of peasant vernaculars, was undoubtedly an important source of Baraga's interest in taking a similar approach with his Indian parishioners in America.

The *Short History* before us is the result of Baraga's own need to give himself a crash course in the historical background of the Native peoples, and also to provide something informative to send back to his parishioners in Austria and Slovenia from whom he drew his financial support. While highly derivative in certain sections, there is also much that is original, coming from his own observations on the Upper Great Lakes frontier on the eve of its transformation from the old fur trade society to one of modern industry and settlement. There is no Rousseau in Baraga, but there is much of the same revised classical stoicism which marks the writings of the earlier Jesuits.

Acknowledgments

I am grateful to the following for assistance in preparation of this book: Regis Walling of the Bishop Baraga Archives, Marquette; Professor Henry C. Wolfart at the University of Manitoba; Elizabeth Delene, Archivist, Bishop Baraga Archives, Marquette, is thanked for her many kindnesses and for getting me around the collection so efficiently; Rev. Alex Sample, Diocese of Marquette; Fr. Vendelin Spendov of Ave Maria, Franciscan Fathers, Lemont, Illinois; Otto Hammer of Calgary for his commentary on the German edition; the staffs of the Bayliss Public Library in Sault Ste. Marie, Michigan; the Sault Ste. Marie

Public Library; the Sault Historical Society, Ontario; and the Manitoba Archives, Winnipeg. Professor Donald B. Smith of the University of Calgary kindly reviewed an early version of the manuscript. Nathalie Zinger of Montreal visited the Ethnographic Museum of Ljubljana on my behalf; Ian MacDonald of Montreal, with Zrinka Ivanovic-Kelemen and Sven Kelemen of Zagreb, photographed various haunts of the young Baraga in Slovenia, as did Jusen Dez of Ljubljana. Dr. Marija-Mojca Tercelj, Curator, Slovene Ethnographic Museum, Ljubljana, is thanked for her interest and assistance with visuals. Marilyn Croot worked on the maps. At the University of Calgary Press, John King, Mieka West, Peter Enman, Dave Brown, and Greg Madsen were always creative and helpful. Thanks also to Windsor Viney and Elizabeth Gusnoski. Special thanks to Walter Hildebrandt, Director, University of Calgary Press, and Frederic C. Bohm, Director, Michigan State University Press, for their support and interest in the project.

A Note on the Translation

The events surrounding the publishing of Baraga's *Short History* are briefly reviewed in the Editor's Introduction. It may be asked why the French edition was selected for the translation. A number of factors were at work: after obtaining a copy of the rare German edition, the present editor asked linguistics Professor Henry C. Wolfart, at the University of Manitoba, if he would briefly review the text with respect to its merits and the nature of the German employed. Some cautious advice was given that there appeared to be a considerable amount of original material in the text and that the German was fairly straightforward but marked by a number of "Slovenianisms." Shortly thereafter, it came to my notice that a French edition had been simultaneously published in Paris in 1837. Comparison of the two texts suggested that they were, for the most part, identical in structure and content. Subsequent review of the excellent analysis of the two texts (and of an abridged Slovenian edition) made by the Slovenian scholar Breda Pozar confirmed that judgment and that the French edition had been prepared from the original with Baraga's approval. The present editor, having much greater facility in French than German, decided to work directly from the French text.

There were some differences in the two editions, however, particularly in Chapter 1; the German version is considerably longer. The Paris editor, with some justification, decided to move certain passages to other chapters, which seemed more appropriate to the content. The anecdote concerning "Old Skrany," which appears in Chapter 11 of the French version, is an example. Other passages cut were repetitive of similar materials found later in the book, such as his comments on child-rearing. In one cut passage, Baraga, rehearses some of his own impressions of Indian character and habits, but these same impressions tend to be repeated here and there in the text. The French edition of Chapter 1 is therefore much tighter and more precise than in the German edition. For the remainder of the book, the changes between the two editions are slight. Any reader interested in a detailed comparison is referred to Breda Pozar's article, cited in the bibliography.

Editor's Introduction

PIETY, PERCEPTION, AND JUSTICE: FREDERIC BARAGA IN THE NEW WORLD

Frederic Baraga (1797–1868) was one of several European Roman Catholic missionaries sent to the American "Old Northwest" after 1830, many of them sponsored by recently established mission organizations such as the Leopoldine Society of Vienna, the Ludwig Mission Central Association of Bavaria, or the Propagation of the Faith in Paris.[1] The "Old Northwest"

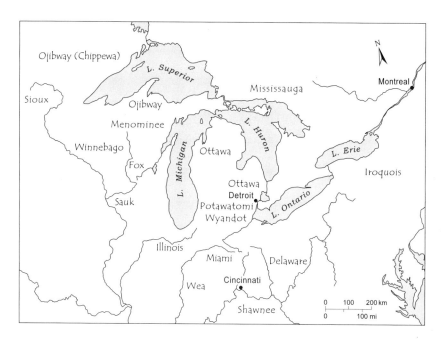

Map 1 Distribution of tribes around
the Great Lakes, later eighteenth century.

was considered to be that vast territory north and west of the Ohio River established by the Northwest Ordinance of 1787. The Ordinance was the basis for what Carlyle Buley called "the first colony of the United States."[2] The new territory embraced the future states of Ohio, Michigan, Indiana, Illinois, Wisconsin and parts of Minnesota. If the American Revolution ended with the Treaty of Paris of 1783, that document clearly did not resolve all outstanding issues between Britain and America. Britain continued to hold many of its military posts in the Old Northwest, pending a satisfactory, if unlikely, resolution of loyalist claims.[3] The revision of the American Constitution in 1787 allowed for some housekeeping with respect to the federal prerogative in dealing with Native affairs. To date, this prerogative had been in question owing to independent actions taken by state administrations or individuals within states who attempted to deal directly with Native peoples in matters of land and trade. The alliances formed between Native tribes and the British during the revolutionary war had left an ongoing uncertainty in American minds about the loyalties of Native

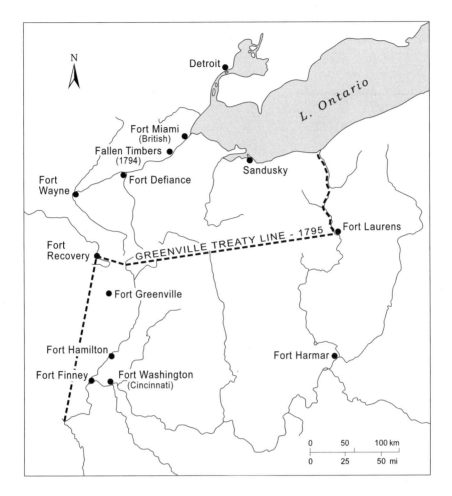

Map 2 Treaty of Greenville Line: 1795.

peoples in frontier areas. For these reasons, President Washington, along with his Secretary of War, Henry Knox, gave renewed attention to framing legislation and policy establishing the conditions for American domestic intercourse and trade with Native peoples, as well as means to exclude British traders from operating on American territory.[4]

Resistance by Native peoples to American expansion west of the Ohio River remained strong after 1787, and it was only as an outcome of the crushing defeat imposed by Anthony Wayne on federated tribes at the Battle of Fallen Timbers in 1794 that formal peace agreements in this quarter were concluded by the Treaty of Greenville in 1795.[5] If the Old Northwest had been a debatable international zone before Fallen Timbers, it was much less so afterwards. The British Military at nearby Fort Miami had refused to give shelter to the retreating Native warriors during the battle, not wishing to create an incident with the Americans, thus indicating to the Indians their probable future value as allies.[6]

With the establishment of Michigan Territory in 1805, treaty-making became the thrust of American Indian policy in the Old Northwest, as in other parts of the republic.[7] The first of several Michigan territorial treaties with the Indians was signed in 1807.[8] Conflicts between Britain and the United States over older established trade patterns continued, augmented by Britain's continued impressing of American sailors into the British Navy as an aid in prosecution of the war in Europe against Napoleon. The practice culminated in the so-called "Chesapeake Crisis" of 1807.[9] The tension increased when a veteran of the Battle of Fallen Timbers, the Shawnee leader Tecumseh, attempted to rally a pan-Indian force of resistance against American encroachment on Indian land, community removal, and abusive treaty rights.[10] These strains eventually flared up into the War of 1812. At locations as far away as Prairie du Chien, in Wisconsin, the war breathed new hopes into some of the inhabitants of the Old Northwest that a territorial realignment might still be possible.[11] With the death of Tecumseh at Moraviantown in Upper Canada in 1813, the hopes of the Indians for a new dispensation were dashed, and with the Treaty of Ghent in 1814, British interest in American territory waned as a result of establishment of a formal boundary delineation process.[12]

Despite the formal border understandings reached after 1814, in the upper Great Lakes area not all was as it seemed with respect to the inner causes of trade friction. There were concealed aspects to the trade in goods and liquor. Owing to the overwhelming political influence exercised in Washington by New York business magnate John Jacob Astor, the control of trade with Native peoples in the frontier zones remained unclear after the War of 1812. Through his American Fur Company, Astor had cultivated relationships with fur traders in Montreal, and by means of these connections he tended to get around the official U.S. Trade and Intercourse Laws. These had provided for the establishment of a system of licensed official traders operating (ideally) only out of American military posts.[13] Apparent British interference with American control of trade in the Old Northwest was actually owing significantly to Astor operating as a fifth column within the highest policy organs of the nation at Washington. There, he worked assiduously out of self-interest to undermine the effectiveness of the American Indian Intercourse and Trade Laws, a policy briefly carried on by Astor's successor, Ramsey Crooks.[14] After 1816, the new federal Superintendent of Indian Trade, Thomas L. McKenney, promoted policies designed to thwart the negative influence of traders on the Native peoples, particularly with respect to alcohol, the effects of which severely limited government plans to control more legitimate trade with Native peoples.[15]

While conflicts with British traders remained, the way was, nevertheless, open for more orderly settlement in the Old Northwest. By the mid-1820s the eastern portions of Michigan Territory were rapidly filling up with settlers.[16] The pressure for additional treaties was constant. Before long, "Indian Removal" clauses started to appear in the terms of treaties. This idea, first broached by President Jefferson in 1803, was not really given force until 1817, with the Cherokee Removal Bill. Well before becoming president in 1830, Henry Jackson was the great advocate of removal based on his experience with the relocation of the southern tribes as a result of the so-called "Georgia Compact" of 1802.[17] As Superintendent of Indian Trade, McKenney generally opposed the idea of removal, but by 1825 he had come to support it in certain circumstances, if it could be done with the consent of the Native peoples.[18] In Michigan, the still-limited demand for land north of Grand River meant that removal was not as serious a threat to Indians as in areas south of that river; but the idea was in the air and was implied by inclusion in treaties of "at the pleasure of the President" clauses.[19] The removal concept was reinforced after 1830 with the arrival of Jackson in the White House. As noted, Jackson had little use for treaties as such, considering them to have been a failure and deeply inconsistent with constitutional principles. While treaties would continue to be signed during his administration, he still continued to be the great advocate of Indian Removal.[20] In Michigan, these removal clauses continued in force until 1854, when it registered on officials that areas to which Indians were to be removed southwest of the Missouri River were actually rapidly filling up with settlers.[21]

It was into this socially fluid and turmoil-ridden frontier that the Slovenian Roman Catholic priest Frederic Baraga was introduced in early 1831, under the authority of the Bishop of Cincinnati. He had come to work as a missionary to the Algonkian-speaking Indians of the upper Great Lakes. Following two years at Wagnakisi or L'Arbre Croche (The Crooked Tree) on the northeast coast of Lake Michigan, he was sent south to Grand River. During his tenure there, the threat of Indian removal first came to seriously occupy his attention, thereafter making his name known to Washington officials.[22]

In Michigan territory, as elsewhere, the baneful influence of liquor and the conduct of unscrupulous traders on the lives of Native peoples were continuing sources of complaint. By 1822, Indian Affairs officers in Washington had received Jedidiah Morse's report on the failures of liquor control on the western frontier.[23] Veteran trader John Johnson candidly described the disruptive role of liquor at Sault Ste. Marie in the early 1830s, a place he characterized as "this den of dissipation and confusion."[24]

The issues of removal and alcohol would exercise Baraga for all of his working life among the tribes of the Upper Great Lakes. Sharing the view of a number of other reformers of the day, Baraga saw no purpose in uprooting peoples who were in the midst of a process of adjusting to allegedly modern European practices. Removal could only postpone a later manifestation of cultural conflict, a view he shared with Jeremiah Everts of the Protestant American Board of Commissioners for Foreign Missions.[25] It was a view he did not share, however, with that other formidable Protestant reformer, Isaac McCoy, who spent much of his career agitating within the Baptist Board of Missions, and in Washington, for establishment of a new Native State west of the Mississippi River.[26]

Baraga much preferred in situ approaches towards the Native peoples. His was a watered-down version of the old *reducciones* or *aldeias* established earlier in South America by the Jesuits.[27] According to his model, Christianized settlements should be established separate from, but within, the flux of ongoing frontier life. Radical geographic isolation was not advocated. He shared with the earlier Jesuits a belief in promoting Christianity in the vernacular as an essential aspect of the saving of Native souls, thereby helping effect such "civilizing" as might be accomplished; Native peoples should retain their own land under title and gradually learn to participate in the wider economy. Baraga and his associates saw Christianity as a prophylactic against the forces of cultural destruction induced by the steady influx of Europeans.[28] Those among whom they made their efforts often saw the missionary presence in much different terms, not always distinguishable from those same forces of destruction.[29]

Such general views of the matter, expressed in both European and Native commentaries, tended to see culture in either/or terms. What often went unacknowledged was an appreciation of the economic dynamics fostered by the fur trade, by which Native and European had long ago become associates in blood, labour, and, in various degrees, culture. European and Native had been influencing each other from the start, and, in retrospect, the apartheid philosophy that informed ideas of removal was as unrealistic as it was irrelevant. While removal was a definite legal threat to Native peoples of the Upper Great Lakes after 1820, an internal drive to "remove" to other areas had, for economic reasons, already been acting as a leaven on Great Lakes Algonkians since the early 1790s.[30] Many had drifted westward and made adjustments to the prairies and to the fur trade opportunities of the greater northwest.[31] This was not always a smooth or peaceful process and its character was often misread by missionaries, as in the case of the Pillager Chippewa of Leech Lake.[32] This group, well west of Lake Superior, was in the thick of intertribal conflict in the traditional border zone between the Dakota-Sioux and Ojibwa. Conflict here was less a consequence of pioneer pressure than of fur trade developments within the old hunting lands of the Ojibwa and Native group movements being made as an adjustment.[33] More seriously, radical downward shifts in the wildlife supply for purposes of both the fur trade and subsistence had come into play. For the Dakota-Sioux, the bison – a resource much coveted in the tribal border zones – was nearly extinct in this quarter by the early 1830s, gradually necessitating a greater reliance on Virginia Deer.[34]

Such nuances were not totally lost on missionaries in the field in the 1830s, but rather than argue for conservation of the older way of life, many in the church looked towards agriculture.[35] This yearning to "civilize" first and "Christianize" second was widespread, but was far from a universal outlook.[36] There were others who did not equate the adoption of Christianity with the parallel project of the adoption of American frontier, or middle-class urban, values. To assume such would be "to overlook the other-worldly orientation of those missionaries who conceived of Christianity as a criticism of Western civilization."[37] Baraga's piety, pastoral gifts, and his abandonment of the things of this world placed him firmly in this latter category. Baraga was by no means unique in this respect, among his Catholic colleagues. Many of the Protestant missionaries in the Old Northwest were American-born, while many of the Catholics were Europeans; as a consequence, there was, perhaps, less of a desire on the part of Catholics to promote outright assimilation to American ways, many of which they themselves found strange.[38] Nevertheless, just how a priest born into modest wealth and reared in the cultured atmosphere of Beethoven's Vienna chose to come to the Lake Superior frontier requires some description.

BARAGA'S EUROPEAN BACKGROUND

Irenaeus Frederic Baraga was born on January 29, 1797, at Mala Vas Castle in the Parish of Dobrnic, District of Carniola, a locality in the modern Slovenian republic, then a part of the Habsburg Empire. He was one of the three surviving children of John Nepomucene Baraga and Katherine Baraga (*nee* Jencic). Rumours used to circulate about Baraga's possession of Royal Habsburg blood, but these have long been put to rest.[39] The elder Baraga was a civil servant and proprietor of a family farm. While the domestic circumstances were not those of wealth, they were yet sufficient to afford an education for the children. Baraga's mother died in 1808. Even before his mother's death, Frederic had been sent to the home of his uncle, Ignatius Baraga, where he was educated by private tutors. In 1809, he departed for Ljubljana, where he lived with Barnard Jencic, an uncle on his mother's side. There, he took classes for another seven years, a period marked by the death of his father in 1812.

The last few years of study had not been easy for the young scholar, for in 1809 his uncle Bernard seems to have run afoul of the French authorities. Baraga had to endure two years of poverty before coming to the attention of George Dolinar, a professor of Canon Law and Church History based in Vienna. Dolinar took the promising university student into his home, and Baraga subsequently took degrees in civil and canon law.[40]

At completion of his undergraduate studies, his knowledge of languages was wide, including French, long the main language of arts, letters and science throughout much of Europe. Baraga had come of age at the height of the Napoleonic influence, just when the "Illyrian Provinces" were being incorporated into the First French Empire. In his schooling he was, therefore, exposed to literary French along with Slovenian, German, Greek and

Latin. Diversity in language was all about him, having been born in one of those interesting pockets of Europe where Romance, Germanic and Slavic languages all rubbed shoulders. This early exposure to languages would serve him well later in North America, when he was required to master those living Algonkian linguistic traditions which flourished around the upper Great Lakes in Ojibwa and Ottawa Native communities.

At the university, an important source of influence on the young man was the Redemptorist, Clement Mary Hofbauer (1752–1820), the head of a congregation that aspired to lead the simple Christian life.[41] The main objective of the Redemptorists was to spread the gospel to the poorest and most neglected folk of the world. As a group, the Redemptorists could trace their origins to the work of St. Alphonsus Liguori (1696–1787) of Naples. After 1732, this pious man had inspired a group of Christians in the vicinity of Scala to undertake pastoral service in the rural areas, for in his view, actions of this type represented the central aspect of religion. About Liguori it has been said that he "never preached a sermon which the simplest old woman in the congregation could not understand." Liguori was an important source of influence on Baraga's thinking about pastoral duty. He was also a man of some standing in the Roman Catholic Church, having been appointed Bishop of Saint Agata del Goti in 1762.[42] At the time of Baraga's decision to go the United States as a missionary in 1829, he was completing the translation of one of Liguori's works.[43]

Clement Hofbauer was born in Moravia (b. Jan Dvorák), where he took up the Redemptorist cause at age thirty-four. When not allowed to establish the Redemptorist Order in Austria under Joseph's system of restriction on new foundations, he spent some twenty years in Poland and Switzerland, fostering the movement. Following Napoleon's dispersal of religious orders in Poland in 1809, Hofbauer returned to Vienna, where he worked on behalf of the Church during the Napoleonic invasion period, attracting a large and diverse following. After 1815, he worked diligently to curb the control of the state over Church matters, and was facing renewed pressure once again from the authorities to leave Vienna, but the Emperor Franz came to his relief following a personal audience with the Pope, and Hofbauer was allowed to establish the Redemptorist Order in Vienna in 1819. Hofbauer's outlook was essentially ecumenical and mission-oriented, and the so-called "Apostle of Vienna" became a main influence on the young Frederic Baraga.[44] In 1817, Professor Vincint Weintridt, a former Jesuit, a student of science and aesthetics, and a friend of Hofbauer, recommended him to young Baraga. Shortly thereafter, Baraga joined Hofbauer's circle.[45]

Baraga's character in these years was undoubtedly shaped with some accompanying inner struggle, for while living with the Dolinar family, he became engaged to Dolinar's daughter, Anna; but by 1821, the year he finished his law degree, the young scholar had broken the engagement and entered Ljubljana Seminary.[46] Verwyst provides a suggestive reference when he states, "In the Austrian metropolis he was surrounded by dangers on all sides, but, thanks to his early training and the nobility of his soul, he escaped the contagion of vice and in the words of St. James, 'preserved himself unspotted from the world.'"[47] There was a profound regret expressed by Baraga concerning his break with Anna Dolinar; but in this same period he also fills his letters to his sister Amalia with the most emotional outpourings of sentiment concerning the nature of love and his growing commitment to the religious life.[48] His commitment became complete; he was ordained in 1823, following which he spent four years as the Curate of Smartno, followed by three years at Metlika. During this period, Baraga's fame as a confessor became widespread among the faithful, while his simplicity of manner attracted many to the church.[49]

Baraga was well suited to the Redemptorist outlook. As a group, they tended to hark back to the reform-minded pietists of the fifteenth century, to the Brethren of the Common Life, and more specifically to Thomas à Kempis (1380–1471), perhaps the foremost representative of that outlook identified with the 'Devotio Moderna.' [50] Reared in the Deventer Windesheim Congregation tradition, the influence of which had spread out from Holland after 1386, Thomas à Kempis achieved a lasting and ever-renewing readership through his book, The Imitation of Christ.[51] The main feature of Windesheim piety was its almost total disregard for dogma or systematic theology.[52] Throughout his career, Baraga would resort for guidance to the writings of Thomas à Kempis and other saints, particularly when he found himself labouring under what he viewed as the burden of administrative duty.[53] Indeed, his movement towards the austerity of a life in which all vanity is purged was strengthened in 1820; he cited Thomas as a motivating source for his abandonment of any future work as a student of the English language: "I was moved to this decision by reading and taking to heart some passages affecting me in the golden booklet of the Blessed Thomas à Kempis."[54] The process was not complete; a year later he abandoned his work as an artist.[55]

Baraga had been born into a Europe in turmoil, but one which, by the time of his early maturity, had given way to the great peace ushered in by the agreements reached during the Congress of Vienna in 1815. The mood of the times was conservative, but it was also a period when certain pre-Napoleonic lessons of the Enlightenment had been selectively learned and incorporated into the restored Habsburg polity. These developments were important with respect to how Baraga came to view his life as a priest in his native land and his decision to eventually depart it for North America. A few words about late eighteenth-century developments in church–state relations may help to clarify Baraga's position.

The Austrian Habsburg lands in the middle decades of the eighteenth century had been marked by war and national reform under the inexperienced but steadily firming hand of the Empress Maria Theresa. Silesia had been lost early in her reign to Frederic II of Prussia and would remain lost at the end of the War of the Austrian Succession in 1748; the inadequacies of Habsburg defences and state finances had been distinctly revealed. In response, the Empress put into motion certain secularizing trends, which would, in due course, significantly clip the wings of the Counter Reformation forces of the Austrian Catholic Church. This had more to do with her wishes to repair Habsburg finances and modernize the Empire against Prussia than with any strong religious convictions of a liberal, let alone Jansenist, flavour. The final ban on the Jesuit Order imposed by Rome in 1773 assisted her in this process.

Having established a national bureaucracy and a standing army, and having reformed many other national institutions, she now moved cautiously, but with strong advice, to curb the Church's influence.[56] Past Church policies were seen as something of a hindrance to the attraction of workers from abroad, many of whom were not Catholics.[57] Prince Kaunitz, Imperial Chancellor since 1753, eventfully urged an expanded policy of tolerance on a reluctant Empress, so that in the 1770s, in the words of Charles O'Brien, "the Counter-Reformation policy of repression decayed, like an old tree rotting from within."[58]

What Maria Theresa had sown, the new Emperor, Joseph II, would reap. Closely involved as co-regent since 1765, Joseph II was free to act on his own in 1780. With promulgation of his *Edict of Toleration* of 13 October 1781, fresh air blew threw the baroque Roman Catholic churches of central Europe, and this was essentially the work of Joseph and Kaunitz.[59] The *Toleration Edict* had great consequences for education. Through the

Figure 1 Joseph II (1741–1790), Emperor of the Austrian Habsburg Empire, at age 23. One of Europe's "enlightened despots," he and his advisors extended the policies of secularization of the Roman Catholic Church initiated by his mother, the Empress Maria Theresa. The unpopular nature of these reforms among many Catholics earned his policies the name "Josephism." (The Mansell Collection, Vienna)

influence of Gottfried van Sweiten (a cautious Enlightenment advocate and the President of the Court's Commission on Education), utilitarian ends of education were pursued, assisted by a judicious use of censorship, which was used as a tool to restrain outbursts by one religious group against another.[60] The fostering of this toleration ethic was made infinitely easier by the presence of personalities within the Catholic Church sympathetic to such a policy. Overlapping with the reign of Maria Theresa and Joseph II was the personality of Franz Stephen Rautenstrauch, the director of the Theological Faculty at the University of Vienna. In the last years of the Empress's reign, he commenced a modernizing reform of the curriculum. Much medieval dross was cleared away, with the result that the "time saved was given to the study of Sacred Scripture and to a new science, pastoral theology."[61] With the Papal dismantling of the Jesuit Order in 1773, a much clearer path was left for those of Jansenist persuasion to influence social policy.[62] Some of these ideas, as received from advisors, were congenial to Joseph. He undertook to see that clerical training became a legitimate reason of state and that monasteries dedicated to the mere contemplative life were closed down, mainly for economic reasons.[63] He initiated the establishment of a general seminary, which his advisors hoped would produce a new breed of clergyman, more open to ideas of toleration and pastoral work. In 1784, Rautenstrauch wrote that "at every opportunity the students are to be instructed in Christian tolerance and to be made accustomed to it."[64] A summary of the official church reform view of toleration stated:[65]

> The truly tolerant person, while true to his creed, does not regard men who profess a different one as enemies of God, truth and virtue; he does not hate, persecute, or condemn them. Rather he loves them as his brothers, as creatures of one and the same God.

Abroad, even profounder forces of secularization were afoot. Just prior to the death of Emperor Joseph II, the storm broke in the form of the French Revolution of 1789. The gradually mounting imperial effect of this event proved to be one of the other great formative influences on the early educational experiences of Baraga. At the time of his birth in 1797, Slovenia, as much of Europe, was starting to come under control of Paris and the "Continental System." By 1809, Napoleon's First Empire had swallowed up Slovenia, if only temporarily, within the so-called "Illyrian Provinces." This name, derived by Napoleon from recollections of the old Roman Empire, designated the Adriatic coastal lands and the territory north of Trieste, including Baraga's native Carniola.[66]

Baraga's character was shaped by several forces in these years. The Josephine reform ideas of toleration and service were reinforced not just by French Enlightenment ideas, which had been moderately infecting Austrian society for half a century, but also by the influence of ecumenical, mission-oriented pietists such as Hofbauer. Baraga was at home in the rich artistic life of Beethoven's Vienna, but this was an aspect

Figure 2 Prince Wenzel Anton von Kaunitz (1711–1794). This diplomat, chancellor, reformer, and modernizer influenced both Empress Maria Theresa and her son, Joseph II. He was open to certain Jansenist and Gallican influences, which gave so-called "Josephism" a bad name among many traditional Catholics. (The Mansell Collection, Vienna)

that he generally curtailed in his personal life as a self-imposed religious obligation.[67] There were many aspects of the so-called "Josephine Reform" which, however, were less palatable to young Baraga. For one, the situation whereby the Catholic Church in Austria had, since the 1760s, been increasingly subordinated to the state (and Rome's influence diminished) did not sit well with him. Rickett has noted that the church "was to be subservient to the state" and that "the crime of heresy was done away with." Religion was to be "regarded as a matter for the individual to decide for himself without State interference." Such ideas may seem congenial now, but at the time there went with them a great bureaucratization of the church and its procedures: "there was hardly a detail of ecclesiastical life that was not affected in one way or another" as a result of the Josephine reforms.[68]

There was some swinging back of the pendulum during the Napoleonic Wars. Count Metternich moved with great caution after 1809, trying to run a course in which Vienna and Rome might reinforce each other's interests against the forces of secularism, nationalism, and revolution. Hofbauer, we have noted, was finally welcome in Vienna. The conservative aspects of post-1815 policy should have appealed to Baraga, but he was ultimately a purist in matters of religion, and he, along with many of his associates, remained offended by Habsburg retention of the Church as a branch of state.[69]

There was, nonetheless, something in the legacy of the Josephine Reforms that could appeal to Baraga.[70] If the predestinarian aspects of Jansenism were not among them, he could at least lean towards certain other aspects of general policy. Blanning has described the Jansenist outlook as follows: "First and foremost it was against traditional baroque piety. Betraying its origins as a movement of the literate elites, it demanded simplicity instead of display, rigour instead of opulence, austerity instead of indulgence, denial instead of sensuality."[71] These are all strong Baragian traits. In addition, Blanning tells us, "the Jansenists were ecumenical: they insisted on the use of the vernacular for at least the Epistle and the Gospel during the Mass; their ideal church was a bare hall."[72] These ideas too could be made sympathetic. Baraga opposed other measures, however, such as any ban on relics and symbols, the veneration of saints, or of downplaying the importance of confession, all elements he took seriously.[73] Still, the improvement of services to the common run of humanity by parish priests, a training in a more fundamental gospel, and the downplaying of the purely contemplative life fostered in certain monasteries would appear to be ideas in line with Baraga's thinking.[74] The pastoral tradition was encouraged, then, not only by Baraga's teacher, Hofbauer, but also by the spirit of certain of the late eighteenth- and early nineteenth-century reforms of the Habsburg Church.[75]

The establishment of the Church as a branch of state was not, as mentioned, something Baraga supported.[76] In a letter to Pastor George Kalan concerning his involvement with the establishment of Sodalities (banned under the Habsburg law), Baraga stated, "It is by no means unknown to me that much has been abolished that was good, and much introduced that does not take the place of the old that was good. Meanwhile, I am not the judge of that, but my duty now demands that I submit entirely to the commands of my superiors."[77] A European's suspicion of the state may explain Baraga's tendency in America to avoid active politics and secular involvements, even to the point of not exercising the democratic vote.[78] The desire to share the simple life and to cater, within limits, to that old Rhineland strain of Catholic mysticism, with its urging of regular contemplation, continued to exercise a strong influence on Baraga, one which he frequently had to curb lest it distract him from his duties as a labourer in the fields. His *Diary* entries in 1860 occasionally hint at a wish to retire from his position as bishop, but these are never developed or acted upon.[79]

Despite his formal education and appreciation of high culture, Baraga took on the disposition of a pastoral priest, and he worked well in that capacity. In the course of his duties in Smartno and Metlika, he published, as had Thomas à Kempis, what was to become an influential and popular guide for the perplexed. His prayer book, *Dushna Pasha* (*Souls Pasture for Christians Who Wish to Worship God in the Spirit and in Truth*), published in Slovenian in 1830, was still in print in the early twentieth century.[80] Baraga's recourse to simple instructional texts in the vernacular for use among his parishioners provides a hint of the approach he might be expected to take in less certain circumstances, as when charged to bring Christianity to the North American Indians of the upper Great Lakes.[81]

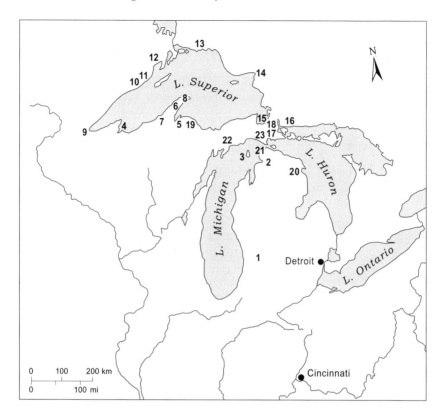

Map 3   Main mission stations associated
with Baraga during his time in North America.

1. Grand River
2. L'Arbre Croche
3. Beaver Island
4. La Pointe
5. L'Anse
6. Houghton-Copper Harbour
7. Ontonagon
8. Eagle Harbour
9. Fond Du Lac
10. Grand Portage
11. Pigeon River
12. Ft. William
13. Pic
14. Michipicoten
15. Goulais Bay
16. Bruce Mines
17. Sugar Island
18. Sault Ste. Marie
19. Marquette
20. Alpena
21. Cross Village
22. Manistique
23. Mackinac-St. Ignace

THE TRANSFER TO THE NEW WORLD

For the first thirty-three years of his life, Ljubljana and Vienna were the main centres of educational influence on Baraga. How he came to serve on the Lake Superior frontier is an interesting story in itself, one that has been told on a number of occasions.[82] Father Frederic Résé, the Vicar General for the Diocese of Cincinnati, had come to Vienna in 1828 in an effort to build support for the extension of mission work in the Old Northwest, that now contentious area beyond the Ohio River Valley. The Vicar sought and obtained an audience with the Habsburg Emperor, Francis I, with a view to advancing his ideas for the establishment of mission societies within the Austrian Empire. Permission was forthcoming, and in 1829 the *Leopoldinen Stiftung* (Leopoldine Society) was founded in Vienna, patterned strongly on the French *Société pour la propagation du foi* (The Society for the Propagation of the Faith), established in Lyons in 1822.[83] During his European travels, Résé was also successful in gaining permission for the establishment of a second organization, the Ludwig Mission Central in Bavaria. The publicity surrounding the founding of these societies appears to have generated a new zeal in Baraga, who, while quite popular among his own parishioners, was experiencing friction with some of his superiors and colleagues, many of whom had been influenced by Jansenism and Josephism.[84]

In 1829, Baraga requested permission to apply to Bishop Edward Fenwick at Cincinnati with a proposal that he enter the American mission field. To his Archbishop he wrote, "Already for many years, I have cherished the desire to go to a mission in order to preach the gospel to the pagans, who as yet do not know God, and to show them, with God's help, the way to salvation."[85] His similar expression of interest to Bishop Fenwick was favourably received.[86]

Baraga's application came in the aftermath of completion of his soon-to-be-popular *Dushna Pasha*. His commitment to distant service of the neglected, combined with disposal of his personal property, had a Thomas à Kempian ring about it. In the first published edition of the *Imitation of Christ* (1471), the title is followed by an explanatory statement: "Here begins a book of consolation for the instruction of the devout, the first chapter of which deals with the imitation of Christ and contempt for the worthless things of the world."[87] By the late fall of 1830, Baraga had disposed of

Figure 3 Trader Louis Campau and his wife, Sophie De Marsac, were Baraga's initial hosts at Grand River (Grand Rapids) in 1833, the location of Baraga's first American mission posting. (Antoine I. Rezek, *History of the Diocese of Sault Ste. Marie and Marquette,* 1907)

his possessions and inheritance and disembarked from Le Havre for the United States. By mid-January, 1831, Baraga was in Cincinnati, on the Ohio River.[88]

Thereafter, Frederic Baraga worked to establish or revive older missions in several locations in Michigan, Wisconsin, Minnesota, and Ontario. He served at L'Arbre Croche (near contemporary Harbor Springs) between 1831 and 1833. Two years were spent at Grand River (Grand Rapids) before moving north to La Pointe on the southwest coast of Lake Superior in 1835. Until his move to La Pointe, his charges had been mainly of the Ottawa Nation, a major sub-group of Algonkian speakers closely related to the Ojibwa (Chippewa).[89] His charges were now mainly Ojibwa, as they would be at L'Anse, some distance to the east, where Baraga moved in 1843. He spent ten years at this location before going to Sault Ste. Marie upon his appointment as Bishop of the Apostolic Vicariate of Upper Michigan, in 1853. By 1856, Baraga and his associates had extended Catholic missionary services around the entire north shore of Lake Superior and east at least as far as Bruce Mines, on the north shore of Lake Huron. Despite changes to diocesan boundaries after 1853, many of the northern

Figure 4 Lewis Cass (1782–1866). First a General in the American Army and then Governor of Michigan Territory after 1818, he was close to Schoolcraft and a proponent of Indian removal. Well informed on Indian history, he was an outstanding example of a proponent of American "manifest destiny" and the assimilationist view of Native policy. (Library of Congress)

missions, for practical reasons, remained delegated to Baraga from the Bishops of Detroit, Milwaukee, and Hamilton.[90]

The upper Great Lakes frontier which Baraga entered in 1831 was far from being a religious vacuum in Christian terms. First, there was the lingering memory of older Jesuit missionary endeavours from the seventeenth century, the influence of which had not totally died out in many Native and fur trade communities.[91]

Second, there was the more immediate context provided by the resurgence of the Catholic Church in this region in the three decades before Baraga's arrival. This revival included not just the efforts of European missionaries such as Gabriel Richard (1767–1832), active around Lake Michigan, but attempts to establish missions at Fort William and far away Red River, where Lord Selkirk had assisted the Roman Catholic Church to become active among the fur-trade labourers of French-Canadian descent.[92] There was also the fruit of the labour of Christianized Natives, such as Baraga's interpreter and language instructor, Jean-Baptiste Assiginack (1768–1866).[93] The latter, born at L'Arbre Croche, had been trained and converted at Oka, near Montreal. He became an active agent of the British and a force of Christian conversion among the Ottawa of the upper lakes, well before Baraga's arrival.[94] The old fur-trade society was also cross-blood society, and conversion and linguistic efforts were greatly facilitated by the work done by established families, such as that of Pierre Cotté at Fond Du Lac and of Pierre Crebasa and Benjamin Clautier at L'Anse Bay.[95]

Figure 5 Chief Andrew J. Blackbird (ca. 1815–1909). A resident of the L'Arbre Croche area, Blackbird wrote *A History of the Ottawa Indians* (1897). He was the brother of William Mactibinessi, who, while studying for the priesthood in Rome, died under what Blackbird took to be suspicious circumstances. He was also a cousin of Augustin Hamlin, Baraga's first Ottawa language instructor. (BBA)

Thirdly, after the War of 1812–14, there was the mounting invasion of Michigan Territory by Protestants and other sects, by means of a steady, westward flow of immigrants from the eastern states.[96] By 1823, representatives of the United Foreign Missionary Society had established themselves around Michilimackinac.[97] More doctrinal complications arose with the arrival of pioneers of adventist outlook, Protestant and Mormon, issuing out of New England and New York.[98] The establishment after 1844 of a "Kingdom" on Beaver Island by the Mormon schismatic, James J. Strang, was eventually seen by Baraga as a threat to the success of his earlier mission work on that island and at Michilimackinac. The Strang social experiment was fairly short-lived and proved eventually to be the stimulus of yet one more occasion of protracted violence against the Mormons during their long and complicated migration to the American West.[99]

As was the case across much of North America, Protestants and Catholics saw themselves in competition for Native souls in Michigan Territory. Baraga and his associates were frustrated at the perceived bias by Federal government Indian Affairs administrators, such as Lewis Cass and Henry R. Schoolcraft, in favour of the Protestant cause. There was, indeed, much validity to such charges.[100] Undeniably, there was a tendency for the Protestant Washington establishment to support removal as an idea compatible with progress.[101] The degree to which such a belief in progress and the inevitability of Native "decline" could mix pragmatically together in analysis, is well illustrated in the writings of Lewis Cass.[102] What was normally lacking in such critiques and resulting policy formulations was an appreciation of the view which Native peoples themselves had of their own connection to place and their long-established tenure upon the land.[103] Nevertheless, Baraga did work well and cooperatively with many Protestant clergy. At La Pointe, he preferred that Catholic students attend the Protestant school rather than no school at all.[104] At L'Anse, Baraga worked consistently well on a number of projects with the Methodist, John Petizel.[105] Even with Cass and Schoolcraft, whom he strongly opposed on the question of removal, he could at least share an interest in the promotion of temperance legislation.[106]

Upon his arrival in Cincinnati in 1831, Baraga's first task had been to undertake training in the Ottawa language, which he did with the

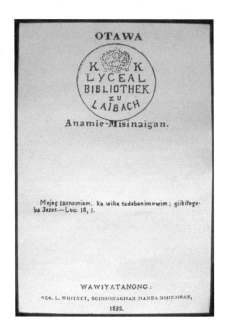

Figure 6 Cover page of Baraga's earliest publication in the Ottawa vernacular, *Otawa: Anamie-Misinaigan*, a prayer book printed in 1832 in Detroit, but bound in L'Arbre Croche by a Redemptorist, Brother Aloysius Schuh. A property stamp of a library in Laibach (Ljubljana) is visible. (C. A. Ceglar, Baragiana, Vol. 1, 1991)

help of two Native Algonkian speakers who were in training for the Church, William Makatebinessi and his cousin, Augustin Hamlin. Both of these men were from the Ottawa Native settlement at L'Arbre Croche (Harbor Springs), some distance south of Michilimackinac, on the east coast of Lake Michigan. In May, 1831, accompanied by Bishop Fenwick, Baraga set out for L'Arbre Croche. He was soon joined by Augustin Hamlin, returned from Rome, where William had died unexpectedly.[107] At L'Arbre Croche, Augustin and Baraga "often worked together on various ventures." Baraga "continued his study of the language, writing the first of his many Indian language books in 1832."[108] Baraga also worked with the experienced Chief, Jean-Baptiste Assiginack, who acted for him as an interpreter and teacher.[109] Assiginack

Figure 7 La Pointe in the 1850s. Protestant missionaries were active at this ancient seat of the Ojibwa before Baraga's arrival. The Madeline Islands were the main focus of settlement and of the fur trade activities of the American Fur Company, active on Lake Superior until 1842. (Wisconsin Magazine of History)

had furthered the local proselytizing activities of another Ottawa Indian, Andowish, after 1824.[110] Andowish, like Assiginack, had been to Montreal, been influenced by Christian circles in that quarter, and subsequently became instrumental in gaining Catholic converts from among the tribesmen and employees of the fur trade around the upper lakes.[111]

Baraga spent over two years in L'Arbre Croche before being reassigned to Grand River (Grand Rapids), a wintering ground for the Ottawas. Because of his growing obstinacy towards the removal policies being applied to the Illinois Indians, Baraga was sent well north of the Grand River in 1833.[112] He first went to Cottreville (Marine City) and then, in 1835, to La Pointe, an active centre of the fur trade already attended by Protestant missions.[113] Following a trip back to Europe in 1837, Baraga returned, accompanied by his widowed sister who had taken vows and now sought to assist her brother on the Superior frontier.[114] Baraga moved to L'Anse Bay in 1843, at the urging of one Pierre Crebassa, where he spent the next ten years.[115] He carried the holy word, often on foot, to other centres such as La Pointe, Fond du Lac, and Grand Portage. A man of great energy, his wide-ranging missionary travels earned for him the name, the "Snowshoe Priest."[116] Knowledge of his enterprise sometimes preceded him, as was the case with Pierre Cotté, a Métis of Fond du Lac; having obtained a copy of Baraga's first Indian *Prayer Book*, Cotté introduced it to the Native Peoples of that quarter well before Baraga himself had ever set foot in the region.[117]

During the 1840s, Baraga collaborated with local churchmen, Protestant and Catholic, in efforts to resist mounting pressure from removal laws, now aimed at displacing Native peoples around the upper lakes. In particular, he worked with the Rev. John Pitezel, a Methodist, in an ingenious scheme whereby the churches purchased the land upon which their missions stood, supplemented by agricultural land, and then deeded the land to the Indians; the removal laws could thus not be invoked with respect to those residing on these lands. In this fusion of ethics with title-in-fee-simple can be found the origins of what eventually became the Keweenaw Reserve at L'Anse.[118] Again in 1861, Baraga entered into a formal contract with Chief Shawanibinessi and his band at Sault Ste. Marie in order to place land for a church on Sugar Island on a sound legal footing.[119]

The official influence of Baraga and his associates slowly spread into the British territories of the north shore of Lake Superior and Lake Huron.[120] While his personal influence was strongest in the upper Michigan

Figure 8 Pierre Crebassa and his wife, Nancy (Roussain) Crebassa. Baraga's friends at L'Anse, they helped further his mission work on the south coast of Lake Superior. Pierre was born in the Red River Country in 1807, was educated in Montreal, and became agent for the American Fur Company at Mackinac. Baraga married the couple in 1837. (Antoine I. Rezek, *History of the Diocese of Sault Ste. Marie and Marquette*, 1907)

Peninsula until 1853, there were other colleagues active in the Sault Ste. Marie area who were preparing the ground in areas further afield. A Slovenian associate active at the Sault during the 1830s, Father Francis Pierz, had established a church there by 1837, and then other missions along the Canadian North Shore.[121] In the 1840s, Fr. M. S. V. Hanipaux undertook mission work in the surrounding areas, including at the *Baie de Goulée* on the eastern shore of Lake Superior some twenty-two miles north of the Sault.[122] August Kohler arrived at the Sault in 1847, and through his efforts a more sustained effort was made to build up the mission at Goulais Bay. Kohler made a census report of the Natives along the eastern shore in 1851, and from this report and from surviving baptismal records, one learns that a good number of people had relocated to the eastern shore from the American side of Lake Superior in the 1840s, probably in response to those same U.S. Government pressures to "remove" which had led Baraga and Pitezel to undertake land settlements on behalf of their Native charges on the south shore.[123] This suggestion is reinforced by the recollections of the Roussain family of Mamainse, north of Goulais, who were related to the old fur-trade family of that name in the La Pointe area – relations and friends of Pierre Crebassa, all well known to Frederic Baraga.[124] On the far side of the Lake at Fort William, Jesuit Fathers Choné and Frémiot were active after 1849, Frémiot in particular playing a role as advisor to the local Indians during the crucial negotiations for the 1850 Robinson-Superior Treaty on the Canadian side.[125]

Following his confirmation as bishop on 1 November 1853, Baraga spent much time at Sault Ste. Marie, the community identified as the See City. Baraga became increasingly preoccupied with the administration of his far-flung bishopric. Mid-nineteenth century Sault Ste. Marie was now a bustling place: the first efforts to straddle the rapids with a canal were underway in response to the mounting demands for the metal and lumber resources of northern Michigan. For the next ten years, Baraga's *Diary* and letters reveal a hectic schedule of travel as he sought to organize and develop his large territory, which now stretched from the north shore of Lake Huron in Ontario to lands well west of Lake Superior.

From his early days as a priest in his native Slovenia until the early 1860s, Baraga published a large and varied group of works.[126] Items published in English were few, his chosen languages for publications tending to be Slovene, German and French. He also published much for Native peoples in the form of transliterated Ottawa and Ojibwa Biblical

Figure 9 Mining community in Northern Michigan, 1840s. (John Pitezel, *Lights and Shades of a Missionary Life*, 1853)

Figure 10 Church of the Most Blessed Virgin Mary, Goulais Mission, 1974. This mission on the east coast of Lake Superior at Goulais Bay, or Kitchi Wikwedong ("in the large bay") was active in a minimal way after 1838. Attempts to establish a church building here were numerous but unsuccessful until late 1862, when Baraga consecrated the structure shown above. (Photo: Graham A. MacDonald)

texts and instructional books.[127] His theoretical works on language started to appear in 1850, with the appearance of his Ojibway grammar, a lengthy work of 576 pages. The "Preface" to this work was a mere page in length: "This is, I think, the first and only Otchipwe Grammar that ever was published in the United States." With a disarming casualness, he noted that, "It was rather a hard work to compose" for "I had to break my road all through." In a distinctly pastoral manner, he observed:[128]

> Writers of other Grammars avail themselves of the labours of their predecessors, and collect, like the bee, the honey out of these flowers of literature, leaving the dust in. I had no such advantage; I had nothing before me. No wonder then, if all be not correct in this first essay.

The *Diary* he kept after 1852 commences on the eve of his elevation to higher Church responsibilities as a bishop. It often reveals him try-

Figure 11 John Bouche, guide to Bishop Baraga at Sault Ste. Marie. Born into the traditions of the ancient Ojibwa canoe fishers of the rapids – "the Saulteurs" – Bouche was skilled with the long-handled hoop-net, still in use in the early twentieth century. (Sault Ste. Marie Semi-Centennial Canal Commission, 1905)

ing to snatch time away from more pressing duties in order to prepare such works as the *Dictionary of the Otchipwe Language*. In his *Diary*, for 11 April, 1853, he recorded: "Today I finally receive the first proofsheets of the *Dictionary* for correction. – Misère! When will it be finished." In 1853, the first edition of the *Dictionary* appeared, a book "explained in English."[129] After so many years in preparation, the manuscript came close to being lost during the course of a perilous trip across Green Bay, Lake Michigan.[130] This work subsequently went through several editions and remains in print.[131]

His pursuit of such utilitarian projects was linked to his belief that pastoral work in Native parishes was best conducted, as in his old homeland, through the use of local and simple vernaculars. Baraga was not alone in

Figure 12 Fr. Albert Lacombe (1827–1916).. This well-known missionary to the tribes of western Canada was a student of the Algonkian Cree language and produced an important dictionary in 1874. In 1884, he helped bring out a new edition of Baraga's dictionary in which aspects of his own studies were fused with Baraga's work. (Alberta Provincial Archives)

Figure 13 Fr. George A. Belcourt (1803–1874). Based in the Red River country of Manitoba and Minnesota between 1832 and 1859, Belcourt also worked on vernacular translations of biblical texts and the preparation of dictionaries and grammars in Algonkian dialects. (Provincial Archives of Manitoba)

Figure 14 Chief Shingwaukonse (1773–1854) and his fourth wife, Ogahbagehequa (b. 1798), in the early 1850s. Father of seventeen children, this important chief of the Sault Ste. Marie Ojibwa was recognized for his leadership and spiritual qualities. He became a convert to Anglicanism in 1833. (Sault Ste. Marie [Ontario] Public Library)

this view, but it was a minority opinion in the mission movement, Catholic and Protestant alike. For allies he might count such as Father George Belcourt at Red River, who had published (unknown for some time to Baraga) his own grammar of Saulteux (Ojibwa) in 1839; or the Baptist, Jotham Meeker, who in Schultz's words, "was almost the complete antithesis of McCoy," his ambitious colleague.[132] Working among the Shawnee in the 1830s, Meeker had come to doubt McCoy's entire approach to mission work, convinced, as was Baraga, that missionaries must master Native languages and remain fixed in their localities long enough to see work through. A printer by trade, Meeker developed a small newspaper, the *Siwinowe Kesibwi* (*Shawnee Sun*) and published a great number of instructional books in Shawnee, Potawatomi, Oto, Creek, Choctaw, Wea and Iowa.[133]

There was, then, considerable variation in basic mission approaches, even among those groups which made considerable room for use of the vernacular. The Protestant Oberlin Mission at Red Lake, founded in 1843, did not prosper, despite the fact that Frederick Ayer and his associates made some

Figure 15 Henry Rowe Schoolcraft (1796–1860). This influential Protestant churchman, Indian affairs civil servant, and pioneering ethnologist was active on the Lake Superior frontier before Baraga's arrival. The two men clashed over matters of Indian policy when Schoolcraft was based in Washington. (Library of Congress)

use of the vernacular. They seemed to favour a process of educational osmosis by which the agricultural example of the missionaries themselves would be the major vector taken towards religious conversion and economic advancement. This meant that most of the energies of the missionaries went into providing for the mere subsistence of the mission itself.[134]

In favouring the use of vernacular in his missionary work, Baraga was conservative in his ambitions and hopes. Utopian schemes were not part of his ideological equipment, but if positive economic and educational results came about from such mission work, all well and good. The merits of his vernacular approach are generally acknowledged and the theoretical works on language remain in use.[135]

His early *Short History*, on the other hand, written for the benefit of his supporters back in Europe, has remained obscure and unavailable to English readers. In composing it, Baraga revealed that he was a churchman first, and certainly not an aspiring ethnologist, as was his contemporary, Henry R. Schoolcraft.[136] The late lecture of 1863 suggests that Baraga had not greatly changed his earlier views on some of the fundamental aspects of North American Indian behaviour and history, but that he was still preoccupied with their physical and spiritual fate under European institutions and practices. Similarly, Baraga's temperance thinking in the 1830s only strengthened over the years; he shared with many of his contemporaries, secular and otherwise, an abhorrence of alcohol and its influence on Native society.[137] An 1862 *Diary* entry states, "... arrived home where I received terrible reports and letters about the drinking of McLaughlin and Konen, which made me decide not to go to Goulais Bay but to Ontonagon."[138] The explanation was, apparently, that Baraga wished to ordain Deacon Patrick O'Flanagan at Ontonagon, so that he could replace one of the two priests he was about to dismiss for drinking.[139] Much as he needed human assistance, he was not prepared to accept it from "backsliders."

Travel, administration, and fund-raising were the constants of Baraga's life as bishop. These activities eventually took their toll, even on his iron constitution. His time was short in 1866 when he suffered the first of a series of strokes while at Cincinnati. He died in 1868, and is buried in St. Peter's Cathedral at Marquette, Michigan, which in 1866 replaced Sault Ste Marie as the See City.

THE TEXT

Baraga published his *Abrégé de l'histoire des indiens de l'Amérique septentrionale (Short History of the Indians of North America)* in Paris in 1837.[140] It had been written as an aid to his own understanding and for that of his followers in Europe. His 1835 *Report to the Leopoldine Society* records that "In the free evening hours of the winter I shall try to write something complete on the manners and customs of the Indians and bring it to the attention of the public."[141]

The imprimatur of the French edition notes that that edition was "Translated from the German." This German text, which was the original, was published in the same year in Laibach (Ljubljana), the capital of Baraga's homeland in Slovenia.[142] A somewhat abridged Slovenian edition also appeared that year from Johann Klemens, the publisher of the German edition.[143] While Baraga would have been quite capable of preparing the French version, he in fact did not. The idea for the Paris project was a last-minute proposition made to Baraga while he was passing through that city, en route for Vienna, in the autumn of 1836. His French publisher, E. J. Bailly, who was then seeing through the press some of Baraga's religious works aimed at his Indian charges, noticed the text of the German-language work on the Indians; he proposed that he bring out a French edition. Baraga agreed, and left the manuscript with the publisher for translation. The name of the translator has not come down to us, but it was prepared in a space of little more than two weeks. Baraga later gave it his approval,

Figure 16 Frontispiece of the original German edition of Baraga's *Geschichte, Character, Sitten und Gebräuche der nord-amerikanischen Indier* (1837).

and then departed for Vienna and Laibach (Ljubljana), the German text in hand. The manuscript was eventually given over to publisher Johann Klemens, church officials having meanwhile given approval to the work.[144]

In many respects, the book takes its place in a long-standing genre of travel and pioneer observations. From the founding of the earliest New World colonies, a demand developed in Europe for the exotic details of Indian life.[145] As with many such productions, Baraga's had a utilitarian purpose, similar to, if not identical with, that of the *Jesuit Relations*, initiated two centuries earlier.[146] The *Short History* was partially a fund-raiser, and it was not accidental that he had the manuscript in hand when he returned to Europe in 1837 to promote his missions. He recapped the themes outlined in the *Short History* late in life, when giving one of his last public lectures, in Cincinnati in 1863. This lecture partially took the form of a memoir but also incorporated, only slightly altered, material from the *Short History*.[147]

It is not clear just how much knowledge about Indian life and tradition Baraga had accumulated before he came to America. While his decision to become a missionary seems to have developed fairly rapidly in 1828, there is reason to think he may have been thinking along these lines as early as 1817. When Baraga was first introduced to Fr. Hofbauer by Othmar Rauscher, Hofbauer is reported to have turned to Rauscher and said, "Are you perhaps bringing me an Indian missionary?"[148] In 1829 letters to his archbishop and to Bishop Fenwick in Cincinnati, he claimed to have been thinking about mission work to the Indians for many years.[149] Should the interest have been kindled in the early 1820s, Baraga would have had considerable time to consult library materials in his homeland. A good number of frontier works, such as Jonathan Carver's *Travels* and John Long's *Voyages*, had appeared in German editions by the 1790s.[150] Baraga's sources, although seldom acknowledged in his text, have been closely documented. We know, for example, that he asked Ramsey Crooks of the American Fur Company to obtain certain titles for him.[151] Baraga's certain use of John Adair's *History* of 1775 served not just as a general source, but also as a foil for his own views on certain historical questions, such as the origin of the North American Indians.[152]

Baraga's *Short History* is just one in a long series of such documents, many of which have seldom been viewed except by those who frequent archives and special library collections, or who have chanced upon them in unusual circumstances.[153] Such works often drew upon that of other authors, with or without due acknowledgement. In format, Baraga's work is arranged in chapters by theme in a manner quite similar to many other contemporary productions, but it is more impressionistic than systematic. Heckewelder is the only name to appear with any regularity, and Baraga clearly drew upon his 1819 *Account*. It is also clear that he drew upon B. B. Thatcher's *Lives of the Indians* (1825) and Colden's *History*.[154]

Baraga prepared the work after he had been about seven years in North America. There is no reason to believe that it was not composed as anything more than one of his working tools, one with a strong pragmatic purpose. The *Short History* was only marginally about North American Indians as a whole; rather, with the exception of the long and derivative "Introduction," it was more concerned with the Algonkians of the Upper Great Lakes. Certain, but my no means all, of his judgments meshed with the emerging viewpoints of the new ethnology and anthropology. Indeed, a flexible view of human adaptability was fundamental to the missionary enterprise itself, which could not, on rational grounds, achieve much in the absence of such a view.[155] If conversion procedures were to be successful, it had to be assumed that, at a minimum, there was a capacity for individuals to rationally modify their behaviour and beliefs. Baraga made the point that he was mainly attempting to describe conditions that had prevailed in the past among the unconverted, or among those who wilfully chose to remain heathen.[156] His main bias was that for Native groups to creatively adapt their ways to modernity, adoption of Christianity was a near essential prerequisite.

The organization of the *Short History* is as follows. The "Introduction" is mainly composed of a loose set of observations and anecdotes dealing

Figure 17 Trader Ramsey Crooks (1787–1859) was in charge of American Fur Company operations on Lake Superior until 1842. Based at La Pointe, he assisted Baraga in a number of ways, including importing reference books relevant to the preparation of his history. (Spokane Public Library)

Figure 18 William Whipple Warren (1825–1853). Born at La Pointe to trader Lyman Warren and Mary Cadotte, he completed his *History of the Ojibway People* in 1852, although it was not published until 1885. The work is rich in oral testimony gathered from many persons to whom he had access by reason of kin relationships and experience. Baraga may have had access to the library of Lyman Warren during the later 1830s. (Minnesota Historical Society)

with the initial discovery of the New World and the settlement period in Virginia and New England, down to the termination of King Philip's War in 1676. The focus is on the east-coast setting, and Baraga touches only occasionally upon other regions of the continent. He identifies 1676 as marking the end of practical influence by the Native peoples in continental political affairs: "The Indians were no longer a historical force in their own country." Subsequently, Indian warfare tended to concern inter-tribal conflicts, feuds, or participation in the armies of the colonial European powers. Baraga concludes his introduction with a discussion of the reasons for the steady decline in Native population since the late seventeenth century, and appropriately gives attention to changes in the traditional economic landscape, forced removal to less favourable lands, and disease. His conclusions were rather prophetic of what became normative expectations and utter-

Figure 19 The Reverend John Heckewelder (1743–1823). An influential member of David Zeisberger's Protestant Moravian Church missionary movement of Pennsylvania and member of the American Philosophical Society, he authored an influential history of the Indians, which Baraga drew upon for his own study. His work inspired the "Leatherstocking" novels of James Fenimore Cooper. (Heckewelder, *History, Manners and Customs of the Indian Nations*, 1876)

ances in the later nineteenth century: "in a few centuries the history of the Indian will be that of a people that exists only in books."

The remainder of the text is composed of fourteen chapters that deal with various aspects of Native customs and ways of life. The topics include a consideration of dress, habitations, hunting, fishing, social practices, warfare, and religion. Drawing on a number of earlier sources, these chapters tend to be a mixture of description, anecdote and interpretation. The chapters on material culture are informative, and the details offered often find support in later scholarship. As a sign of his interest

Figure 20 Alexander Henry the Elder (1739–1824). An experienced free-trader from Montreal, active in the upper Great Lakes area after 1760. Baraga drew upon his popular *Travels*, first published in 1809. (Alexander Henry, *Travels*)

in these matters, Baraga conveyed a number of artefacts back to his home province of Carniola, where they became the basis of a European collection that is still extant.[157]

Much of Baraga's *Short History* relates to functional areas of everyday life. In his treatment of "customs and manners," many European prejudices and assumptions may be noted. One finds references to the "sluggishness" or "indolence" of the Indians, phrases much employed by travellers, fur traders and missionaries of all stripes. The notion that the only productive human being was one seen to be hard at work at standard European agricultural and industrial chores was a difficult perceptual hurdle for many non-Natives to climb over.[158] Centuries of making a living through variations of the "seasonal round" informed the behavioural traditions of Amerindians. The associated traditions of such ways of life made room for time in the day or month when movement and actions were seen to be counterproductive, wasteful of energy, and just bad survival technique. Regardless, the kind of open communism which allowed "seasonal round" societies to work, while often gaining notice by missionaries, did not always convince them of its relevance, so preoccupied were they with their ambition to foster new forms of economy amongst their wilderness charges.[159]

Baraga's observations on Native demography also reflected much of the general thinking of the times.[160] His stated reasons for population decline among the Indians since European contact were sound enough, showing an appreciation for the role of disease in the decimation of numbers, along with altered conditions of economy. He held the view, as did many others, that most Native cultures were probably destined to disappear altogether, although he contended that there was hope for those who adopted temperance, Christianity and a settled way of life.[161] On the question of alcohol, Baraga was firmly of the view that it was one of the great agents of Native social destruction. After several centuries of contact with Europeans, Native leadership and organization had, as a result of these interconnected causes, suffered a serious eclipse.[162]

There indeed appears to have been a developing crisis in Native leadership by the 1830s in the Upper Great Lakes region. Vecsey has described how traditional authority was being split in a variety of ways under the treaty system and through the influence of traders and missionaries.[163] An obvious loss was diplomatic, in the larger sense: Native leaders were no longer sought out for their war-related alliance capabilities. As treaty-making progressed, artificial forms of band leadership were established at the behest of governments in order to deal with the mechanics of treaties.[164] Secondly, commercial traders tended to establish their own hierarchy of Native contacts, geared to their suitability as hunters and traders. The natural talent in a given individual that previously might have led to his election as chief now tended to become the rationale for his recognition in trade.[165]

Understanding much contemporary Indian social organization to be weak, Baraga nevertheless saw in the records of past performance signs of past vitality. In a striking passage on government, a formal method for the recording of oral traditions and important speeches is outlined in some detail. There were other modes of preserving the past as well; in a commentary on aboriginal tattooing, for instance, he describes how the practice took on exaggerated proportions in the hands of one venerable warrior: "his high deeds in combat with his enemies were drawn on his skin, with the result that he represented his biography."

Baraga gave consideration to the heroic nature of warfare in his study. It is less the material aspects of warfare and more the psychological and ceremonial ones that command his attention. Having argued that since the late seventeenth century, standing armies were no longer a factor of Native life, the discussion now shifts to the more sensational aspects of blood-feud battles and ceremonial torture. The author punctuates his discussion by making distinctions between those groups still pursuing traditional customs and those who have left them behind in the wake of adopting Christianity.

In his consideration of Native government, Baraga develops a modest theory of natural aristocracy. His description contains much of interest concerning the role of speech-making and the veneration of elders. The manner in which oral tradition is actually perfected as a mechanism for transferring information between the generations is described with originality.

The final chapters, dealing with disease, cures and mortuary customs, are full of interest, both for the anecdotal content and for the manner in which Baraga reveals his own scepticism concerning medical claims and practices generally. He writes of "those who impose themselves, by their chatter, upon credulous and ignorant people alike."

As might be expected, Baraga took much note of social and religious values as practiced by Native peoples, and as in the writings of

Figure 21 Johann Georg Kohl (1808–1878). Geographer extraordinaire and a talented travel writer, Kohl wrote an important book on the Lake Superior Indians, *Kitchi Gami: Wanderings Around Lake Superior* (1860), published in both German and English. He met Baraga on a number of occasions, but regrettably little record of their conversations survive. (H. A. Schumacher, *J.G. Kohl's Amerikanische Studien*, 1885)

many other frontier missionaries and travellers, Baraga describes such ideas as the "Great Spirit," notions of the afterlife, and the details of ceremony. Typical of European writers, much attention is given over to detailing the more flamboyant aspects of practices associated with the Sun Dance and other rituals. The content of Native religion was described by Baraga with a mixture of curiosity and dismissal; the positive elements guided by the "Lord of Life" were, in his view, compromised by other, pantheistic aspects.[166]

We now know that under the conditions of fur-trade competition and frontier expansion, the role of traditional shamans had been modified as intercessors with the manitous, particularly with respect to the important "Hunter's Medicine" as defined under the system of the syncratic Nativist religious order known as the *Midéwiwin*, or "Grand Medicine Society."

Shamans had been particularly important in Great Lakes Algonkian culture as the Ojibwa Chief of the Marquette area, Charles Kawbawgam, recalled late in the nineteenth century.[167] The great river-oriented fisheries, particularly at Sault Ste. Marie and La Pointe, facilitated the promotion of a wide variety of social functions at certain seasons of the year. Remnants of the shattered Huron nation helped introduce the relatively short-lived "Feast of the Dead" around Chaquemegon in the later seventeenth century. Other functions, associated with the Algonkian *Midéwiwin*, reveal it to be of rather recent and syncratic origin.[168] Baraga's success in understanding the *Midéwiwin* went only so far, according to his contemporary, trader Benjamin Armstrong, who claimed to have been inducted into the *Midéwiwin*.[169] Consequently, Baraga showed little interest in the origins of the *Midéwiwin* or in the possibilities of much more ancient, localized, Aboriginal spiritual experience which have captured the attention of twentieth-century scholarship.[170] The implications of trader George Nelson's 1823 *Journal*, with its revelations about conjuring and the "orders of the dreamed," would have registered on Baraga as deterministic, in the same way that Jansenists were suspect, owing to their flirtations with predestinarian thinking.[171] It is interesting however, that Baraga rendered in his *Short History* the precise mechanism of "the orders of the dreamed" through an anecdote about a young Indian whose dream of destiny was that he must commit several murders – and did.

If Baraga was reticent to explore vestiges of Native religious expression owing to his own religious commitment, he revealed a fledgling interest in exploring the farther reaches of human antiquity around Lake Superior, the possibilities for which were only beginning to be suspected by geologists.[172] There are certain aspects of his book that reveal him to be on the edge of a modern understanding on such questions as Native origins. Disagreement over the nature of the Indians still represented a serious split in the public opinion of Baraga's day. The missionary class, on the whole, and many of liberal outlook, were advocates for the recognition of the kindred humanity of the Native peoples. Politicians, administrators, frontier developers and intending settlers were often, to one degree or another, opposed to such a view; if this was not always expressed by their words, then it certainly was by their actions. The Jacksonian project of "removal" essentially equated Native people to the status of so many cattle.

Questions had long been asked about the origins of the American Indians. In trying to preserve the integrity of Bishop Ussher's Biblical

Figure 22 Marquette, Michigan, about 1840. Marquette became the See City in 1866, replacing Sault Ste. Marie. Bishop Baraga is buried in Marquette's St. Peter's Cathedral. (Antoine I. Rezek, *History of the Diocese of Sault Ste. Marie and Marquette*, 1907)

calendar, dating the creation of the world to 4004 B.C., many eighteenth-century writers, such as John Adair, opted for a theory of Native origins linking them to the "lost tribes of Israel."[173] Such views were becoming more difficult to retain. Geology was making rapid strides in clarifying the genuine antiquity of the Earth and of the human race. Lyell's *Principles of Geology* (1830) synthesized what had been in the air since the early eighteenth century, thereby reducing Bishop Ussher's biblical time scale to something of antiquarian interest.[174] The new history was putting all of this aside in response to the questions raised by geology and language. Close students now favoured an Asian cradle for the Native peoples. Such had, indeed, been suspected by the Spanish Jesuit, Acosta, in the early sixteenth century.[175] While in Acosta's time, deference to religious sensibilities continued to govern the public utterances made by many scientific enquirers, evidence was accumulating, throwing up disturbing inconsistencies with respect to the historical time scale implied by the Book of Genesis. Acosta's view was given a distinctly modern push by Isaac de la Payrère in 1665, and advanced by Lafitau in 1724.[176] By the second quarter of the eighteenth century, then, the notion that the Indians bore some connection with the "lost tribes of Israel" was starting to wear thin. The theory still had a future, nevertheless; it was strongly advertised in James Adair's influential *History of the Indians* (1775) and even between 1830 and 1848, in Viscount Kingsborough's life-consuming work, the monumental *Antiquities of Mexico*.[177]

By the turn of the nineteenth century, many members of the American Philosophical Society had abandoned all such middle-eastern notions and opted for the view that Native peoples had crossed over from Asia via the Bering Land Bridge into Alaska. This idea was promoted by Heckewelder in 1819, and it was the view adopted by Baraga.[178] It was an idea with a long future, one not entirely disposed of today, although much modified.[179] Baraga did not merely inherit this view, but maintained it based on his own reading. In a letter of 1843 to the Archbishop of Vienna, Baraga stated, "I cannot refrain from mentioning the questions that are being asked about the origin and descent of the Indians in America." Under seven headings, he went on to briefly analyze the reasons why, given "the proofs cited," with respect to the Indians being descended from the Israelites, "not one is conclusive, and most of them, if not all, are entirely erroneous."[180]

For Heckewelder and his associates, an important element impinging on the question of origins had been the factor of

Figure 23 Benjamin Armstrong (1820–1900). Born in Alabama, Armstrong went north and became a trader in the upper Great Lakes area. He married a niece of the influential Chief Buffalo, was adopted as a son by him, and claimed in his Memoirs to have been admitted into the Midéwiwin, or "Grand Medicine Society." He knew and respected Baraga but disagreed with Baraga's interpretations of Native religion. (Armstrong, *Early Life among the Indians*, 1892)

language.[181] Thus, in his *Notes on the State of Virginia* (1787), Thomas Jefferson urged that the systematic compilation of vocabularies of the Native tribes would be most useful for comparison with old-world languages, with a view to a construction of "the best evidence of the derivation of this part of the human race."[182] By the late eighteenth century, then, attempts to link Native peoples with Old World, Biblical populations based on parallels in appearance or specific ethnographic traits were no longer satisfying to students such as Jefferson, who sensed that there was great time depth implied in the customary use of a language. The comparison of New World languages was, therefore, coming to be considered essential in order to trace the supposed earlier connections with Old World groups.

By 1850, when Baraga had started publishing his own works on language, this notion had gathered some momentum. In the "Preface" to his *Dictionary of the Otchipwe Language* (1853), Baraga made a gesture towards

Figure 24 Chief Buffalo (ca. 1760–1855). Known as Kechwaishki, Beshkike or Le Bœuf, this war chief of the Chippewa was signatory to the 1842 Treaty of La Pointe and worked with his adopted son, Benjamin Armstrong, to achieve a revision to the removal terms via the new 1854 Treaty. He is buried near Baraga's first church on Madeline Island and is reported to have converted to Christianity on his deathbed. (Wisconsin Museum of History)

Schoolcraft, approving his recognition "that the true history of the Indian tribes and their international relations must rest as a basis upon the light obtained from their languages."[183] Owing to the extensive geographical distribution of Algonkian speakers, many missionaries working in the northern and eastern portions of the continent became familiar with variants of this language family, and the widespread distribution of such speakers did not go unnoticed by these field workers.[184] This appreciation of linguistic and cultural diversity within a larger framework of "others," conveniently called "Indians," goes against the observation of those who argue that Europeans saw New World peoples as a uniform and indistinguishable horde.[185] On the contrary, from the first New World landings, records and accounts of diverse languages and practices proliferated along an upward curve. The term "Indian" was a necessary descriptive generalization, just as "European" (or some equivalent in the language of any given indigenous group) was necessary in the minds of the "others" to describe these newcomers.[186] With increased local knowledge, Indians were quickly recognized by some regional name and Europeans, in turn, were recognized as "English" or "Spanish."[187] It is not surprising that by the early nineteenth century, something called "ethnology" was in the air in America, with its mounting preoccupation with classification and description, nor that some of the members of its early organizations were staunch imperialists such as Jefferson, Cass and Schoolcraft, or missionaries such as Heckewelder.

The experience of northern missionaries reflected a long tradition of observation on linguistic diversity in the New World. By way of introductory remarks to his *Key into the Language of America* (1643), that enterprising and ever-dissident Puritan, Roger Williams, disclosed a variety of motives for the work in hand. Addressing his "Deare and Welbeloved Friends and Countreymen, in old and new England," he noted that "This Key respects the Native Language of it, and happily may unlocke some Rarities concerning the Natives themselves, not yet discovered." Addressing the utility of his *Key*, Williams observed that there is "a mixture of this Language North and South" and that "their Dialects doe exceedingly differ," and yet not so much that "a man may, by this helpe, converse with thousands of Natives all over the Countrey." This can assist the larger purpose: "by such converse it may please the Father of Mercies to spread civilitie (and in his owne most holy season) Christiantie; for one candle will light ten thousand, and it may please God to blesse a little Leaven to season the mightie Lump of those Peoples and Territories."[188]

Variations on this series of motives would be reiterated time and time again over the next two-and-a-half centuries by imperial and government officials, church officers and educators. The terms "savagery," "barbarism" and "civilization" became common in the works of colonizers, enlightenment writers, and missionaries.[189] Such utterances were often tinged with a romantic flavour and may have, as with Lafitau, demonstrated a strong curiosity

Map 4   Contemporary Slovenia and Baraga's birthplace, Dobrnic.

about parallels that might be drawn between the Indians and "barbarian" peoples described by ancient classical authors such as Julius Caesar.[190]

More recently, some have detected a "civilization-savage" syndrome in New World commentaries, a syndrome viewed as implicit in the observations made by any number of Europeans encountering those experienced by them as "others."[191] It would be an error however, to think that some of these observers were not well aware of the ambiguity of their perceptions and the bewitchment of language which informed their own writings.[192] Lahontan, for example, indulged in popular literary sport when trying to fathom the gulf of misunderstanding separating Native from European by showing how flimsy European assumptions were, when viewed critically from a hypothetical Native perspective.[193] As Enlightenment writings shaded into Romanticism, the term "savage" took on some entirely positive aspects, particularly in the works of Rousseau and Chateaubriand, who were certainly not the first to promote the vision of the "noble savage" but merely the most famous. The term "savage" has had many contextual meanings in the literature.[194] It has already been noted that many missionaries viewed their own work as reflective of their own, personal critique of western civilization itself.

The lure of the frontier for men of the cloth was undeniably of a different order from what it was for most "soldiers of fortune," or those drawn by the fur trade and various other resource enterprises, yet there was a common thread. By definition, Europeans crossed the Atlantic to further some substantive purpose, be it searching for gold or for the conversion of souls. The assumption was that a moral bond could be constructed between Native and European. In some quarters that bond was the ethic of slavery.[195] The early colonists and the northern fur traders, especially, learned early that as a matter of practical survival, whatever differences existed in ways of life, they were not so severe as to preclude the cementing of human relationships and the fusion of blood.[196] Many missionaries, while seldom doubting the correctness of their own religion, were frequently open to, and aware of, the relativity of such terms as "savagery" and "civilization," and might be quick to point out that there was seldom any group monopoly in the exercise of barbaric or civilized behaviour. Cultural differences were real, but the proselytizing class did not doubt that the differences could be overcome in areas where they counted, nor that Native peoples could be brought into the true fold. Was there not, they asked, much historical evidence for gradual "barbarian" transformation in the Old World?

By the early nineteenth century, the great assumption of many Europeans, and particularly of clergy, was that Native peoples were living in some remote age, in a kind of state of suspended cultural animation, and therefore needed assistance to "catch up" with European practices.[197] Fur trader and explorer Sir Alexander Mackenzie shared this view, and reflected that missionaries should have "begun their work by teaching some of those useful arts which are the inlets of knowledge, and lead the mind by degrees to objects of higher comprehension."[198] Approaches toward Euro-Native consolidation were, it was suggested, to be both technological and spiritual.

It was a logical enough vision of a closed system. If it was possible for one group of "others" to "catch up," it was just as possible for the "civilized" to revert back as "backsliders," to use the favourite term of many a clergyman. The guardians of the first settlements in old Quebec were acutely aware of this possibility; unable to comprehend that a working man might want to belong to any other culture than his own, their worst fears were readily confirmed by the rise of the *coureurs de bois*, young men all too ready and eager to "go native" and experience a different social order.[199]

For many European colonials, the veneer of "civilization" was thin and, hence, eternal vigilance over all members of civil society was necessary. In forever going on about "savagery," the typical colonizer often did so while looking back nervously into a distant mirror which reflected what he supposed his own culture had left behind. Upon further contemplation of that image, the more acute were often led to an uneasy awareness that the distance between past and present was short, and perhaps not even real. In his *Short History*, Baraga described the aftermath of the 1622 uprising of Opechankanow: "The colonists who escaped the massacre all fled to Jamestown, where they dreamed only of taking revenge upon their enemies. History proves that they were very well able to imitate, even surpass, the examples of treason, revenge and slaughter which the savages had bestowed upon them."

SHORT HISTORY OF THE
NORTH AMERICAN INDIANS

 ## Introduction

The history of the peoples of America begins on the
12th of October, 1492. This was a decisive day for
America, the most important day in its annals, when
Christopher Columbus discovered this part of the
world, until then entirely unknown to the peoples of
the other hemisphere.[1]

Christopher Columbus, a Genoese by birth, had
thought that by always sailing to the west he would
arrive in the oriental Indies by a more direct route,
and consequently in much less time than by the previously followed route around the Cape of Good Hope;

he resolved, therefore, to send an expedition to ensure the possibility of such an enterprise.

In order to undertake it, he sought the support and protection of the Genoese government, but he was received as a dreamer and his plan was rejected. He then presented himself in Portugal in order to request the co-operation of the Royal Court, but his representations there were no more happily received. He then sent his brother, Barthélemy, to King Henry VII of England. Barthélemy was taken prisoner en route, and languished long in irons, with the result that several years passed before he could fulfill the mission he had been charged with by his brother.

Firm and resolute, Christopher Columbus pondered long upon how to get around these obstacles; he thought only of the execution of his plan and presented himself at the court of Spain. King Ferdinand was not willing to give any cooperation whatsoever to such an enterprise; as did everyone else, he treated Columbus' plan as a dream and considered its achievement quite impossible. The genius of this great man grew in the minds of his contemporaries, although he was unable to find at sovereign courts anyone prepared to comprehend his project.

After a delay of four years, one capable of rebuffing a man of less perseverance, he finally found in King Ferdinand's Queen, Isabella, a sup-portive woman and a zealous partisan of his plans. She sold a part of her jewels, and saw fit to equip three ships, the Sancta-Maria, the Pinta, and the Nigna.[2]

With this small fleet, Columbus set out from the coast of Spain on Au-gust 3rd, 1492 and sailed consistently in the direction of the Occident over an immense ocean that no vessel had ever crossed. His purpose was to ap-proach the oriental Indies, but Providence opened the path to a new world entirely unknown to civilized peoples.

For two months he had great difficulties during the passage, such that the greatest discouragement and the deepest displeasure set in among the crew; it became necessary for him to summon up all his spiritual resources in order to restore calm and ensure that no one renounced the enterprise. However, all his reasoning and authority did not long calm the crew. A general murmur was heard, one which rose to such a pitch that discour-agement and desolation approached despair among the men. In the midst of these obstacles, Columbus remained firm and steady, always trying to instill calm among his companions. He was finally constrained to promise them that if in three days land was not spotted, they would return. But that

Providence which decreed that they should arrive in this region and then spread the news to the civilized world, also granted that they should, on the 12th of October, 1492, before the expiration of this deadline, discover an island to which they gave the name, San Salvador.

A general rejoicing was heard; they all fell to their knees, and thanked God for the happy success granted to their enterprise. At the same time they entreated their captain, whom they now recognized and admired for his genius, to forgive them for their delinquent behaviour. Columbus, dressed magnificently and with naked sword in hand, went ashore first and was then followed by the entire crew. They prostrated themselves on the ground of this new world and Columbus took solemn possession of the country in the name of Queen Isabella.[3]

The Spaniards and their leader were not a little surprised to find that the inhabitants of the island were a race of men different from all those that they had ever seen before. They were of a coppery colour, naked, without beard, and wore long, black hair. But even greater was the astonishment of the Spaniards in learning that they prayed to the Sun as their principal divinity.

After having been employed for several weeks in reconnaissance in the interior of the newly discovered country, and having visited several other neighbouring islands, Columbus then disembarked for Europe. During the journey, he was assailed by a horrific storm that threatened destruction. At the height of the storm, Columbus, with admirable presence of mind, wrote a short account of his expedition which he carefully placed in a cask to defend it against the fury of the waves, in the hope that it would one day fall into some navigator's hands; in the event that they were to perish in this storm, the world would at least learn of his important discovery. The storm abated, however, and Columbus approached Spain on the 15th of March, 1493.[4]

The path to the New World, once traced by Columbus, was not long in attracting peoples of different nations, eager to exploit the new discoveries and to create new settlements.

It is established in history that after the discovery of America, all that part of the world was seen to be inhabited, but as to when and how these first inhabitants became established is what no author has yet demonstrated. The history of the American peoples before the discovery is entirely unknown to us, and will probably always remain so.[5]

The question of the origin of the Indians of America is resolved in different ways by English historians. It seems to me, however, that one would not reasonably doubt that they have come out of Asia, the region out of which all human races have come, the more so since the Bering Strait separating Asia from America, is in some places no more that forty English miles, a shorter distance than some Indians often cross in their canoes; they could well, therefore, easily pass between Asia and America. In addition, the Bering Strait is frozen in winter, and the Indians are accustomed to making trips on lake-ice of more than forty English miles.[6]

The northern coasts of America were explored only in 1497 by John Cabot. He had been sent to America by the English King, Henry VII, who also wanted to have his share of the New World discovery. He first approached the island of Newfoundland and before long had discovered the terra firma of North America, becoming the first European to visit the new continent, but he returned soon after to England without having established a colony.[7]

In 1524 the French King, Francis I, sent to the New World a Florentine named Verrazzano to take possession of a part of this country in the name of the Crown of France. He approached Florida, and after having surveyed and visited the coasts of North America, he returned to France, also without having attempted to establish a settlement.[8]

The year 1584 marked the first attempt at colonization in North America. Walter Raleigh, an English gentleman, became the head of the colony; they established themselves in Virginia, to the number of one hundred and eighty men. Its duration was quite short, for the colonists, instead of concentrating on agriculture, dreamt only of the search for gold and money. Their provisions were soon squandered, and in order to live they were, in turn, constrained to begin trading with the Indians: this they could not undertake for any great length of time; they therefore abandoned the colony and returned to England after a stay in America of less than two years.[9]

During their sojourn, these colonists had taken up the North American Indian habit of smoking tobacco; similarly, the Spaniards had long ago adopted the same habit from the South American Indians, and upon their return to Europe the colonists transmitted to their compatriots this practice, so well regarded by the savages.

All attempts to base a durable colony in North America failed until 1607, when the foundations of a stable settlement were finally laid in Virginia. In this year also commenced the history of the Indians of this part of America. The history of these peoples before this period is entirely unknown, owing to the lack of historical documents of any kind.

Christopher Newport, at the head of one hundred and five English colonists, took up land on the coast of Virginia, close to the mouth of a great river that he named the "James" in honour of the King.[10] They ascended the river until they arrived at a superb valley in which they determined to remain. The settlement that they began to build also honoured the King of England, and was called Jamestown. Other English folk came, increasing their numbers, and giving the colony an imposing aspect.

Seeing the rapid increase in the number and power of the colonists, the neighbouring Indians began to develop anxieties about their country. Without declaring an open war, yet they did not hide their hostile intentions against the colony. The colonists were in turn, therefore, obliged to surround Jamestown with palisades in order to repel attacks by their savage neighbours.[11]

One of the principal colonists, John Smith, with some of his companions, journeyed a day's travel into the interior of the country.[12] At a certain distance from the colony, they were suddenly attacked by savages who had watched them from the woods. A violent struggle ensued, but the English, inferior in number, either fell under the assault of their enemies or were taken prisoner.

What happened to John Smith in this confrontation merits recounting. Injured by an arrow at the beginning of the altercation, he seized his Indian guide with his left hand, and made a shield of him against the arrows of his enemies; holding his musket in his right hand, he reduced four approaching Indians to the dust. While all were engaged in the fighting, he beat a steady retreat hoping to escape danger, when suddenly he found himself in a marshy spot where he sank down so much that defence became impossible, and he fell into the hands of the Indians, who were impressed by his bravery. To escape the unavoidable death confronting him, he offered to the Indians, with admirable presence of mind, a magnetized needle in a box of ivory and, through signs interspersed with words, he began to explain to them the outstanding properties of this magnetized needle. Amazed, they attentively took account of the box, but soon their interest reverted to their distinguished prisoner. They tied him to a tree and began to pierce him with their arrows, when suddenly the Indian who held the compass in his hands shouted to others, "Let him live awhile and bring him to our King." They untied him from the tree and conducted him in triumph to their chief, Powhatan. The latter convened them in council, and as a man who by his courage and skill could be very harmful to the savages, the prisoner was, by the rules, condemned to death. Smith was conducted immediately to a place of torture. Here there was a large stone upon which the miserable soul was obliged to place his head. Powhatan wished to take on the function of executioner; a huge club was brought to him and he had already raised his powerful arms over the head of the European he was about to strike, when all at once he heard a scream of fright. It was his daughter, the young and beautiful Pocahontas, who, at his feet, was protecting the head of the convict. She then turned a beseeching look on her surprised father and asked him, in quiet but very eloquent words, for the life of the prisoner. The heart of the barbaric savage was not closed to all noble sentiment, and being overcome by this gesture, his arms fell without force. The same sentiment seized his tribesmen. Smith was pardoned and soon regained his liberty.[13] This circumstance re-established friendly and peaceful relations between the colonists and Indians, a peace which lasted two years.

Powhatan was one of the most remarkable of the North American chiefs. He exerted unlimited power over all the different tribes of the regions that today compose the state of Virginia. These numbered about thirty at the time of the arrival of the first English colonists; each had its true chief, but Powhatan exerted his supremacy over all. The chiefs of the thirty tribes were required to pay annual dues in furs, deerskins, corn, copper, etc., and these chiefs were made to deliver these dues by members of their tribe.[14]

Powhatan had four residences in which he lived at different times of the year. His palace consisted of a high and very large Indian lodge, approximately one hundred feet long. He resided there with his guards, his woman and his servants. His guard consisted of forty or fifty of his greatest and most vigorous warriors. At night, four of these warriors watched the four corners of his residence. From time to time, on the half-hour approximately, they called to each other in order to remain awake. When one of them did not reply, he was cruelly struck by an officer of the guard.

This powerful Indian king had another fortified lodge, made with the trunks of trees joined together and surrounded by high fences; it contained his treasure. This lodge was almost one hundred and fifty feet long, with a proportional width. Here were preserved his furs, skins and other items received in tribute, as well as his bow and arrows, his shield and club. In order to inspire a certain respect for this structure in his subjects, he had carefully placed at each of the extremities, an idol; these roughly worked figures, represented a dragon, a bear, a leopard and a man.

He had a great number of women in his residences. One of his women always sat to his right and another to his left. Before each of his meals, one of the women brought him water in a wooden vase in order for him to wash his hands, and another would present him a duvet, which served in place of a napkin to dry his hands. When he became disgusted with his women, he gave them to his warriors, and took others.

In 1609, hostilities resumed on the part of the Indians, and Powhatan conceived a plan with his subjects by which, united, they could destroy all the colonists at a single blow. Happily for them, the noble Pocahontas became aware of her father's cruel project. The Indians had resolved to fall upon the whites during the night when they would suspect no danger, and to kill them without exception. On a stormy and sombre night, Pocahontas secretly slipped out of her father's camp and went to Jamestown and revealed the terrible plan to the colonists. They hastened to put defences in place, and when the savages found the English villains ready to receive them, they hurriedly fled into the forest.

This remarkable young Indian remained at Jamestown for some time, and soon after wed one of the main colonists by the name of Rolf.[15] This marriage was celebrated with the greatest pomp, since it was the first such marriage of a European in North America. Some years after, she went with her husband to England, embraced the Christian religion, and received baptism in an Anglican church. She then returned to Virginia, where she died soon thereafter. Her descendants are now numbered among the most distinguished families of the country.

The commander of the colony did not fail to notice the pleasure the Indians had taken in seeing an Englishman marry an Indian, and urged several of the colonists to contract marriages of this type. The Indians, after the re-establishment of the peace, came with their daughters and offered them as wives to the colonists; but none of the latter wished very much to be associated with the Indians, and the former concluded, naturally, that these foreigners were scornful of them and disliked them.

In 1620, the second North American English colony was founded in the lands known today as Massachusetts. When the colonists arrived there, they dispatched some of their companions to discover a favourable place for the foundation of their colony. They had proceeded only a short distance when they met a horde of savages; the appearance of the Europeans frightened them so that they quickly withdrew and did not reappear among the colonists. The colonists found some baskets of corn, which they took, in order to sow in the spring. After much searching, they found a place that appeared favourable as a base of settlement; there, they began to build a town which they called Plymouth.

Although the Indians never made excursions out from their new places of residence, the colonists remained in continual fear of their savage neighbours. To remove themselves from that disagreeable situation, they sought to make a treaty of alliance with the Indians, and the parties finally came together in the month of March, 1621.

Samoset, one of the local chiefs, provided the occasion on which to conclude this treaty.[16] One day, he came from the interior of the country and after a journey of five days, came to Plymouth; upon his arrival there, he shouted to the colonists, in English, "Welcome, English! Welcome, English!" They were not a little astonished by this friendly salutation from the savage, and hearing it expressed in the English language. He stated that he had lived for some time on the coast with English fishermen, and that he had learned some of their language. He then added that the place where they were settled had formerly been populated by Indians, but that five years ago a terrible plague had raged among them, such that not a single man, woman or child, had escaped the havoc.

The colonists treated this Indian, so well disposed in their favour, with much respect, and sought to attach him to their party for greater advantage. They quite succeeded in this. He came back to see them often and one day brought with him their Supreme Chief or King, Massasoit.[17] The latter, however, did not dare to enter colonial settlements again and stopped some distance away with his elite guard of sixty Indians. The English, on their side, did not have complete confidence in this savage. A reciprocal distrust kept them at a distance for some time. Finally, the colonists sent an Indian to Massasoit, one who was known to him, to ensure him of their friendship. Massasoit sent him back, informing them that he desired to speak to an Englishman of the colony. The colonists sent one of their principals, authorizing him to take to Massasoit a rich store of presents. He accepted these presents from the English with friendship and placed them in the hands of his guard and presented himself in the colonial town. He was received with the greatest honour and with testimonials of friendship, and they concluded a treaty with him that lasted for more than fifty years.[18]

The colonists at Jamestown, Virginia were not so well pleased. The settlers were multiplying in number and continually spreading out across the country. Their greater numbers rendered them secure: suspecting no danger, they did not dream of watching the movements of the Indians, and although surrounded by a people whose experience had made them familiar with the spirit of malice and revenge, they neglected all precautions which prudence and foresight prescribed to a people in their position. The Indians who served them as hunters, meanwhile, had obtained firearms and were not long in putting them to their own purposes. The confidence they were granted was such that they were allowed to come and go to the settlements at all hours. This gave certain treacherous Indians the idea of forming a well-designed plan, the execution of which would result in annihilation of the colonists.

Unfortunately for the latter, the Indians also had a chief capable of driving such a destructive project with address and consummate skill. This chief was Opechankanow, successor to the dangerous Powhatan, who had died in 1618.[19] Opechankanow had all the necessary qualities to be a chief of the savages. He combined courage and strength with a large physique, prudence and consummate skill. He was, besides, a man with roots in a more civilized tribe from the south, without doubt from the empire in Mexico. He enjoyed a reputation among the Indians of Virginia such that all the different tribes of this state submitted without opposition to his command. English writers of that time also called him the Emperor of the Indians.

As soon as Opechankanow achieved supreme authority in Virginia, he resolved to bring about the destruction of all the English colonists of that state, as their presence represented not a small obstacle to his ambition.[20] Four years were spent in meditating upon the best ways of carrying out this murderous plan, and with so much caution and discretion that the colonists had not the slightest suspicion. All the Indian tribes that lived in the vicinity of the colonists became, little by little, accomplices to this bloody project, except for some tribes residing on the sea coast and who were entirely devoted to the English. It is remarkable that the proponents of this scheme were able to plan it so secretly and with such caution over four years, in a way that no individual of the peaceful tribes came to perceive the ways of the world.

For each tribe, he designated the place where it was to conduct its operations, because, as we have already mentioned, the colonists had spread across the country and possessed many villages and small towns.

The 22nd of March, 1622 was the day fixed for the execution of this barbarous action. On the morning of that day, each tribe resorted to its designated place. The colonists so little suspected the destruction that threatened them that on the morning of that sad day, all Indians who came to take up their positions were welcomed with the customary benevolence.

Noon was the designated hour for the start of this dark undertaking. Although the Indians did not have precision watches, they knew very well how to distinguish the height of the sun at midday. That day, those savages avid for murder observed the course of the sun with that impatience which passion always excites in its slaves as the crucial moment approaches; as soon as it had reached the middle of its course, they unleashed themselves from all sides upon the disarmed victims of their barbarity and killed, without distinction, all the English they could find. Several small villages of colonists were so destroyed that no individual escaped death. In one instance some three hundred and forty-seven men, women, and children received the death blow.

The destruction of the colonists would have been general had it not been for an Indian convert to the Anglican religion, one aware of the project and its time of execution, who warned the English, thereby saving Jamestown as well as several neighbouring villages; in these places, the colonists retreated from the armed murderers, and at the same time, the Indians, having made their preparations with such secrecy and skill, no longer demonstrated so much courage for the implementation of their plan, and took to flight before encountering serious resistance.[21]

The colonists who escaped this massacre all fled to Jamestown, where they thought only of taking revenge upon their enemies. History proves that they were very well able to imitate, and even surpass, the examples of treason, revenge and slaughter that the savages had bestowed upon them. They, in their turn, resolved to destroy the Virginia Indians to the extent possible. They enacted shooting regulations against them, as against wild animals, and when the former retired to the forests, the English, no longer able to pursue them, employed more imaginative ruses to draw them out. They promised them their friendship and a reconciliation of the past, and with such an apparent hypocrisy and lack of sincerity, that the Indians put aside all fear and returned to their residences. The English held out to the savages the opposite kind of consideration which the latter had extended to them. Just as the Indians lived with increased security, seeing that the

English now treated them with greater friendship than before, they were suddenly attacked from all sides, and all whom the English could get near, perished. They escaped in small numbers into the forests, where many of them died from hunger, so much so that several tribes disappeared entirely from the face of America.

In 1635, a new establishment was formed in that country that today bears the name of Connecticut. Soon, the neighbouring savages began to molest the colonists, fermenting all sorts of cruelties against those they found in isolated situations. Thus, one day they fell upon twelve English folk some distance from the colony, killed three, and watched the others escape. Another time, they attacked a group of colonists going to tend their fields, killed six men and three women, and took two girls and twenty horned beasts.

In 1637, two years after the founding of this colony, savages under the leadership of Chief Gassakos determined to extinguish at one blow this rapidly developing community.[22] They gathered in a camp of sixty lodges which they surrounded with several ranks of fences and which they turned into a kind of fortress. The colonists placed themselves in a state of defence, and although they numbered only ninety men, supported by seventy Indians who were attached to their settlement, they resolved to advance upon their enemies and to attack them in their trenches. On 26 May, 1637, they approached the Indian fortress during the night. They advanced with great stealth, under orders from Captain Mason, hoping to surprise their enemies, when a dog gave a bark so loud that the Indians arose frightened and shouting, "Owanoks! Owanoks! English! English!"[23] Instantly, all the Indians were under arms and defending their fortress with such courage that the English, instead of rushing them, sensed that they were themselves in danger of being crushed by their numbers. In this moment of perplexity, the besiegers discovered a passage that took them through the fences into the fortress, and they set the Indian lodges on fire with brands.

A fierce wind immediately spread flames everywhere. A terrible spectacle ensued in which seventy Indian lodges, wherein women and children were hiding, were set afire, the miserable inhabitants falling prey to the flames. Those who sought to escape from their huts were annihilated without distinction by the English, who in this circumstance surpassed the savages in their inhumanity. Most of the men became undone in witnessing this atrocious scene, hearing the shouts and horrible wailings of their women and children being devoured by flames, or from their falling under the blows of their enemies; only a small number of them were able to effect an escape.

The English, gaining this advantage, pursued their purpose. When they reached their enemies, a sustained combat commenced. The Indians, whose rage was stretched to the breaking point, defended themselves with fury. But as their arms were so inferior, they could not hold out against the colonial regulars, and were so mauled by them that, of the several tribes, there remained only two hundred individuals who surrendered to the English and sued for peace. These then resettled among other tribes and with their friends.[24]

After this bloody encounter, the colonists enjoyed a long period of repose with their savage neighbours. To achieve yet greater tranquility, all of the North American English colonies sought to enter into a treaty of alliance. The leaders of the colonies worked for three years establishing the basis of this arrangement; finally, an agreement was achieved, and the treaty was signed on 16 May, 1643. According to this treaty, the colonies were committed to reciprocally provide troops, arms and provisions, in cases where Indians moved to attack any part of the allied territory of the colonies.[25] When this news came to the attention of the Indians, they saw that they had little to mount against the English, and several of their chiefs came to ask for the friendship of the colonists.

The peace and security that the colonists had assured for themselves by this alliance, lasted without interruption for more than thirty years. For all that, the Indians did not cease to detest them, and to wish for their entire extirpation, but they felt too weak to attack, for they saw too well that their efforts had been useless against the separate colonies, and that they could now anticipate little success, since they would encounter a united force.

They did see, however, with the greatest displeasure, the daily spread and strengthening of the English, who were expelling them increasingly from the interior of the country; they saw a reduction in their hunting grounds and their fisheries, the main sources of their subsistence, and this was becoming more worrisome with the rapid increase in English population; they saw their natural liberty, to which they were accustomed, continuously restricted by the neighbouring enemy which was engulfing them. And what was more disturbing was the natural conclusion to be drawn: that this distressing situation would only continue for some time. All of this was disconcerting and becoming unbearable to the proud descendants of the ancient masters of the country.[26]

As each tribe, taken separately, was too weak to attack the colonists, they entered into alliance, according to the example provided by their enemies, having in mind the project of destroying the common threat by gathering their forces together. This alliance was fully concluded in 1675.

The main author of this union was a powerful and distinguished Indian Chief, the son and successor of Massasoit. His Indian name was not known. The English called him King Philip.[27] He was a man of great natural gifts and qualities, having the strength required to lead the savages. Prudence and personal skill were combined in him with a natural and forceful eloquence.

After having long stirred up the minds of the Indians against the English, and having drawn into his alliance, little by little, nearly all of the neighbouring tribes in the colonies, he was not unhappy to find an opportunity to initiate open hostilities at his pleasure. He gave three of his subjects an order to kill one of the Englishman whom they often visited. Some time later, these three murderers fell into the hands of the colonists and were executed. The savages used this incident to excite in their subjects a thirst for revenge and an irreconcilable hatred against the English. The firsts hostilities began on June 24, 1675. On a Sunday, the Indians encountered a large number of Plymouth colonists returning from church. They attacked and killed nine, but the others took flight and were saved.[28]

All those colonists in the state who bore arms quickly gathered, and on the 28th of the same month they initiated a campaign against King Philip under the leadership of Captain Hutchinson.[29] The Indians, unaccustomed to finding themselves confronted by such a large force, retreated in an effective manner by putting all English houses in their path to the torch, and by massacring their defenceless inhabitants.

On the 17th of July, the English appeared where Philip was camped with his warriors in the great marshy Forest of Pokasset. They hastened to one side and attacked the enemy very sharply. The Indians retreated to the interior of the marsh and defended themselves quite well, as the troops could only manoeuvre with difficulty in the forest marsh, while the more lightly equipped Indians could not have found a more favourable battlefield. Towards the evening, the Indians withdrew further into the marsh, the English having attacked them during the day with little effect and having sustained considerable losses.

Seeing that it would be impossible to crush their enemies, the English adopted a plan to block them and to starve them out. King Philip soon discovered the intentions of the English troops and quickly retreated with his warriors. He departed for the area that today forms the state of Massachusetts, where he demonstrated the skill necessary to persuade other Indian tribes to enter into his alliance.

The English General then sent a deputation to the king of the savages to negotiate a peace. But these envoys were received in a way deserving of enemies, which is to say, by a rain of arrows. Eight of them fell dead on the spot, and eight others were mortally wounded; the small remaining number made their escape. But this was not enough for the savages; they wished to destroy the entire deputation. They pursued the runaways, who had been fortunate enough to gain refuge in a nearby English village. The frightened town residents retreated in great haste to a large fortified house that they forcefully barricaded. The savages arrived in the village and ravaged it completely, encountering no obstacles. The sole and weak resistance offered came from the windows of the house where the colonists were sheltered. The savages put all of their effort into setting the house on fire; but they did not dare approach too closely. They launched brands and blazing arrows towards the roof, and for two days and nights they exhausted all of the methods at hand. Finally, they obtained a wagon found in the village, filled it with flammable materials, and after having set it on fire, pushed it towards the house with the aid of several poles attached to it. The fire then began to spread. Frightened screams arose while the savages surrounded the place and made ready their bows and arrows in order to shoot at the first to appear.

In this moment of terrible and imminent danger, they could no longer count on human assistance; Providence came to the aid of these miserable colonists. A drenching rain began to fall, such that the fire was soon extinguished. The savages did not abandon their cruel intentions until a company of English soldiers suddenly arrived and attacked, and then allowed them to escape after having killed a large number.

In September, savages ravaged and burned a great number of villages in the country that today forms the state of Connecticut. Many colonists perished in these fires. On the 18th of September, Captain Lathrop, having led eighty men and a convoy of several loaded wagons of wheat to the inhabitants of a decimated village, was attacked upon his return by eight hundred Indians, who killed him and seventy men, and they would have killed them all if Captain Mosely, in the vicinity with an English force, had not quickly arrived, attracted by the noise of the muskets. His soldiers were not numerous, but they were so aggressive that they soon put the Indians to flight after having dispatched ninety warriors and wounding forty others.[30]

In October, the army of King Philip received powerful reinforcements through the arrival of another tribe, come to join him. Philip then sent three hundred of his warriors to Springfield, one of the more important colonial towns, in order to set it aflame. Under the cover of night, they slipped into the town with torches and set fires at different spots. But they were soon discovered: the English took up arms, and that same night British troops arrived in the town, which they secured and preserved from destruction. Thirty-two houses, however, fell prey to the flames before the fires were extinguished.

King Philip and his wild hordes then ranged widely over the country, killing and ravaging wherever they were able. Before long they had attacked, pillaged and partly burned nine towns, and destroyed a great number of defenceless inhabitants who had been taken by surprise.[31]

It is true that the Indians treated the English with barbarity, but it is also true that English sustained the Indians in their rage by their previous treatment of them, which the Indians considered to be quite atrocious. To illustrate, one day some Englishmen heard the story that Indian children could swim naturally by instinct. To convince others, these men went and overturned a boat in which the wife of an Indian chief was crossing a deep river with one of her children. They attempted to save them both, it is true, but the child died shortly thereafter, and the chief, avid with rage and anxious for revenge against the colonists, fanned those sentiments to a flame in all of his subjects.[32]

The English now resolved to engage their enemy in a decisive combat. On the 19th of December, 1675, Governor Winslow of Plymouth, at the head of eighteen hundred regular troops, and one hundred and sixty Indians who had come into service, marched to Virginia against the far more numerous forces of King Philip, camped not far from an Indian fortress.[33] This stronghold was constructed on a hill in the middle of a marsh, and was surrounded by a double walled enclosure. The exterior of this enclosure was formed by a hedge of thorns, branches and trees, approximately sixteen feet thick and which rose to a very great height; high, thick fences defined the inner enclosure. The savages had been at great pains to construct this fortress, but had imprudently left in the enclosure a passage way which was easy enough to discern. The English were not slow to discover this passage and rushed into the fortress in a torrent. A bloody combat began, but as the English could not penetrate all at once, the first to enter were soon overwhelmed by the greater numbers; others began to retreat, when suddenly the English found a passage on the opposite side through which the Indians were able to pass.

All the English soldiers then broke into the fortress, and a terrible massacre began. At the same time, the English put the Indian lodges in the fortress to the torch, causing here in Virginia the same fearsome spectacle that in 1637 had been imposed on Connecticut, with this difference, that the current scene was even more terrible. Six hundred Indian lodges were put in flame; shouts of distress from miserable women, invalids and the elderly rang out from under the ruins of the huts, mixing with those of the wounded and dying warriors, painting the saddest picture yet offered to us in the history of these peoples. It is painful to have to cite such horrors induced by a civilized nation.

The number of Indians who withdrew into the fortress rose to approximately four thousand. Seven hundred warriors were killed, without counting the three hundred wounded who died shortly thereafter; three hundred were taken captive along with an almost equal number of women and children. This ignores the many who perished in the fires. As for those who were fortunate enough to escape from the fortress, they sought their salvation in flight. Among them was found King Philip. The English lost but ninety men, mortally wounded. One hundred and fifty of them received lighter injuries.

This defeat of the Indians was decisive. They did not, in fact, cease all hostile acts, but they could no longer initiate important undertakings; it was not just that they were almost entirely annihilated, but also that they now knew and feared the courage, resilience and the superiority of the English in war, so much so that they consequently despaired of conquering them or of ambushing them in the countryside; on the contrary, they saw them increasing and strengthened by new arrivals in the colonies. The Indians no longer dared to attack the enemy openly, but made frequent surprise attacks against villages and small, defenceless towns upon which they inflicted the most atrocious cruelties. During the winter of 1675 and 1676, they killed, pillaged and ravaged all who fell into their hands. Twelve towns and villages of colonists were attacked by savages and partly destroyed, some from top to bottom, and the greater part of their inhabitants perished, being cruelly massacred.

In the spring of the year 1676, Captain Piercy, at the head of a force of fifty Englishmen and twenty Indians in their service, were attacked by their enemies; all fifty Englishmen and the greater portion of the Indians were killed; some of the latter were able to make an escape.[34] In the month of April of the same year Captain Wadsworth, marching at the head of fifty men, suddenly found himself surrounded by Indians. He, with all his soldiers, were killed on the spot, or taken to die by fire, following a horrible martyrdom.[35]

The winter and the spring proved favourable for these Indians who had endured much cruelty from the colonists. But the following summer saw an end of this terrible war, with the death of the vindictive King Philip. In order to strengthen his troops, this perverse man had taken urgent steps to engage against the English an Indian tribe which had not yet moved against them, and to bring it in line with his stated ends. He secretly brought about the death of several Indians of this tribe, and blamed these murders on the English. The truth was soon known, however, and he was obliged to escape with such of those Indians who consented to remain attached to him.

As soon as the English learned where he had fled, a body of elite soldiers was dispatched to put an end to his life, if possible, and to his crimes. Philip was, according to the custom of the Indian warriors, hidden with his people in a marsh. The English arrived at the marsh during the night, and not wishing to advance further, they surrounded it and waited for sunrise. Philip soon learned of the imminent danger and, without flinching, moved all of his forces to a spot he thought safe from the English. But an Englishman and an Indian were hidden there, and when Philip approached, the Englishman relaxed his guard: his musket misfired; the Indian opened fire as well, and his ball pierced the heart of King Philip.

When the savages saw that their king was dead, they all took to flight. The commander of the English troops then gave the order to his Indians (more deserving of King Philip, had he been the victor, than by an officer of the regulars) to cut off the head of the Indian Chief and then draw and quarter him. The Indian who received this order then advanced and addressed this speech to the corpse: "You have been a very great man, and you have made the world tremble before you, but however great you have been, I do not hesitate now to cut you into pieces."

So perished an Indian hero, one who had been endowed with extraordinary valour and with those rare and natural qualities that make a great general. The advantages of a well-directed military education, along with a great theatre for his exploits, caused his name to be celebrated in the larger world.[36]

In some provinces of the colonies, Indian hostilities continued, but now that they no longer had a chief and daily came to better understand the impossibility of struggling against such numerous troops of regulars, they started to come into the towns from all quarters in order to request that a peace be concluded with them.

From this time on, the Indians of North America were no longer a historical force in their country, and became a people without importance, whose role it was no longer necessary to mention in historical and geographical works except to speak of the singularity of their morals and customs.

When in the future the North American English Colonies found themselves at war with France, and later with Great Britain, the motherland, the two parties sought to employ Indians to strengthen their troops. But they played a secondary role in these wars, always being mixed in with regular troops, and under orders of their officers; the history of warfare never, in fact, mentions or speaks of their numbers. The circumstances of these conflicts do not pertain so much to the history of Indians, as to that of the English and their colonies in North America.[37]

As for wars between the Indians, these were not wars properly speaking, but excursions of murder and robbery, the relation of which can not follow a consistent course, as do the wars of civilized nations, but that which can be related, is drawn from accounts of some extraordinary events which one can call anecdotal history, the most remarkable of which are cited in this brief work. Since the death of King Philip, whose warring spirit and forceful eloquence had united the Indians, it has not been possible to identify an example of such a standing army in North America.[38]

What was their manner of waging war? When a tribe finds itself in conflict with one of its neighbouring tribes, usually there has occurred a murder or some breach of conduct concerning hunting rights; chiefs from different locales and tribesmen capable of bearing arms, convene at a spot where, after various ceremonies and war dances, they speak among themselves and then conduct a kind of council on the causes of the division which has arisen, and on the conduct to be adopted by the warriors. Each then returns to his community, where they convene in bands of ten, fifteen or twenty men, and these are then persuaded to go and annihilate a portion of the enemy. They depart for the territory of the hostile tribe, where they then attempt to surprise and to kill isolated individuals, families or small bands of the tribe. If they succeed, they return in great haste to their own country, in order not to expose themselves to attack or be vanquished by a larger party. Should they take an Indian of the enemy tribe captive, they take him in triumph to their country where they kill him, as we shall see later, by means of the most terrible tortures.

The various North American tribes enjoy little repose under these conditions, and their country remains an unceasing witness to atrocities of all kinds. This year, as I write these lines, the Ojibwa who reside in the interior of the country westward from Lake Superior were attacked by their neighbours, the Sioux. The hostilities had been caused by various encroachments by the Sioux Indians on Ojibwa hunting grounds, trespasses that were of the greatest prejudice to the latter with respect to the beaver-skin trade.[39]

Before ending this rapid sketch of North American Indian life I must make some observations on the diminution of the population of the Indians. It is a remarkable fact, however presented, that the number of Indians of North America has decreased by a great proportion since the establishment of the colonies in this country, and continues to decrease.

When the first European colonies were founded at Jamestown and Plymouth, there were approximately two million Indians in North America; and now in all the tribes one can count but three hundred and eighteen thousand. Some of these tribes are quite feeble and some are so weakened that they number but five or six hundred souls.[40]

There follows a list of the Indian tribes that are found today in North America, and the number of individuals that compose them, according to new statistics compiled with much care.[41] As the population on the coasts of North America expanded with the arrival of Europeans, the Indians were obliged to keep at a distance and they moved towards the interior of the country, and although the Europeans did not force them there directly, they were not often seen, owing to their need to live by the hunt in the forests, the one kind of life which they favoured.

In many parts of North America, where the initial arrival of colonists created a prosperous population, one no longer sees a single Indian. This is so for much of the east coast. The government of the United States has worked for a long time to remove the Indians from state spheres.

Serpens	27,000
Tschoktaw	20,000
Crik	20,000
Tcheroki	15,000
Blackfoot	15,000
Otchipew	8,000
Siou	15,000
Pauni	12,000
Assiniboy	8,000
Winibigo	6,000
Sac	6,000
Potewatami	5,000
Osages	5,000
Kriss	5,000
Krow	4,500
Manomini	4,200
Otawa	4,000
Arrilpaha	4,000
Seminol	4,000
Tschikaswa	3,600
Algonkin	3,000
36 small tribes count	41,600
Tribes of the West and the Northern groups	80,000
Total:	**318,900**

It is not only in times past that the North American Indians have decreased; it is an established fact that they are decreasing in a significant manner year by year. According to all probabilities, in a few centuries the history of these Indians will be that of a people that exist only in books.

In my opinion, these are the causes for the rapid diminution of the Indian population.

First, there exists a great difference between the country in which they resided before the arrival of Europeans, and that in which they reside today. Formerly, the greatest number of Indians lived in regions situated in south and eastern North America, and a very small number were dispersed in the arid areas of the north and the west. Regions to the south and east are extraordinarily fertile and enjoy a healthy and agreeable climate. These areas naturally attracted the Indians, and there they prospered. Furthermore, despite their extreme sluggishness, they never completely lacked for nourishment in these lands. Without agriculture, the earth would still provide all sorts of tuberous plants that they could eat. Forests and bushes were sources of savoury fruit, and on the edges of rivers, one could find an abundance of grapes, which in their native state, came to full maturity, as one still notices today.

The game was so abundant in these naturally fertile areas and in the immense sheltered forests that the Indian could, without difficulty, obtain provisions of meat; when he wished a change, it was to be found in the fine fish from the many rivers.

When one now compares the miserable position of the Indians in our day with the contentment enjoyed by their ancestors, it is easy to understand why their numbers have so declined, and decrease day by day. The impoverished Indian people, the ancient masters of this country, are now confined to the most inhospitable regions of the north, where, owing to their laziness and their natural indolence, and as a result of the poor quality of their lands and the rigor of the climate, they have descended into a miserable state of culture, barely sufficient to sustain life during some months of the year. The Ottawa tribe alone sustains agriculture of some importance, one whose products suffice to provide a living; these Indians find themselves, naturally, in a more favourable position, and are the most civilized of North America. But agriculture is practised very weakly by all the Indians of the north and west.[42]

Furthermore, the northern regions only produce native fruits, and the hunting there is far more time-consuming, and far less abundant, than in parts of the east and the south. I am often a witness to the misery of Indian life in the North. It is not at all rare among them, when they are unable to kill any game, to go three, four, or even ten days without food. In these cases of extreme famine, they sometimes resort to eating one another and feeding upon a host of things of an unhealthy nature. There are many Indians in the North who literally die of hunger, and that has been related to me by many eyewitnesses. One can therefore not doubt the miserable position in which the Indians find themselves, nor that it is one of the main causes of their continuing decrease. Another great cause of this decline, I am quite convinced, concerns the incredible quantity of brandy that culpable fur traders give to them and which the latter consume with zeal. This passion is widespread among the Indians without exception, because wherever they dwell there comes the fur trader to exchange his brandy for precious furs. Prior to the arrival of Europeans in this country, this poison was entirely unknown to them; but unhappily, today it is so widespread that there are regions where the Indians are in a perpetual state of drunkenness. When they are in this state, they commit a host of murders, and a murder among the savages usually entails much else; for it is the barbarian custom that the relatives of the victim will pursue the murderer until he has been given the death blow; and then the relatives of this man seek in turn to take revenge upon his death, and so it continues. A train of Indians lose their life in such drunkenness, by drowning in water, by fire, or by other accidents. And even if they do not die in this state of drunkenness, such excessive abuses brought on by pernicious drink does not fail to shorten their days, for the savages are different from civilized peoples who may drink from time to time and for some hours; for they continue to drink brandy ceaselessly, as long as they have it. And as they often buy entire casks from the fur traders, they may drink for four or five weeks, day and night, until the cask is empty. It is easy to conceive that such excess destroys even the strongest constitution, and one finds among the elderly only a few who are healthy.[43]

Indians who have converted to the Christian religion renounce entirely such drunkenness and observe temperance; all the more admirable, for the Indians before their conversion, almost without exception and particularly so the women, had an extraordinary propensity for this vice. These Indian converts could make those civilized peoples blush who attempt to convince the drunkard, without shame, that it is impossible to renounce the habit. How many Indian pagans have I not seen perish during their best years, victims of this unfortunate passion for drink. All wars that savages have made between themselves, before the arrival of Europeans, could certainly not destroy so many as this terrible poison.

The third cause of their decrease is, without doubt, the great number of epidemics that since the arrival of the Europeans have so terribly ravaged them. The malignant smallpox has, above all, depopulated a great number of their territories. Indians do not have the habit of taking precautions or of nursing themselves when they are sick; they expose themselves to humidity or to a cool temperature, and often take on a mortal sickness, indispositions that would present no danger for a civilized man familiar with nursing procedures.

I have heard from different Indian witnesses at Arbre Croche and in the country where I now reside, the relation of events many years ago when smallpox so terribly ravaged the Indians that it carried off in the space of a few months half of the population. They consider that in this period one could find entire villages where not a single resident had escaped death. This disease, just one of many others, was entirely unknown to the Indians before the arrival of Europeans.[44]

These are the obvious causes of the decrease of the Indian population; and as these causes still exist today, one can have no doubt that this decline will continue.

Manners and Customs

1

Manners and Customs
of the North American Indians:
Nature and Character

*T*HE INDIANS OF North America are in general well formed and of an average size. As in Europe, the people of the regions closer to the pole are smaller. It is very rare to meet among them men of notable obesity; during the entire time that I have spent in this country I recall encountering but two women who were somewhat corpulent.

The colour of the Indians is in general coppery, especially as men reach a mature age; that of the young people is of a less deep taint, and the children are born, in general, as white as in France or Germany; but it may be noticed that they have the habit of remaining bare headed and exposed to a fiery sun, which darkens them rapidly; particularly so when one adds to this the widespread custom of daubing the body with grease, and the passing of entire days in their huts around a fire in the midst of the thickest smoke.

They all have black hair, and I have not seen an example of a young Indian with blond hair. Accounts left by the first explorers to penetrate North America portraying the Indians as a naturally beardless people were erroneous; it is true that one does not see them fully bearded, but that is because the young men take the greatest care to pull out or to burn the first fuzz which covers their chins. They do this in order to be able more easily to paint the entire body.

The Indians are not content to pluck the beard; one sees many who extract the hair, little by little, so as to give a clean-shaven appearance; it is not uncommon to meet young people who are almost entirely bald. Old men who no longer have hair are given greater consideration than others, and one must confess, indeed, that this circumstance gives a great sense of dignity to meetings of the elders.

The manner of Indian walking is of a singular nature; their feet always following directly one ahead of the other, with the result that the path of an Indian traced on the snow presents only a single line; it is almost impossible for a European to walk on some of their paths.

Their senses are incomparably acute. Their sense of sight especially seems to be without limit; during my trips on the lakes, I have often had them point out to me individuals they recognize on the shore, while for me, even with the help of a telescope, I would not have even been able to assert that there was someone there. Not only do they notice a staggering number of distant objects, but neither does anything nearby escape their exceedingly acute attention.

One day, a European stole from the lodge of an Indian a piece of venison that the latter had hung there. On returning to his place, a quick glance was sufficient for the Indian to recognize the larceny and its author; he left hurriedly and gave chase to the thief. On the way, he met some traders whom he asked if they had passed a small, elderly European, accompanied by a small dog with a short tail; the former replied affirmatively and asked him to tell them how he had knowledge of all these details. "The thief is small," he replied, "because he was obliged to climb up on a block of wood to reach to the height of the piece of meat that he stole from me; he is European, for his tracks left on the sand do not admit of any doubt; he is old, the smallness of his steps and the numerous stops which he has been obliged to make, are the proof. He is followed by a small dog having a short tail, because it is easy to distinguish the places where it has stopped and relieved itself on the sand." Upon uttering these words, the Indian resumed his pursuit and soon caught up with the thief.

Indians convey an overall appearance of indolence and laziness; they often remain for weeks before the fire, smoking their pipes, until hunger forces them to seek food; but once outdoors, as will be seen later through a description of their hunting practices, they are tireless. However, they are in general far more agile than hardy. Their swiftness in running is prodigious; they may cover eighty to one hundred miles in a day, and do so for several days in a row. During the war between England and France, an Indian charged with an important mission and strongly pressed, covered in the space of two and a half days, running night and day, a distance of two hundred and eighty miles, that is, close to one hundred leagues.[45]

Indians have, above all, an admirable talent for orienting themselves during their long runs through the forests; when the sun is hidden, the incline of the crests and foliage of certain trees indicates north to them; even during the darkest night, their hand is still sufficient to discern the same indication by feeling the froth that develops on one of side of the trunk and upon the roots of certain trees and plants.

The North American Indians have an extraordinary capacity to endure insults; outwardly insensitive to all such outrages, they inwardly meditate upon ways to appease the furies of their vindictive impulses. Unhappy about what has offended them, months and entire years do not weaken the recollection of this insult; he will receive his enemy with the greatest signs of affection, but when the day of revenge comes, the enemy will fall pitilessly under his blows.

The Indians are very hospitable; hosting is a sacred thing among them, and the exercise of this virtue often establishes a rapport between families which extends from generation to generation.

During a long journey, an Indian exhausted by fatigue, hunger and thirst, came to pass close by the hut of a Canadian; to the former, who sat at his door, he prayed grant him a bit of food, and above all a little water to quench his thirst. The Canadian replied to him abruptly that he could not be at pains to amass provisions for barbarians. The Indian withdrew, saying nothing, and without too much trouble, was able to return to his home. Some time later, the Canadian, having gone hunting, lost his way in the forest. The day was already waning when, happily, he appeared before a lodge. It was that of the Indian he had formerly repulsed so thoroughly. He went and knocked at his door and asked that he point out the path to his house. The latter, whose perceptive eye immediately recognized the Canadian who had so blatantly ignored his request, assured him that he was still far away, that it would be impossible to return before nightfall, and that he would certainly become lost again in the forest. He promised at the same time to accompany him to his house the next day. The Canadian consented to remain, and his host served him as well as possible. The next day he accompanied him to his house. They were just on the point of arriving when the Indian stopped and was recognized by his companion. The Canadian, knowing the vindictive Indian character, was not just a little terrified; but the Indian, whose disposition in favour of hospitality rose above any propensity for revenge, said to him quietly, "Banish all fear, friend, I will not harm you; go in peace, and learn at least what the savages know about hospitality."

The sense of valour among the Indians has degenerated greatly in recent times. The Osages and those of the Sioux tribe are today the most warlike and the most courageous. There are some less warlike tribes that are remarkable for their good and peaceable character; the best are the Manominis, the Ottawas, and the Algonkins.

Dress of the Indians

2

Dress
of the
Indians

EFORE THE ARRIVAL of Europeans in North America, and for some time after their coming, the entire mode of dress of the Indians consisted of animal skins. When the English arrived in the country, they soon noted that the women dressed with much more care than did the men. The Indians would wear their clothes for a long time before changing them. As the Europeans gradually became accustomed to their manner of dress, they came to find their own mode of dress so impractical that, for day-to-day work, they incorporated some of their styles. They adapted animal skins against the rain that kept the outfit quite dry. When they went out to see other colonists, they did not fail to wear European garb, but they were in the habit of removing these again when they returned to their homes.

Today, the Indians of North America garb themselves with materials manufactured by the whites, brought in to the most distant northern regions by fur traders who, in exchange, receive very precious furs. The further one advances towards the north, the rarer becomes European dress among the Indians. There, they dress mainly with the skins of the beaver; it is the garb of both men and women. They also make covers for their bedding by stitching them together with the sinews of young deer. In summer, however, they dress with materials provided by the fur traders. But even when the Indians are dressed in white men's materials, they may be distinguished from all other civilized peoples by the design of their outfits. Indian women make all of their clothing, and those of their spouses, for among the Indians there are neither tailors nor shoemakers. They are very ingenious in the invention of all types of small, light-hearted ornamentation that they add to their outfits. Women also make the shoes for all of the family, and they make these alone, without the help of the men, who only dress the buffalo and deer skins which provide the material from which the shoes are made. It is true that skins tanned by the Indians are not so beautiful and flawless as those prepared by tanners in civilized countries; however, Europeans are always surprised by their first sight of a skin which has been tanned by Indians and in which the differences between that of a skin prepared by a skilled European worker are often imperceptible.

It is a curious thing to watch the preparations made by a sporting young Indian, especially when undertaken in a village other than his own. His shirt is mottled in lively colours. He wears over it a kind of scarlet spat, adorned with a multiplicity of small glass beads and ribbons of all colours which hang around the leg; this spat ascends until over the knee, around which are attached a small group of handbells destined to attract the attention of all who pass by this popinjay.[46] His shoes are covered with glass beads and by so many ribbons that one hardly can see the leather underneath; sometimes his outfit consists of a blue or red robe festooned in the most ridiculous manner with variegated ribbons and false braids. On top of it all he wears a red belt; on occasion, instead of clothing, he simply wears a red or blue robe over his shoulders. It is not rare to see suspended from each of his ears at least a half dozen large buckles of silver, a large silver ring in his nose, and two or three circles of silver around his arm.*

He places an otter skin on his head, or a large cloth of various colours, in the manner of a Turkish turban. He adds to it, with daubs of red green and yellow colours, figures of the most ghastly type.

Such is the toilet of a young Indian master who enjoys some measure of wealth, but vanity is far from being so common among the Indians as among the whites. The portrait that we have drawn of them here is rarely encountered: in general, Indians are dirty and quite slovenly in their habits. Often, when they put on a new shirt, they never take it off and wear it until it falls off in scraps: and then they go for a long time without a shirt, wearing only a robe of wool (a kind of hanging wardrobe). In summer, the shirt is often their single garment, and when they take their leave, they are content to attach this covering around their shoulders.

The Indians do not adopt a common hairstyle; they may put some plumes of various colours in their long, thick hair. The better dressed wear a high, cloth gaiter, or one made from an old blanket, but never pants, and an outfit also made from an old blanket which they press around the kidney area with the help of a leather belt. Their outfits are very dirty and full of vermin, and when nearby, one is struck by a disagreeable odour. They wash their shirts but rarely, and even more rarely their hands and face.

---

* The Indians pierce great holes in their ears such as can be easily penetrated with a finger.

It is necessary to notice, however, that what we have related applies only to the pagans. Once Christianized, they are observed to become attentive to cleanliness and tidiness of dress, in which they avoid flirtatious effects, for they are severely cautioned against them. As soon as an Indian who possesses silver earrings, nose rings or bracelets, embraces the Christian religion, he is obliged to exchange them immediately for more useful garb; he can no longer use body paint nor place feathers in his hair.

Pagans and Christians always carry a large bag of tobacco made with the skin of a domestic or wild cat, a young otter, or any other animal of this sort; they attach it to their belts, behind the back. They always carry a large sheathed knife suspended from their belts.

The Indian woman's mode of dress is no less singular than that of the men: they wear, as do the latter, various coloured shirts and a type of short garment which they wear around the body, almost similar to one worn by Europeans when they go to work. These clothes are made from a woollen cloth, or from various coloured materials. As with the men, they wear a high spat, which they adorn in a most remarkable manner; it is similar with their shoes. In winter, they wear a kind of woollen coat or an older cloak; they never wear anything on their heads, not even feathers in their hair; to this day, I have not seen a single Indian woman who has painted her face; one encounters this practice more often, and always among smaller groups, towards the western and northern coasts. When they are preparing to depart, they fix around their head a woollen scarf, and in this case not only in winter, but also in summer, when they suffer from heat. When coquettish women go out, they drape themselves gaily with a large blue or red fabric cloak.

I have frequently noticed that the limited vanity that prevails amongst the Indians is more noticeable in the men than in the women. Flirtatiousness in an Indian woman consists in wearing very fine cloth, and in attaching to her shoes, strands of glass-beaded ribbons. The women wear many earrings and sometimes bracelets, but never nose rings.

The colours with which men paint their face are strong and varied, and they purchase them from the fur traders. While they are in mourning or tormented by hunger, they paint themselves in black; when in joy, they treat of the entire face with a dye of vermilion, tracing black or deep brown lines here and there, sometimes adding yellow or black dots, all of which bestows upon them the most frightening aspect; they always carry a small round mirror in order to glance at themselves from time to time.

Heckewelder, a Hollander by origin, who has lived a long time among the North American Indians, recounts the following, heard from an Indian chief.[47] Having spent a day in the hut of this chief whom he was visiting, he found him occupied in pulling the few strands of beard that grew here and there on his chin. The Indian asserted that he was making these facial preparations because it was necessary if he was to be painted in the finest possible manner, in anticipation of the great Indian dance to which he was invited that evening. At this point, the European did not wish to disturb him in this important occupation, and he returned to his abode. The Indian did not delay in presenting himself at the home of the Hollander, in order to return his visit, so he said, but indeed, rather more to be admired by the European. The latter was surprised indeed to see three different faces that he had skilfully and carefully superimposed upon his face in different colours. He had, among other things, painted his nose in such a manner that when one looked at him directly in the face, one would say that he had a very long nose, quite gnarled, and ending in a large knot. One side of his body was painted in red, and the other in black, and the eyebrows were all different on one side from how they appeared from the other, with the result that when one looked at him directly, it was an entirely different man from the one looked at from the left: it was, he said, a masterpiece, and in it he could not have been prouder. He had taken a small mirror in which he viewed himself incessantly; he said finally to the Netherlander, "How do I look, my friend?"

The latter replied, "If you had made this work on a piece of birch bark, it would please me infinitely."

"It is not therefore to your taste, such as it is?" asked the Indian. "And why?"

"It is," replied the European, "that I am not able to recognize you in your triple face." Thereupon the Indian returned home, somewhat discontented.

There exists in this country another manner of preparation which one calls tattoo. This custom has in fact become less frequent than in earlier times, but one can still find its occurrence

In order to execute a tattoo, the Indians make a black powder from the bark of a certain tree which they have burned; they then attach several nails together in the form of a brush, and after having pierced the skin until some blood runs, they spread the powder over these lesions and leave them to dry, the residues of which become embedded in the skin. Before the arrival of Europeans in the North of America, the Indians used sharp stones or pointed fish teeth for tattooing.[48]

When they tattoo, they draw all kind of animals, birds or fish on their skin. In some Indian tribes, it is common to have a communal mark, the figure of an animal; all then wear the conventional sign.[49] Among the Indians, there are tattoo masters who often come from a great distance to tattoo a warrior or an illustrious chief. Years ago, there was an intrepid warrior Indian chief who was constantly warring with the neighbouring tribes, and he had received many injuries. He fetched a master tattooer and had him tattoo the most horrible designs around all of his scars in order to render them all the more visible. In addition, he had all of his body tattooed to such a degree that no place was exempt; his high deeds in combat with his enemies were drawn on his skin, with the result that he represented his biography.

Habitations and Food

3

Habitations
and Food of the
North American Indians

$\mathcal{T}$HE LODGES OF the Indians still take the same forms they had at the time of the arrival of Europeans in this region. The descriptions that the first English historians gave of the North American Indians are still quite accurate today.[50] It may be noted that Indian converts to Christianity, having adopted a regular and civilized way of life, build houses similar to those of the settled people of this region. But idolatrous Indians always construct small, quite miserable hovels in the manner of their ancestors.[51] They sink long, flexible poles into the ground in the shape of a circle which form arcs attached together at the peak. They then cover this weak structure with great mats of birch bark or with a kind of reed, or again, with skins of buffalo which they stretch around the poles. At the peak, they leave an opening that serves both as window and as chimney. They also leave on one side an opening through which they come and go. In the middle of the hut a large fire burns continuously, around which on mats or tree boughs, they sit and smoke tobacco. The smoke is often so thick in these poor huts that the people can hardly see.[52]

Indians never stay long in the same place. They establish themselves, according to the different seasons of the year, in different locations where they hope to find the best hunting and the most abundant fisheries.[53] When they travel from one place to another, they take all their wealth and all they own, and they pack it in a canoe with their hut, and depart for the place where they hope to find the means of subsistence. In winter, they load all onto a small travois, which they often harness to their dogs. Three or four families often reside in a small and miserable shelter, without counting a certain number of dogs that the Indians keep for the hunting of their food.

When the Indians note an enemy tribe in their vicinity, they gather together in large numbers and construct their lodges close to each other. Sometimes they surround their village with two or three fence rows, ten or twelve feet high, which makes for a good fortress. In the middle of such a fortified spot, there is always designated a central location for the great fire, around which they perform their war and sacred dances.

The furnishings of the Indians are rather meagre. They have neither chairs nor table in their huts; they sit and eat upon the ground. An Indian can remain a whole day sitting on the ground, something that would be a great affliction for a European accustomed to sitting in chairs. They do not have wooden beds, nor beds at all, for they always sleep on the bare ground or on mats, and cover themselves with but a single, often well-used, blanket, even during the depths of the winter. On the other hand, during the night they maintain large fires in their lodges, and whoever wakes up first, must attend the hearth.

In connection with furnishings, one finds a great difference between those of the Christians and those of the idolatrous. The cabins and dwellings of the Christians are almost of the same quality as the houses of the civilized inhabitants. One notices among them tables, chairs and beds. It is not uncommon, however, to see older Indians give up a convenient chair and go and sit on the ground, a place they favour owing to the habits of their childhood. They often do the same when they visit civilized dwellings. When offered a chair, they will accept it and sit down, but soon afterwards they give it up in order to sit on the floor. The vessels of the Indians are very simple: their plates, especially in the north, are commonly made of birch bark which they have stitched together with the help of delicate roots of certain plants, and which have been coated with pitch in order to render them waterproof. They also make dishes and spoons from wood, a type of work at which some Indians excel. Their battery of kitchenware consists of two white tin or cast-iron pots. Before the arrival of Europeans, their kitchen vessels were made from clay, as one may note from the fragments that one finds here and there in the crust of the earth. Northern Indians today still use cooking pots made from tree bark. In doing this, they heat stones and put them in the pot, and when the stones have cooled somewhat they remove them and replace them with other hot stones, repeating this operation until the water is boiling, and until the dishes they are preparing have risen to the desired degree of concoction. Several eye witnesses, long in the service of the northern fur-trade companies, have assured me that by this method the Indians prepare their food very quickly.

Before the arrival of Europeans in North America, the Indians did not have the use of iron; to make their vessels, they employed hard stone tools that they could sharpen so well that they were used to make their bows and arrows, and even to cut their hair. Today, as fur traders search out Indians in all quarters and conduct their trade for precious pelts by exchanging those articles most necessary for the convenience of life, all Indians possess those indispensable wares of iron such as the axe, the knife, scissors, the gun and other weapons.

The food used by Indians today is commonly what it was before the arrival of Europeans. As formerly, hunting and fishing provide their main sources of subsistence. Agriculture is much neglected by the Indians, with the exception of those who have been Christianized, and some families who have adopted a civilized way of life, and who are now often the owners of very extensive fields. Even before the arrival of Europeans, they undertook some cultivation. The history of the English colonies in North America suggests that upon their arrival, they noticed, more than once, Indian corn sown by Indians in their small fields.

Indian corn, the potato and the pumpkin are the principal, or rather unique, objects of their agriculture; and if one sometimes finds beans and peas in Indian fields, this is only by exception; but one never encounters wheat or rye or other cereals of this type; they are not yet so advanced.[54]

Their agricultural implements consist of a hoe, with the help of which they churn up a bit of soil and make small holes in which they put some grains of corn or small potatoes.

They have neither barns nor cellars in which to store their produce; the Indian women make bags with bark linings which they fill with their crops and which they then bury in the ground.

As they have no mills for grinding their corn, they crush it on tree trunks with the help of wood pestles. These pestles are today the same sort that they had at the time of the arrival of the Europeans and consequently conform to descriptions given by some of the first colonists; the manner in which they are made is still the same today. To this end, they take a piece of wood from a tree trunk, a bit over two feet long and a foot in diameter, and with the help of coals, which they take care to keep renewing, they burn a large, deep hole near one of the extremities. This is their pestle. They do not pound their corn several days in advance; they prepare only what is necessary for a meal; and when they are inclined to travel, they load the pestles in their canoes and take them with them.

Indians have no regular mealtime and they rarely eat together. In the morning, they will cook a pot full of pounded corn, fish, meat, or whatever one wishes, and set it in a place in the lodge designated for that purpose; then each takes as much as he pleases and when he so desires. They eat everything without salt.[55] One sees a few Indians who, after having lived among the whites, do make regular use of salt. A certain amount, also, is imported for them for their food when served hot or cold. Especially during their travels, one notices them swallowing hot vitals in a way that a European would not be able to tolerate; on the other hand, one often sees them, in the course of their navigation, taking their pot from the boat, and letting it trail in the current for their daily food, although it is often entirely covered in ice, especially in the cool mornings of the spring or at the end of autumn when frosts have already set in.

What an Indian is prepared to consume is remarkable; but it is also amazing how long he can go without nourishment, not suffering any great pain. To remain five, six, and even ten days without is not a rare occurrence.

I know a young Indian who, several years ago, became lost in the forest while travelling with his father. The latter went to great lengths to find him but this was in vain. Finally, he continued along his way and returned to his home. He recounted the misfortune that had befallen him, and several young Indians, along with their parents, resolved to take up the search for this unfortunate one. All the effort they expended over several days was equally useless. A few days later, the father of the young man went hunting and searched the country high and wide. One day, he came to the spot where he had lost his son, and he determined to at least find his remains in order to give him a proper burial, but instead he found the young man alive. He was sitting on the trunk of a tree and his gaze was fixed on the ground. They counted the days from the moment he was lost, and they concluded that he had been in the forest all of twenty days with almost no food.

Indians feed upon many things that are repugnant to the taste of civilized peoples. They eat not only dogs and cats, but also wolves and carrion. When they see a dead fish floating on the water or thrown up on the shore, they eat it without revulsion; it is similar for all dead animals that they find in the forest, some so decayed that they are already imparting an odour. I have seen thousands of examples during the mission trips I have undertaken, but on the whole, the Indian converts abstain from such practices.

Indians do not eat butter, milk, or cheese; one sees little of such which they consent to taste, even when it is offered to them.

One of the principal Indian food resources is the wild rice that they collect in autumn in such great quantities that they retain a store of it throughout the winter and even into the spring. It is found abundantly, especially at the edge of the rivers that flow into Lake Superior. It grows equally well on northern lakes and rivers. Wild rice greatly resembles oats, with this difference, that it is green instead of yellow, even when it has been dried. This rice is an excellent food, although quite delicate. I find that it somewhat resembles the taste of our barley.[56]

Hunting, as we have said, is one of the main means of subsistence for the Indians; in the interior they live only by the hunt; they are greatly impoverished, and are exposed to very cruel famines; it is not rare that they eat each other, or that a great number die of hunger. We will speak later of the hunting practices of the Indians.

Indians who reside on the shores of the North American Great Lakes live almost entirely by fisheries. These lakes are prodigiously stocked with fish. In Lake Superior there are places where, at certain times, two Indians fishing in a canoe for two or three hours in the morning take five hundred large fish; one of them directs the canoe, and the other stands in the bow with a net which he dips continuously into the water. He will maintain this as long as the fish continue to reward his effort.[57]

One must also note as an important Indian food resource, although only during limited times, the wild sugar which they produce from a sugar bush. For about two months in some areas, the Indians, especially the children, eat little but sugar and syrup. In my view, it would be impossible for a European unaccustomed to this sugar to consume it and no other food for a period of two or three weeks; for after a certain quantity is taken into the stomach, it produces an unbearable heat, and in the mouth it dries and clogs with an excessive bitterness. It is necessary therefore to be reared to it from childhood. However it has, when added to coffee and tea, the same taste as white sugar and is just as strong. As the Indians collect far more than they can consume during the time of the harvest, they sell the excess to the fur traders, who give them in return other provisions, or blankets, clothing, firearms and other objects of this sort. It is therefore with good reason that Indian sugar is counted among the principal food sources of the Indians.[58]

The Ottawa tribe, which is without doubt the hardest working, is also the one that harvests the most sugar. There are at Arbre Croche Indian families who harvest, in most years, close to two thousand pounds of sugar. The Ojibwa give themselves over to the harvest of the sugar crop; but the more one advances northward and towards the edges of the West, the less one encounters Indian sugar, since in some of these regions the sugar bush grows less abundantly, and therefore they do not go to much pain to harvest it.

Indians prepare their sugar in the two months of March and April. In the southern regions of North America, sugar time has already begun by the tenth or fifteenth of February, but it ceases earlier by the same proportion. Each Indian chooses a place where he wants to make his sugar; it is usually in the centre of a place where many sugar bushes are growing. He builds a hut approximately twenty feet long by fourteen wide. The lengthy portion remains constantly exposed to the air from one end to the other, in order to give passage to the smoke, since for almost the entire length of the hut a great fire is maintained day and night. At each extremity is found a door, and on one side are hung their blankets and all else they have, since at this time the hut also serves them as a habitation.

As soon as this hut is finished, other preparations are made; wood has to be gathered in advance, since in the making of sugar it is consumed in great quantities. Then they make barrels out of birch bark for use in gathering the juice from the sugar bush; they finish by carving notches in the trees, and in these notches they place small pieces of wood, the magnitude of a large knife blade, along the length of which the sugar sap flows into the barrels prepared for this purpose. In the smaller trees, one makes only a single notch, while in the larger ones, three or four may be made. In the spring, as soon as the soil and trees begin to germinate, the sap of the sugar trees starts to flow; sometimes it flows only drop by drop, sometimes it precipitates as a stream: usually it flows only during the day and but rarely at night; it never gushes excessively except when having been frozen during the night the sun warms it the following day. When it has been warm for several nights running, the sweet liquor ceases to flow until it freezes once again during the night.

When the barrels are entirely full, they are emptied into a huge vat or into a trough which the Indians make from immense tree trunks; it is then subjected to the action of fire in great pots which are lined up beside each other to the number of twelve, fifteen, and even twenty, until the aqueous parts have evaporated and there no longer remains in the pots anything but a thick, brown syrup. They then pour the syrup into a single pot where they boil it anew until it becomes close to a solid state. With the help of great, wooden spoons, they put it into large vases, also of wood, and they stir it until it has cooled and changed to a powder of a white-yellow hue, which is Indian sugar. It is then wrapped in large, birch-bark canisters which hold from fifty to one hundred pounds, and then covered.

The sap from the sugar bush is as clear as spring water and has an exceedingly agreeable taste. But the more one drinks, the thirstier one becomes. This sap ceases to flow on the fifteenth or twentieth of April, and the Indians then abandon their sugar huts.[59]

Some English authors have proposed that the North American Indians in general, and above all those of the most barbarous tribes, are cannibals, but on the contrary, they have the greatest abhorrence of human flesh.[60] What has no doubt given currency to this opinion, is that there are examples which demonstrate that Indians have sometimes partaken of human flesh; but this situation usually occurs only during the greatest famines and where the life of a man was sacrificed in order to save several others.[61] One could cite instances of the same nature among civilized peoples to which one would never imagine assigning the term "cannibalism."

A sad example of this type is presented here as occurred many years ago in North America. In the depth of a severe winter, an Indian undertook a long journey to visit her parents' community; the snow was already deep when she set out on her way, but nothing would divert her from continuing her senseless project. What was even more imprudent was that she had taken with her all three of her children. They suffered much during their walk through the deep snows, and became more miserable since they had taken but few provisions with them. They had walked for several days when a heavy snowfall made it impossible to continue. The woman then made a hut with branches of trees, lit a good fire in the centre, and resolved to wait there until a more favourable time, or at least until the snow was frozen and they could consequently continue their trip. They were very economical in order to save their limited provisions as much as possible, which they finally exhausted entirely. She was then obliged to cook the froth, roots, herbs and barks of trees to maintain herself and her children.

However miserable this nourishment was, it nevertheless would have sufficed to sustain their lives until the spring, except the snow resumed falling heavily and for so long that it rose to a depth of six feet. It became impossible to obtain enough subsistence in this way, and it became necessary to spend all of their time and energy in gathering the wood necessary to maintain their fire. Add to this that hungry wolves prowled night and day around their hut, and their terrible cries constantly kept her and the children in fear of being ravaged.

In this terrible position, she and her children having spent several days without food of any kind, and finding herself in clear danger of dying of hunger with them, she took the course of killing one of her children to save her life and that of the other two. After a long and terrible deliberation, she finally decided upon the smallest, and with shouts of desperation gave him the deathblow. She now had, in truth, a source of subsistence and could struggle once more for some time against the rigors of famine, in the hope of being saved by a change in the temperature, or by some Indian hunter who might come to pass by. But it also increased her danger from being devoured by the wolves. The latter were attracted once again and in greater numbers by the odour of roasted human flesh, and they descended upon the small hut with such rage that only by continuously hurling fire brands at them could they be prevented from entering.

The terrible lengths to which she had to go in order to survive increased her fatigue, and she found herself in a position rendered ever more dreadful by the growing rage of the wolves. She was already nursing the idea of executing her second child when suddenly a human voice rang in her ears. There were two Indians on snowshoes coming towards the hut. The joy with which she received them is impossible to describe. They hastened to make her a pair of snowshoes, and bore up in their arms the two children who were in a state of great deprivation, and in few days they arrived at the home of the woman's parents.

Today one still hears about similar situations in which Indians have found it necessary to kill and eat their own. But that does not mean that such actions to which they are pushed by famine are not undertaken with the greatest horror.

Travellers who come from the more northerly regions, after having spent several years there among the Indians, contend unanimously that even the barbarous peoples of the North look upon those of their comrades who have partaken of human flesh as branded. They contend also that an Indian who has once so eaten, is looked upon by others as a dangerous man whom it is necessary to defy, owing to his desire for more. It has even come to pass that such persons have been put to death for committing this crime.[62]

A learned traveller reported upon a horrible event of this type that took place on the north coast of lake Superior, where he had stopped for some time to go fishing during his North American trip. The group of fishermen was composed of Canadians and Indians. One day, an excited young Indian emerged from the forest and joined them. He reported that his family had remained back in the forest, because hunger had rendered them so weak that they found it impossible to continue to travel. The appearance of the young Indian was frightening, and his breath so repulsive that one could not remain close to him. The Indians soon began to suspect him of recently partaking of human flesh, and of having fed upon his family whom he stated he had left in the forest. The greatest agitation arose among the assembled; they began to press him with new questions and demanded to know of him if he had partaken of human flesh. He denied this to be the truth, but in such a manner that the suspicions of the fishermen only increased. The Indians resolved to assure themselves and retraced his tracks until the following day they arrived at the place where he had passed the night. There, they found the still fresh hand of a man, and a skull. They needed no other evidence: they returned to their camp, and showed him the miserable remains of his barbarous meal, and he was obliged to confess his guilt to these horrors.

He recounted how the family to which he belonged was composed of his uncle, his aunt and their four children. Of the four, one was a boy of fifteen years. He then told how his uncle, after having trailed several animals, but having failed, had lost all courage and that he had pleaded with his wife to kill him. She refused to do this, however, but the son and the nephew of this unfortunate man were unable to resist the hunger pangs devouring them, and they resolved to dispatch him. This they in fact did, and his body provided them with food for some time. After having eaten their father and uncle, they killed, one by one, the poor woman's children.

Finally, seeing that they were unable to find any wild animals, they adopted a plan to take what remained of the human flesh and depart for Lake Superior where they might count on making a fishery. They then took to the trail, abandoning the miserable woman, their mother and aunt, to their terrible fate, they who, in their exhaustion, were incapable of following them. The road was long; their provisions were soon exhausted, and hunger pressed them anew. The barbarous Indian then killed the sixteen-year-old, his only companion, and the hand and the skull which were found were the last remains of his body.

The Indians shuddered at hearing the account of this miserable one who sought to exonerate himself from the awful necessity to which he had been reduced, but they did not feel anything for him but the deepest horror. They resolved to put him to death; and one Indian, having slipped out to conceal himself behind the lodge where he had been resting, split his head with an axe.[63]

Arts

4

Arts
of the North
North American Indians

*B*EFORE EUROPEANS APPEARED in this country, the use of iron was unknown to the Indians, all of their implements, and even their arms, having been made with hard stone or with animal bones.

Their hatchet consisted of a long stone, sharpened on one side, and firmly fastened between two pieces of wood. They sharpened their arms with grinding stones found in great numbers in North America. These axes were, indeed, insufficient to cut trees, but they were quite capable of splitting dry fallen tree trunks. The more northerly Indians, rarely visited by the white man, still use axes of this kind. Their knives were also made from stone, as well as their fleshers and their lances.

Their science of these arts was very simple and but little advanced among the ancient Indians. One is surprised however, in seeing the results that they achieved when one considers the implements at hand. With their stone tools they made all types of small furniture, bows, arrows, snowshoes, sleds and even boats.

These boats of the ancient Indians consisted of a great dugout trunk of a tree, and were approximately twenty or thirty feet long and three wide. It was, assuredly, not an easy thing to construct such boats with these imperfect tools. If they were not able to completely sever a large tree trunk with a stone axe, they made a small fire around the trunk, taking care to prevent the tree from becoming completely engulfed in flame.* With the help of fire and the stone axe, and after much tedious work, they are able to dig out the tree; they then burn it anew at the two extremities, thus marking the length which they wish to make the boat. Then they raise the block slightly, beneath which they place pieces of wood, and began to gouge it out. This operation is again undertaken with the help of a small fire and stone axes.

---

* The ancient Indians did not know about the use of iron, nor consequently that steel served to make fire between a tender and hard piece of wood. The northern Indians make it this way still today, and eye witnesses assert that for them it is achieved instantly.

It is easy to imagine that a craft made in this manner is a crude production; but it was not less useful for all that. The Indians undertook very long journeys in these boats; they served equally well for fishing, except that they were smaller and lighter.

The modern Indians, especially those who reside on the shores of a great lake, and who are now in possession of all the necessary iron implements, make a kind of boat which, when seen for the first time, excites the imagination of the outsider. They are made of large, tough sheets of birch bark, sewn securely with strong bush roots: the stitches are coated with a pitch which renders them impenetrable to water; across the superior portion of the boat there are two, strong, light wood poles, to which are solidly attached sheets of bark. The interior is lined with sizable wood shavings as thick as a knife blade which are kept in place by large semicircles of light wood placed in a way that assures that the birch bark does not break when one enters the boat.

These boats fulfill their purposes perfectly. First, because one cannot avoid when travelling in the North America interior by boat having to cross portages from time to time, in order to get from one river to another, when the course ceases to be navigable, and to thus find a way to continue the trip by water. One may in this manner cover several hundred leagues continuously by water, with the exception of the portages, which are in general quite short, often only a quarter of a league. When the Indians or traders of the country come to one of these portages during their travels, they transport not only their goods, but the boat itself. These boats are so light that two Indians can easily carry one that is thirty feet long and five wide. A single man has no trouble in carrying a canoe of average magnitude, that is to say, twelve feet long by approximately three wide. In addition, these boats are able to carry greater cargoes than the heavy wooden boats used by the ancient Indians. A large birch-bark boat can support a weight of from forty to fifty quintals, the crew included.[64] When Indians want to load a boat heavily, they place along the bottom fifteen or twenty long sticks in order that the weight is spread more equally across all points.

Finally, Indians can travel much more rapidly in these light boats than in the heavy structures that served their ancestors. On the largest, a small pole is added with a sail, fifteen feet high and about twelve feet wide, and with this assistance they are able to make fifty or sixty miles per day when the wind is favourable. When a storm arises on these large lakes, such boats are far more secure than boats made from wood. Although these storms are of great violence on the vast Lake Michigan, and still more terrible on Lake Superior, there is no danger of perishing in a birch-bark boat when one knows how to direct it, and Indians excel in this art.

When they approach the shore, it is necessary to take the greatest care to ensure that the frail boat avoids being punctured by a stone. When the shore is rocky, they stop at a certain distance, jump into the water and unload the boat, without bringing it to the shore. When they have European passengers in the canoe, they carry them on their shoulders to the shore. When the unloading is finished, they then transport the boat by hand to the shore and carefully place it on the ground.

If, as a result of improvidence, the boat hits a stone, breaking the bark and allowing water to enter, they are forced then to hastily make for the shore and unload. They then light a fire to dry the damaged part of the boat, stitch over a new piece of birch bark (in the same manner that one makes a patch for an outfit), cover the sewing with pitch, and resume the voyage. The Indians, in addition, never undertake an extensive trip without taking along pitch and birch bark.

Indians of the Sioux tribe, and those who generally reside in regions where one encounters large numbers of buffalo, use the skins of these animals to make their boats. The form is almost the same as that of the birch-bark boats. The buffalo skin boats have the advantage of being less fragile than those made of bark.[65]

Another very ingenious invention, and a very important one to North American Indians, is the snowshoe, without which, especially in the north where the snow often rises to six or eight feet in depth, it would be impossible for them to sustain life, since hunting would be entirely closed off. Instead, with the help of their snowshoes, they are able to travel distances as easily and rapidly when the snow is eight feet high as when it is only half a foot. When the snow is somewhat crusty, the foot sinks only to the depth of two thumbs; and even when it falls freshly and that consequently one would not fail to sink to the ground, the snowshoes do not sink more deeply than three thumbs.

Indians travel very rapidly on these snowshoes; I have seen some who covered fifty miles in a day. To use them well, however, it is necessary to have been reared to them from childhood. A European who does not have the habit becomes extremely fatigued. The snowshoe, used by a man, is approximately four feet long and a foot wide at the centre. It consists of a strong circle of hard wood, in the interior of which one finds two strong struts fixed in the sides of the circle, and covered in total by the interlacing of sinews of hide. A snowshoe of this type is not only strong and light but allows the snow to fall off and easily pass through it, consequently not accumulating on the shoe. Bands of leather serve to attach the foot to the shoe, in a manner, however, that the heel is not constricted, and so that the toe of the foot acts upon the racket.[66]

Another invention, very useful although less ingenious, is what one calls the dog sled. These dog sleds consist of a light, large board, seven feet long and a foot wide. This board has a curved form, and into each side are sunk small batons designed to hold on the sled the goods being carried. These narrow sleds are durable and useful in country where it is necessary to travel continuously through forests in which no path has ever been cleared.

The Indians harness dogs to it. (Often they pull the sled themselves). One cannot believe what cargoes these small animals can transport on these sleds. It is not uncommon to see two large and strong individuals dragged with the greatest speed by only two dogs.

The Canadians who prosecute the fur trade make use of the dog sled even more than the Indians. A pair of strong, trained dogs can cover, with a man and considerable baggage, forty-five to fifty miles in a day. They can even cover this distance six or seven days running, of which I became convinced this winter when I received a message that had come one hundred and eighty miles in four days on a sled harnessed with two dogs, and these dogs appeared so little fatigued that he was still able to travel for a few more days with them. He returned, indeed, after only a one-day rest.

One encounters a large number of reindeer in North America, especially the more one advances towards the pole. Indians have not, however, made use of them in the same way as the Lapps, this animal which is so useful to those inhabitants to the north of our hemisphere. It is necessary to attribute the cause only to their laziness and to their indolence; because the whites there have often used them, and they know very well the quantities that can be transported by these other northern peoples.[67]

5

Hunting Practices
of the
North American Indians

*A*S HUNTING IS the main occupation, and in some tribes is still the only occupation, they are exposed to it from childhood. The ancient Indians generally had only the use of the bow and arrow with which to pursue game. As they had no knowledge of the use of iron, they attached to their arrows sharp, pointed stones; and as in North America one comes across many copper mines and finds quantities of virgin copper in the forests as well as on the banks of lakes and rivers, the ancient Indians also armed their arrows with points made of this metal.* Today, almost all Indians have the use of firearms. There are, however, still some Indians, mostly the smaller tribes in the North, which continue to employ the bow and arrow with the help of which they kill as much, and even more game than do the southern Indians with their guns. There is nothing so formidable as the power with which Indians shoot an arrow, and the skill with which they undertake their task.

It is quite a simple task, because Indians continually employ the bow and arrow. Hardly has a child learned to walk when his father makes him a small bow and several small arrows which the child soon tries to shoot; as he grows, he is given a larger bow, and it ends in his making his own bow and he is then trusted to possess a beautiful, strong bow with which

---

* Approximately two days travel from the mission of Saint Joseph, on the edge of Lake Superior, at a small river which flows into the lake, there has, since ancient times, been knowledge of a huge lode of most beautiful, virgin copper, thought to be without parallel. This lode is in the form of a lentil; it is approximately six feet in diameter, and its height at the centre is almost three feet. How has this huge mass arrived there? Nobody is certain. It was without doubt a volcanic explosion that threw it up onto the surface of the Earth. In 1826, the governor of Detroit sent two large merchant vessels with forty men to remove this piece of copper; they spent an entire day of fruitless effort to move this mass, and were obliged to abandon it to the glory of posterity.

he spends his days in the forests pursuing birds: he shoots a great many of these which serve as food for his parents, brothers and sisters.

Many years ago, a French missionary took a North American Indian with him to Europe. During his visit in France, he spent a day at the country estate of a rich proprietor. The latter was delighted to see an Indian with bow and arrows in hand. He had a certain number of peacocks that were widely distributed over his large estate. He urged the missionary to ask the Indian if he was able to hit one of these peacocks with an arrow. The Indian replied with a slight grin; he was surprised, no doubt, to be asked to do such a small thing. The proprietor then told him to shoot one of the peacocks. The Indian took his bow and the bird fell, pierced by an arrow. The proprietor saw fit to remark that this could only have been chance, and that the archer would not always be as fortunate. He therefore asked him again to shoot one of his arrows at a peacock. The Indian replied that it would be a pity to kill such beautiful birds uselessly. "Shoot away," said the Frenchman, "it may be that you will not hit him at all." The Indian released his arrow and the second peacock fell. The still incredulous proprietor again attributed this second kill to chance, and it was necessary for the Indian to shoot a third, in which he was not less fortunate, for the European to become fully convinced of his skill.

Indians are in general lazy; but when they go hunting it is astounding for a European, and quite remarkable to notice with what tireless zeal and speed they pursue a wild animal. But what is still more astonishing is the skill with which they detect tracks. Not only do they see them where a less trained eye would never suspect them, but they also follow them for days without losing them. Even in the darkest night when, for example, a wild animal comes to pass close by their lodge, they distinguish it immediately without seeing what kind it is. They have such a knack for noticing tracks and for recognizing the tread of an animal, that for them it is a quite simple matter, and that they find our inexperience in this as ridiculous as their skill to us, appears remarkable.

In the course of an obscure night some years ago, a European fired upon an Indian dog, and wounded it mortally, believing that it was a wolf. The dog dragged itself up close to the hut of its master who soon realized that the European had shot his dog. He was convinced that the foreigner had done it deliberately, and that he had thereby insulted the Indians. They went to him the following morning, assembled in a large number around him, and demanded an explanation of the outrage that he had inflicted upon them.

The European justified himself by saying that if he had shot the dog, it was because he had taken it for a wolf; because the night had been so sombre, it had been impossible for him to distinguish the object before him. The Indians asked him if the darkness of night had prevented him from noticing the difference that exists between the track of a dog and that of a wolf. The European replied that he had not noticed that, and added as well that he did not believe that there was anybody in the world capable of grasping this difference. At these words, a general laughter burst out among the Indians. They spoke with the deepest contempt of the inexperience of this white man, and allowed this miserable fool (as they called him), his liberty.

Indians are courageous and formidable, but at the same time, very prudent during hunting. They adopt this attitude to avoid being torn to pieces by the extremely ferocious great North American bears; yet it is rare for an Indian hunter to perish in this manner, because he always carries a great knife in his belt with which to defend himself if a wounded bear charges him.

Indians make use of all types of traps and pits to capture bears, deer, beavers, otters and other animals. The ancient Indians also trapped them; those used today are iron traps, which they buy from the white men.

Indians are very superstitious: there are some, for example, who believe that wild animals understand when words are addressed to them. Heckewelder, whom we have already quoted in the course of this work, recounts a very singular instance of an Indian hunter.[68] The former had shot a bear of a prodigious size and mortally wounded it. The bear was heard to give a plaintive groan and rolled to the ground. The Indian advanced towards it quietly and addressed it with this speech:

> Listen, my friend the bear, you are a coward without heart, and in no way a hero as other bears are recognized to be. If you were a hero, you would now show heroic courage instead of self pity, groaning like an old woman. You know, although your tribe is in a perpetual war with all Indian tribes, what we all have waiting for us as the lot of war. If you had hurt me, I would have suffered with firmness and courage, and in death I would be an intrepid warrior; but you, you lie down groaning, without thinking that your cowardice shames your tribe.

Heckewelder himself heard this singular speech, and after the Indian had given the bear the death blow, he approached him and asked him if he believed that the animal had understood him. "Without doubt," replied the Indian. "Did you not notice with what astonishment he looked at me, when I reproached him for his cowardice?"

In North America's virgin forests one finds trees of an extraordinary circumference; they often become hollow when they are old, and bears use some of them when they retire for the winter. When the Indians notice that a bear is located in a hollow tree, a number of them gather and cut all around the tree; but as they often have only very light axes, it is not easy for them to fell a large tree, for these trees, hollow at the top, are healthy near the roots.

An Englishman, long resident among the Indians, related the following story. He had lived for a long time in the lodges of the Ottawas. One winter, having gone into the forest, he saw a huge tree which attracted his attention; he came closer and noticed that the bark of the tree was heavily scratched; he also saw a cave on a certain height of land. He concluded that a bear was passing the winter in this tree. He then returned to the lodge where he lived and shared his discovery with the Indian family, and proposed that they go and fell the tree in order to kill the bear. At first, the people were little disposed to undertake this work, since according to the account of the Englishman, the tree was approximately twenty feet in circumference, and consequently, more than six feet in diameter, the axes of the Indians being small, approximately a pound and a half in weight. However, the prospect of finding a large, well-fattened bear in the tree encouraged them.

All of the family came the following morning, and, upon seeing the monstrous trunk, were a bit inclined to give up their enterprise. However, they decided to set to work; they laboured with ardour in as great a number as they could at one time, and when they tired, others replaced them. By the evening of the second day the tree finally fell.

All waited with close attention. The Englishman placed his gun close to the opening of the tree, and to their great happiness they saw a bear of extraordinary size come out. With his first shot the Englishman brought him to the ground. When the bear was dead, the old mother of this Indian family approached it and, with all sorts of grimaces, kissed it one hundred times and asked for a thousand pardons that they had come to disturb him and to take his life in his winter quarters. The bear was so large that it weighed five hundred pounds, and so fat that, in places, its grease was six thumbs deep.[69]

6

Hunting
Practices
(Sequel)

*B*ESIDES BEAR, WHICH is found in remarkable numbers in the immense North American forests, there are other animals hunted by the Indians: beaver, otter, porcupine, wildcat, wolf, deer, the stag, elk, reindeer, the great American elk, or moose, the buffalo and the wild bull, without mentioning the many small animals which the Indians trap rather than by shooting with guns.

The beaver, owing to its precious fur, is one of the main objects of the Indian hunt; they are found in great numbers in most northern regions. It has become quite rare in the central parts of North America. Every year, Indians take a considerable quantity, however, but one no longer sees very many in the central or coastal regions of the south.

The beaver has extraordinarily delicate senses, and Indians are obliged to take the greatest precautions in trapping or shooting them. All the world knows that this animal builds a lodge in which it resides; it establishes this habitation against the edge of a river or a small lake and it leaves but a single opening on the side facing the water. When it hears the slightest murmur in the vicinity, it dives into the water to the bottom and swims towards the opposite bank, or to any other distant place, where it remains hidden until the danger is past. When a beaver takes flight, it makes a loud noise that sounds the alarm, signalling his neighbours to take flight.

The Indians work hard at trapping the beaver rather than shooting them. Most Indians today use iron traps with a bait treated with Water of Cologne, or any other odorous water, which helps attract the beaver from afar.

When the edges of rivers and lakes frequented by beaver are frozen, they gnaw a hole in the ice, through which they may flee in the case of danger. The Indians attend to several holes in the same stretch of ice at a certain distance from the beaver houses. They withdraw then, and after giving them time to return to their lodges, they approach on foot; the beavers flee again under the ice while Indians wait with their clubs beside the openings. As the beaver cannot remain for long underwater, it soon surfaces for air; but when it does it receives a blow from an Indian, which kills it instantly.

After the beaver, the fur of the otter is that most sought after. The Indians hunt them very intently. It is hard to believe how resistant these animals can be. Indians claim that even the strongest man would not be able to kill an otter without the use of arms. A white man who has long lived among the Indians, heard this so stated one day and wished to convince himself by firsthand experience. He went forth to find a live otter and sought to kill it solely with his hands; he was cruel enough to try and suffocate and strangle the poor animal for an entire hour; but his efforts were useless, and he was obliged to concede that it was necessary to use arms to kill this animal.

The American porcupine is the size of an average dog, only it has very short legs. His quills are white and about three or four thumbs in length. Indians hunt them in great number, and without traps, because this animal is so extraordinarily lazy that when stalked it does not even seek to escape when it sees an enemy advancing. It remains in the same place for two or three whole weeks, and after having gnawed the herbs or the small plants found close by, it will often go several days without food before determining to seek it further afield. Sometimes, it climbs into the lowest branch of a tree and gnaws it until he falls with it to the ground. Indians have reported this as eye-witnesses; the laziness and the imbecility of this animal is thus proverbial with them. The flesh of the porcupine is very savoury; Indians notice, however, that those who partake often feel a great weariness in their limbs and a great propensity for sleep.

The Indians dye the quills various colours and make use of them in the ornamentation of their shoes or other different items.

An Indian dog never approaches a porcupine more than once; as soon as the latter sees a dog within reach, he trains his quills on its muzzle and even the eyes, leaving it in a miserable condition.

The wildcat is also an object of the Indian hunt. In general, it is excessively fat. Indians, as well as the whites who live among them, regard its flesh as very fine, and indeed, it has a very delicate taste.

Indians often hunt the wolf, and are very content when they have killed a few of them since these carnivorous animals do them harm by encroaching on their hunting grounds. It has already been mentioned that Indians eat wolf meat, not only when famine presses them, but whenever they can obtain it.

One encounters innumerable hordes of tawny beasts. The deer especially are in such great numbers across the continent of North America that in some regions, the Indians live almost exclusively upon them, and

Colour Plate 1 The young Frederic Baraga: a self-portrait, ca. 1826. Baraga had considerable talent as an artist but gave up his involvement as a matter of religious conviction by 1830. (BBA)

Colour Plate 2 Jean-Baptiste Assiginack (ca. 1768-1866). This influential Roman Catholic member of the Ottawa Nation was born at L'Arbre Croche (Harbor Springs), Michigan, but spent much of his life on Drummond and Manitoulin Islands. After 1831, at L'Arbre Croche, he became an important associate and friend of Baraga, serving both as translator and a lay clergyman. (Paul Kane ca. 1845; Royal Ontario Museum, 912.1.4)

Colour Plate 3   Mala Vas. The birthplace of Frederic Baraga in central Slovenia. (Photo: Dusan Jez, Ljubljana, 2001)

Colour Plate 4 The landscape around Metlika, Slovenia. Baraga served in this vicinity as a parish priest between 1828 and 1830. (Photo: Dusan Jez, Ljubljana, 2001)

Colour Plate 5 Birch bark vessel decorated with dyed porcupine quills, presented by Baraga to the Slovenian Museum in the late 1830s. (Ethnographic Museum Slovenski. Ljubljana, E-2886)

Colour Plate 6 Tobacco Pouch: woven wool and strings of white beads, presented by Baraga to the Slovenian Museum in the late 1830s. (Ethnographic Museum Slovenski. Ljubljana,   E-2868)

Colour Plate 7 Bishop Baraga's residence in Marquette. He lived here from 1866 until his death in 1868. Close to St. Peter's Church, it currently houses the archives of the Bishop Baraga Association, established in 1932 to promote the cause of Baraga's canonization. (Photo: Graham A. MacDonald, 1998)

Colour Plate 8 Memorial to Baraga in Dobrnic Church. (Photo: Dusan Jez, Ljubljana, 2001).

often they kill six or eight in a day. Among the northern and western Indians, who are still very primitive, it is common for them to drink the hot blood that issues from the mortal wound of a deer.

The Indians also go deer hunting during the night; in the better places, they may kill them far more effectively during the night than during the day, and the darker the night the better. Here is how they take them. After having prepared torches which burn slowly, producing a constant, clear light, they put two persons into a small boat, at the head of which they attach a torch; thick branches placed behind the torch serve to conceal one who is armed with a gun; the other places himself in the rear of the craft, which he directs with the greatest caution, and in complete silence. At night, the deer resort to certain spots on the edges of the rivers to cool down and search out lush pasture. The Indians post themselves at these places, and when they see a deer, they approach it in silence. The animal is happy to see the light and in its dazzle it does not see anything but the torch, and remains immobile in this satisfactory state until the Indian, coming closer, makes it pay severely for its pleasure.[70]

The moose is rare in North America, there are none but to the north; one encounters a few in the Michigan Territory.

The elk is much more numerous, especially in the western parts of this continent. One encounters entire herds of these beautiful and superb animals. The antlers of the elk are very long and have more points and are larger than those of the deer. This animal becomes dangerous when it is wounded. Indian hunters have, as a consequence, sustained accidents of the most serious nature.

They run with incredible speed, but not for a great length of time; old and modern voyageurs suggest that Indians urge the elk to run, not that they can equal it in speed, but because they can run further for a longer period, and then by shooting their arrows they bring them down. When an elk sees an Indian, it takes off with such speed that in the twinkling of an eye the hunter loses sight of it and remains behind it for several miles, and any European who has not witnessed it would not believe it possible for a man to follow the faint tracks of this animal. But the Indian continues at a fair pace until he comes upon it once again, some hours later. The elk resumes its flight and the Indian doubles his pace, catching up to it more promptly than the first time. The hunting continues thus during all day, until finally the miserable beast can no longer run as rapidly as the Indian who, coming close, dispatches it.

It is not the same in the hunting of reindeer, because this animal can run for a much longer time. It resides in the northern regions. In America, one does not find them below Lake Superior, but the more one advances to the north, the more numerous become the reindeer herds.[71] It is not rare to see over a thousand at one time. The North American Indians have never made use of the reindeer as do the Lapps, but they do take it to be one of the most important objects of the hunt, and in regions to the north, reindeer meat is the standard food of the people, and similarly, the skins serve for garments.[72]

Indians of the areas where reindeer are numerous know the habits of these animals through long experience. They know that in summer they migrate to the north, often as far as the edges of the Icy Sea; in autumn, one sees them re-descend to more southerly forests. The Indians have noticed that reindeer make this double migration regularly every year in great herds. They have noticed also, that during their journey these animals do not fail regularly to pass by certain places. The Indians then gather in large bands and wait for the animals at these locations, where they often execute a horrible slaughter.

Indians have invented all sorts of ways to kill large numbers of reindeer. When, for example, they have discovered a place where these animals customarily pass, they prepare a strong and high enclosed palisade of tree branches, through the middle of which runs the trail. These enclosures are very extensive and often they are two or three thousand feet around. The Indians take care to leave an opening to the enclosure. Along the two sides of the trail that leads to this opening, the Indians place branches of trees in the form of a corridor which widens as it moves out from the opening. In the interior of the corral they create small, strongly interlaced hedges and fences. When all is prepared, they retreat some distance to their huts and await their prey.

From there they can see when the reindeer, following their normal course, slowly begin to appear within the corridor that leads to the opening of the enclosure. The reindeer then move rapidly into the corridor that opens before them and they are guided hurriedly into the enclosure, where they hope to find sanctuary. The Indians enter rapidly and close off the entrance and prosecute the hunt within the enclosure, the reindeer falling en masse, hit by the bullets of the hunters, or becoming entangled in the laces. They are thus able to kill at once a large herd of these animals. An enclosure of this type is used for several hunts.[73]

The greatest of all the tawny beasts of this part of the world is, without doubt, the great American moose, or Original, whose size is larger than the greatest horse. The antlers alone may weigh over fifty pounds. It is also the most solitary animal, and most rapid in movement, and the most difficult to seek out. I have often heard Indians confess that there are few among them clever enough as hunters to kill one of these moose. Its vision, its hearing and its sense of smell are equally formidable, and more attuned than those any other animal of this region. When a slight wind blows up-wind of the hunter, he senses the enemy, well before the former has been able to see and hear him, and it escapes with the speed of lightning. The Indians, when they find tracks of a great moose, try to approach him from down wind.

The speed of the moose is quite remarkable. Although it is the fastest of all the animals of this region, it never gallops but always trots. Hunters are particularly able to kill it in places where the animal is accustomed to come to quench its daily thirst. When an Indian discovers one of these places, he hides as completely as possible and fires on the moose when it comes down to the water; but often the latter senses the presence of an enemy from afar and makes his escape.[74]

To the west and north of this continent, buffalos are the main object of the Indian hunt. There are in these areas such vast plains that, when at their centre, one sees nothing but grass and sky in all directions. The most perceptive eye can discern neither hills nor trees upon the horizon. Across these plains are spread innumerable herds, often composed of more than ten thousand buffalo. The Indians of these quarters dwell in the forests on the edge of the plains and hunt these animals, by which they live exclusively.

There are also in these regions other smaller prairies and grasslands where less numerous herds linger.

Indians of the western areas have horses, which they commonly ride without saddles. This serves very advantageously in the buffalo hunt since this animal, which is very heavy and runs quite rapidly, can not, however, match in speed the Indian horses, which have been trained deliberately for such hunting.

Buffalo often migrate in huge herds from one plain to another seeking good pasturage, and the Indians follow them. When these animals encounter a river, the entire herd crosses it by swimming and continues its course. During the winter, they usually dwell in forests in order to be less exposed to the winds of the plains, and because they also find there more abundant food. When they move during the winter and come to a river, they all want to cross the ice en masse; as well frozen as North American rivers become in winter, yet even the hardest cannot support the weight of one of these herds when it is too numerous; it usually breaks up, and the greater portion of the animals then perish.

It may be noticed that in such a trek, where whole herds of these heavy animals advance in tight columns, the first are obliged to move, willingly or unwillingly, especially when the herd is being pursued.

This circumstance is often a source of profit to the Indians when they pursue a herd of buffalo close to a place where one finds a precipice formed by a cliff. They then choose among themselves the best runners; these men wrap themselves in buffalo robes, complete with horns and ears, and so disguised, slip ahead of the herd to the edge of the precipice. The other Indians widely circle the herd, with the exception of that side where the men disguised as buffalo are located and, little by little, they approach them. When the buffalo begin to see the Indians, they become anxious and prepare to take flight. The disguised Indians then run in great haste towards the precipice while the others raise a terrible shouting, which totally terrifies the buffalo, such that the whole herd flees rapidly, following the direction of the disguised men preceding them and who they take for some of their own. When the Indians reach the cliff they hide in a crevice in the rocks that they had located in advance. The first buffalo arrive at the edge before which, greatly scared, they retreat; but they are no longer able to stop. The great mass that presses them from behind cause the first to fall over the precipice to a certain death. The barbarous savages thus often destroy, at their pleasure, an entire herd; but they do not consume but the hundredth part, and do not delay their departure in order to always have fresh meat.[75]

Indians of the west, as we have already said, hunt buffalo communally, while mounted on their horses. They make use of the bow and arrow, because they find it inconvenient to load a gun while on horseback. When they encounter a herd in the forest, they drive it slowly ahead of them towards the plain. They then ride into the middle of the herd, disperse it, and choose the largest to shoot with their arrows. They continue their pursuit until they exhaust their arrows. There are still today in the American northwest, archers who are strong enough to pierce one bull through another with one of their arrows.

When Indians are in search of a herd of buffalo, they often sleep on the ground in order to listen for them; and when a great herd is in the vicinity, they recognize its movements as far away as fifteen or twenty miles. An Englishman who has spent thirty years among the Indians states that having once gone with them on a buffalo hunt during the night, they had distinguished the sounds of a herd that was eighteen miles distant. The following day, they rode their sure horses in the direction from which they had heard the noise, and arrived on an immense plain that had the appearance of a sea. They were still ten miles away from the herd, but they could just see it as a long, black line on the horizon. These intrepid Indians, although not numerous, rode straight towards the herd, which they soon reached on their swift steeds: they killed a considerable number, and some just for pleasure, which they left where they lay and searched instead for calves, the flesh of which the Indians prefer in some seasons to that of the buffalo. One can say, without exaggeration, that the Indians kill more buffalo for pleasure than they consume for their food.[76]

Besides buffalo, one also finds in the virgin forests of North America wild bulls, but they are very rare. When an Indian has discovered the tracks of one of these animals, he always takes some companions with him, because a man alone would not be capable of killing this monstrous beast. An Indian of Arbre Croche, who has spent fifteen years of his life among the savage barbarians of the north, told me that Indians where he lived, one day killed a wild bull whose skin was so great that it covered all the ground in the hut where they lived. I concluded also that at the neck, it measured twelve feet long and eight feet wide.[77]

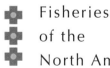

7

Fisheries
of the
North American Indians

*A*FTER HUNTING, FISH is one of the principal and most abundant resources in the life of the Indians. North America counts immense and numerous lakes, most filled with beautiful and very delicious fish. Indians residing on the edges of these lakes feed on nothing but fish. The implements which they use in prosecuting the fishery are spears, or small types of harpoon, hooks or nets. Earlier Indians, who did not know the use of iron, made their hooks with animal or fish bone. They prepared their nets with the delicate filaments from inner green tree bark from which they made plaits. The Indians to the north and west often still prepare their nets in this manner.[78] Today's Indians use iron lances and hooks obtained from the whites in trade, and their nets are manufactured from thread.

Lakeside Indians live by fish, winter through summer. When the lakes are frozen, they open up holes in the ice approximately a foot in diameter, and lie down by the side of the opening, holding their harpoon at the ready, and when a fish passes by, they spear it. These lakes are so rich in fish that an Indian commonly takes twelve or fifteen large fish per day. Sometimes it happens that they take thirty, fifty and even a hundred. I know an Indian on an island who, a few years ago, speared three hundred fish in a day. These fish are firm, large, and are a kind of pike; the smallest weigh from ten to twelve pounds, the greatest from twenty to thirty.

To better attract such preying fish, Indians make small wooden fish of some six to eight thumbs in length which they hollow out and in which they place some lead. They then attach these small fish to a strong cord, and sink them into the water through the opening made in the ice; they take care to pull the cord from time to time in order to keep the bait in continual motion. When a pike passes close by, it does not fail to go after the artificial fish; but the skilled Indian spears it before it has had time to realize its error.

They also tend their nets beneath the ice, thereby taking a great quantity of fish. These nets are, in general, three hundred and sixty feet long and five feet wide. It is not an easy thing to tend this huge net beneath the ice. I have been able to understand it well only after having been a witness to it. They first make a large opening in the ice, and then, in a straight line of some three hundred sixty feet, they open several smaller holes, approximately twelve feet apart. These holes serve to run a long cord under the ice, with the help of a pole, until the last opening is reached. There, one pulls out the pole attached to the cord. To this rope is attached one end of the net, the other end of which is attached to another rope held in the hands of an Indian standing at the first opening. They then carefully let the net slip into the water and it is pulled with the cord, little by little, by the Indian near the last opening until the net is positioned completely under the ice.

As fish do not, in general, swim near the surface of the water, the net is placed at a depth of ten to fifteen feet. In order to do this, the Indians attach to the lower extremity of the net, at specified intervals, small stones whose appropriate weight lowers the net, while to the upper portion, opposite to each of these stones, they fix pieces of light, dry wood that cause the net to rise and in consequence, remain taut. The two ropes are then fixed to poles placed at the openings at both ends. The stitches in the net are made such that an average sized fish can enter with its head as far as the gills, but without being able to withdraw. They tend their net until the evening, and pull it in again the following morning; they never fail to find ten, twenty, and even fifty fish.

Indians of the West know of a certain root which they pound after having dried it, and which they then dissolve in water. They then spread this over the water at a place in a lake or a river known to be rich in fish, and in few moments fish are suddenly made so dizzy that they ascend, as if dead, to the surface. The Indians then grab them with their hands, and throw them into their boats until they have sufficient; they leave the others in their giddiness, which wears off before very long.

Some small tribes of western Indians, residing on the shores of the Pacific Ocean, take whales with the help of great harpoons attached to long ropes. To these ropes the Indians attach, at regular intervals, twenty or thirty skins of dogfish inflated as bladders designed to slow down the wounded whale in its attempt to escape, and to prevent it from diving to the bottom.

A traveller has given some details on the intrepidity of west-coast Indians in the taking of a great prey fish. This fish lives in the sea and is very large and dangerous. During the summer, it remains near the coasts, between the rocks and from behind which it watches for its prey. When an

Indian goes in search of one of these fish, he takes a sheet of red cloth and swims underwater, until he comes across one of them. He then holds his red sheet ahead of him and the fish opens its jaws large enough to seize the prey that it believes it sees. But at the same time, the Indian sinks his arm into its muzzle, seizes it, and after a persistent struggle, drags it between the rocks onto the shore.[79]

At certain times of the year, some Indians also use small, round nets that are approximately five feet in diameter and three feet deep. With the help of these nets, they often take in some places and at some periods, several hundreds of fish, five to eight pounds, in the space of a few hours.[80]

Marriage and Education

8

Marriage and Education
of the Young Among the
North American Indians

*T*HE PRACTICES OF the Indians with respect to marriage, differ according to the various tribes. Usually, all matters are arranged by the parents of the two parties, and often the young couple is united, notwithstanding the lack of feeling which the two spouses may feel for each other. The wisest Indians, however, investigate the inclinations of their children before negotiating their union.

The mother of the young man usually makes the first enquiry. She goes to the lodge of the mother of the young woman to whom she has chosen to betroth to her son, taking with her a small present, usually a leg of deer or a slab of bear, which she gives to the mother, taking care to draw expressly to her attention that it was her son who killed the animal. The mother of the young woman understands immediately what she is called upon to say; and if the young man pleases her, she prepares a dish from produce of the fields (for as we have already stated, agriculture was left to the women and the girls) and brings it to the mother of the young man, making her understand that it was her daughter who harvested it from her field. All of this indicated that on one side, the young man was a good hunter and would always provide his woman with sufficient provisions of game; and that on the other side, the young woman would tend to the fields, and would not fail to provide her husband with the earth's produce.

Thus was prepared the contract of marriage, without a single word about marriage being spoken; for among those Indians where this custom is practised, the mere exchange of presents signifies formal consent. In the case of a refusal, it is true that the mother of the young woman accepts the present, but by not giving anything in return she ceases the diplomacy of negotiation.

If the youth no longer has a mother, she is replaced by the father or by one of the parents of close relatives. There is a mutual exchange of other small presents, and the marriage is concluded without ceremony. The young man takes his bride to his lodge or goes to reside in hers.

In some tribes, it never transpires that a young man, by himself, chooses or requests a young girl in marriage; he depends entirely for that on his parents, his close relatives or those of his betrothed. In others, on the contrary, it happens from time to time, usually exceptionally, that a young man seeks a woman on his own. In this case, the young Indian declares, in concise terms, his intentions to the girl. When she gives her consent, and if there is no opposition on the part of the parents of the two parties, she removes immediately to his lodge and becomes his woman, without any other procedure. But if she refuses, it will only rarely happen that the Indian will make a second request.

In some other tribes, it is the custom that a young Indian, after having chosen a betrothed, goes to her tent and sits on the ground next to her. The young girl knows immediately what is implied. If she accepts, she remains quietly seated; the young man knows that his request is accepted, and the marriage is concluded. But if she does not wish to marry the young man, she rises quietly, goes to sit in another spot, or goes out of the lodge. The young Indian understands this gesture very well and no longer returns to sit by her side.[81]

All North American Indians are in the habit of mutually presenting small gifts after having concluded a marriage. In case of rupture, the presents are returned, and when one of them has already been used, it is necessary to replace them by others of similar quality.

There are tribes where the Indians are in the habit of asking for the agreement of the chief of the tribe, without the consent of whom, the marriage is null.

Among some peoples of the north, the young Indian always goes to the house of the betrothed and lives with her parents and relatives who continue, however, to treat him in all respects as an outsider, until such time as the girl delivers her first child. Only then is he admitted to the family and recognized as one of its members.

Marriage among the North American Indians is no more than the temporary and voluntary union of a man and woman. As soon as this type of life pales upon one of them, he goes and returns to his parents or relatives and resides with them, or departs to remarry elsewhere. In truth, in some tribes many considered it shameful if a man abandoned a woman, or if a woman removed herself from her husband; but one must grant, however, that neither one nor the other had the right to force a spouse to return to continue a common life. When an Indian marries, he is not committed to remain all his life beside the woman, even though when he makes the commitment he looks at it as such.

The Indians of all tribes, despite some differences found between them in language and other customs, are all in agreement on this point, and hold firmly to this practice, some representations of which whites have been able to adopt in this respect.[82]

An Englishman who has spent much of his life among the Indians, one day offered some observations to them on the excessive liberty which reigned among them in their marriages. An aged Indian replied to him as follows:

> You whites are in the habit of courting a young woman for a year or even for several, before obtaining her in marriage; and when once you have her, and you finally notice that she is a wicked woman who nags and torments you from morning until evening, you are not less obliged to keep her always; you have books which charge you not to banish your woman from your home, wicked though she is, or to seek some better woman. The Indian is better advised, my friend; when he sees a girl who appears good to him, he goes and asks her, or has her asked by others, if she wishes to be his woman. If she accepts, he takes her; if she refuses, he goes and seeks another and marries her. He is sure to have a good woman, because she knows too well that if she becomes irritating her husband would not hesitate to send her away. She likes to eat a good piece of game; she knows that the Indian is a good hunter who will always provide her, and so she does not fail to do all that is possible to live in harmony with him.

Thus reasons the savage who knows neither the law of God nor human law. It is more uncommon for the woman to leave her husband than for the latter to leave his woman; because the Indian woman is very dependent upon her husband, especially in tribes that live only by hunting or fishing.

When they have children by each other, they rarely separate. When such happens, however, the father takes with him as many of the children as he wishes and leaves the others to the mother. Often he leaves all to her and hunts alone far removed from them.

Besides this unlimited liberty granted to the two spouses, to separate from each other according to their caprice, and to remarry elsewhere, polygamy is a custom in all Indian tribes without exception. All Indians can marry as many women as they wish. One finds few, however, who have several women, because they would have too much trouble providing food and dress for them.[83]

According to what we have stated, one sees that those romantic passions which come so often to form or break the knots of marriage among civilized peoples are unknown among the indifferent inhabitants of North America. One can cite only one example of this type that merits relation owing to its singularity.

Many years ago, there lived on the shores of the great Lake Superior a famous Indian Chief, named Wawanosh, whose reputation as a warrior and hunter, was spread far and wide among the Indian tribes.[84] A paramount dignity had been preserved from time immemorial in his family, and he was very proud of his origins. He joined to the advantages of his birthright, his personal attributes which bestowed upon him the greatest consideration in the eyes of members of his tribe. He was of great size, and his magisterial bearing commanded respect. Nothing equalled his strength and courage. His poised bow was feared and recognized everywhere; Wawanosh alone could bend it. In addition, he was very reflective, prudent and wise, and all neighbouring tribes admired his wisdom, as much as they acknowledged his valour. This remarkable man had a unique daughter who, by the fine virtues of her sex, was almost as famous as her father. When she had reached eighteen years of age, a great number of the most promising young men of the tribe appeared to ask for her hand, but were repelled by the proud chief, who believed that they were all beneath such an honour. A new claimant, one of the most handsome and noble of the young men, then came to ask the father for the hand of this much-courted girl. In truth, he feared being repelled also, as the others; but as he had taken care to make advances to insure the sympathy of the girl, he hoped by this intercession to obtain the consent of the father. He therefore went to find the old chief and supplicate him to give his daughter in marriage to him.

"Listen to what I am going to tell you, young man," said Wawanosh:

> You ask for my girl; she is the most precious jewel that I possess on this Earth. Many claimants have already come to address me making the same demand: more among them have a right than you to claim the honour of becoming my son-in-law, and yet none has become so. Have you thought well, young man, about who you want to have for a father-in-law? Have you well reflected upon the great actions that have raised me to my position, and which have rendered my name fearsome to all enemies of my nation?

What chief of neighbouring tribes is not proud to be the friend of Wawanosh? What hunter is prepared to bend the bow of Wawanosh? Which warrior does not burn to attain the glory of Wawanosh? And what accomplishments have you, young man, to claim the honour of becoming my son-in-law? Have you ever distinguished yourself by some act of daring against the enemies of your tribe? Have you reports in your house of the signs of victory? Have you ever, when submitted to torture, to hunger, to fatigue, given some proof of heroic endurance? Your name, has it ever crossed beyond the limits of the hamlet where you were born? Go therefore, young man, and make yourself a name, and then come to ask for the alliance of Wawanosh.

The young Indian now knew the conditions to which he would have to aspire in order to obtain the amiable daughter of the famous Wawanosh. He resolved therefore to attempt a daring act that would bestow heroism on his name, or that would cost him his life. He gathered his young friends and companions and imparted to them his desire to distinguish himself by a warlike enterprise against the enemies of their tribe; and he spoke to them with such passion that he inflamed in them the same ardour. Eight days later, he found himself at the head of a large band of young Indians eager to take the measure of the enemy, so to later speak of their great accomplishments. They provided themselves with arms and provisions, painted themselves in a most horrible manner, and departed for a designated place in order to perform their war dances: it was a beautiful green; it ended on one side at the shore of Lake Superior, which rolled in over the finest, white sand, and at the other, in a thick forest of oak and firs. At the centre of this spot stood an old fir tree around which the Indians were in the habit of gathering for their war dances. It was around this fir that the young chief gathered his warriors. An elderly Indian beat the measures on a drum.

After the dance, which lasted two days, they marched towards the territory of a neighbouring enemy tribe. The young chief gave a tender farewell to Wawanosh's daughter, and they pledged to each other reciprocal fidelity. Then he departed for combat. They soon arrived in enemy territory and attacked one of their bands. The combat was bloody, the determined chief was distinguished for his valour, and the enemy had begun to retreat, when an arrow mortally wounded the poor young man. His companions redoubled their efforts and put the enemy entirely to flight.

When Wawanosh's daughter learned of the death of the noble young man, she remained immobile and did not utter a single word, since Indians rarely effuse in vain complaints. Some stifled sighs and tears were the lone marks of her pain. She ate rarely and very little, and no longer uttered a word. Her father reproached her often for her conduct and sought to amuse her, but it was of no use. She no longer wished to remain in his lodge, and passed the greatest part of the day in the woods. She lost weight to such a degree that she seemed to be little more than a skeleton. Soon afterwards, this extraordinary young woman died. Too late, her father repented of the conduct that his pride had imposed upon him with regard to the noble young man.

There are only a few things to note concerning the education of the Indians; they like their children incomparably more than the latter do their parents. But their love is only natural; the reason is not for nothing, and the children are abandoned to their caprices and innocent wishes. The latter do not fail to notice this, and take onto themselves all the authority, such that in most Indian families, the children give the orders, and it is the parents who obey. Corporal punishments are employed but rarely. Most Indians view it as shameful to punish their children. I have often seen Indian women throw a bowl of cold water at the heads of their children, and I learned that this was a technique employed by mothers to correct their children, and that the latter fear this more than physical punishment.

Sometimes they also punish their children by depriving them of food. This is not just a simple way of correction to curb rebellious children, but it is also to harden them to become accustomed to endure hunger with constancy, to which their sluggishness and improvidence so often exposes them. The Indians give a name to their children shortly after their birth. It is usually the name of a wild animal, a bird, a fish, etc. But only a few among them keep their first name until the end of their life. Often, they change it themselves after they have reached maturity; also, they often receive some other name from their companions, on the occasion of some courageous action or after having been exposed in some remarkable situation.[85]

Indians do not go to the pain of teaching things to their children, until they are in control of their sight and hearing. When hunters and warriors give an account of their adventures, the young Indians listen with much attention, and they are thus initiated into a knowledge of those occupations which one day will be theirs. When a father makes a birch-bark canoe, snowshoes or other items, the children watch him, and look for ways to imitate him; similarly with the small girls, when they see their mothers occupied with the work of their sex.

Religion

9

✚ Religion
✚ of the
✚ North American Indians

*A*LL TRAVELLERS HAVE noticed this great truth, that there exists no people on the Earth without some kind of religion. All the Indians tribes of North America have their religion as well, which is not, however, the same among all of them. They all believe in the existence of a Supreme Being, which they designate as the Great Spirit or the Master of Life; but the other points of belief and practice and religious ceremony differ considerably.[86]

Their traditions concerning the creation of the Earth, on the deluge, and on certain others events of the Ancient Testament vary accordingly as did the imagination of their ancestors who transmitted these traditions.

Indians of the Delaware tribe (a tribe of little import today) believe that they formerly lived within the Earth, and only by good fortune were they later able to come out. An Indian of their tribe one day discovered an opening in the surface of the Earth. He climbed towards this opening, and kept climbing for a long time until he finally reached the surface. He was struck with wonder at seeing the beautiful country he had come to discover, and even more surprised at seeing all the types of animal that dwelled on the Earth. He set out to explore some of this beautiful country, and was very happy to find a deer that he took with him back down into the Earth. His neighbours gathered round him and learned of the wonders he had seen. This account, but even more the flesh of the deer which they had found to be so excellent, persuaded them to leave their sombre surroundings and climb to the surface of the Earth, in order to go hunting for the animals which lived there.

Indians from another tribe in the Missouri country, believe equally that they find their origins in the interior of the Earth, but they do not speak in the same way of the mode of their deliverance from this dark dwelling place. They believe that a vine planted by their ancestors grew to such a great height that it found a large opening located at the top of their underground dwelling, and which no person had ever been able to reach. As the foot of the vine was very strong, one day a young man had the courage to keep climbing until he reached this opening. He reached the very summit and then descended to the surface of the Earth. He admired the beauty of nature and the brightness of the sun, but especially the herds of buffalo that he saw around him on the plains. He was able to kill one of the buffalo, and he took a piece of it with him. He hastened then to return to his residence and gave to his tribe a brilliant picture of the beauty and fertility of the Earth and of the wonderful hunting that one could undertake there. All the tribe resolved immediately to depart from their dull habitation, and the project was put into motion. Unfortunately, he encountered among their number a very strong woman who also wished to go to the promised land; she seized the foot of the vine and began to climb; but her extraordinary weight broke the stock, which fell to the ground. The Indians, not able to leave, and deprived of this unique road to salvation, were obliged to remain underground, where they still live today.

The tradition of the deluge is generally retained among the Indians, but is so altered and in so many forms that one is at pains to recognize it.

Some tribes believe that after three generations of the first family, a universal flood engulfed the Earth and destroyed all of the human race, and that after the waters had subsided, certain animals (without doubt those which lived in the water) were changed into men, in order that the Earth would become newly populated.

Others tribes relate how a distinguished Indian was warned in a dream by the Great Spirit that a great flood would cover the Earth. A man of wisdom and foresight, he immediately constructed a raft with the trunks of trees, and when the flood became general, he took animals of all kinds onto the raft with him. He spent several months on the raft until he began to lose courage; the animals that he had taken with him, animals which had the gift of speech, started to murmur among themselves against him. The Great Spirit finally created a new land that the man then came to approach with his animals. The latter persevered in their displeasure with regard to the man, and were soon on the point of exciting a revolt against him under the leadership of the bear, when suddenly they all lost their capacity for speech, and fell into the state in which they are still found today.

All North American Indians, except for some individuals, believe in the immortality of the soul, but they differ among themselves as to the destination of the soul after death. It is believed by some that, after the death of a man, his soul remains for a long time on the earth in the company of its nearest relatives who sense and hear it, although nobody can see it, and that in times of danger it comes to the aid of its kin. But sooner or later, it is obliged to commence a long journey to the country of the spirits, in the direction of the setting sun. This trip is very tedious and takes several months. The soul is obliged to pass more than once, through very rapid rivers on a single plank, and often finds itself attacked by savage dogs and others fierce animals.* As the Indians imagine that during this trip the soul experiences once again all the needs of a man on Earth, they take care to provide their kinsman with all necessities which they themselves take on their journeys; they also place in the tomb food provisions, arms, a gun, pipe and tobacco. This practice is general among peoples of North America. Some Indians have the habit of adding a bottle of brandy.

All Indians, with some individual exceptions, believe in rewards and punishments in the other world. But opinions differ as to the quality of these other-worldly rewards and punishments. If an Indian was recognized as a sharp hunter and intrepid warrior, he is, in their opinion, deserving of eternal rewards. Those who were compassionate towards the unfortunate, the hospitable, and those who continually suffered, are also assured of rewards. Indians believe as well that some animals will live again for the pleasure of the chase; such is the general picture the Indians describe of the plenitude of the other world: one will live in a country characterized by a most pleasant climate. The land there is perpetually green, with very sweet-smelling flowers which never wilt, with superb forests filled with game of all kinds, and lakes with gentle waves wherein feed the best fish, separated here and there only by the green plains of this happy country. The chosen Indians fish and hunt there eternally without sorrow and fatigue, as on the Earth, but instead with a renewing pleasure.

Having arrived in this country, the soul is obliged to pass over a weak plank that spans an immeasurable gorge. The good make this journey without fear and without stumbling, and then enter into the realm of happiness. But the malevolent, such as murderers, thieves, cowards, etc., carry with them the weight of their iniquities: this weighs upon them and causes them to stagger to such a degree that they finally lose their balance and fall into the terrible abyss where they remain confined forever. This is the idea by which they are sent to hell. But as to the torments that the sinners endure in this gorge, the Indians have no fixed idea. They state only that the evil ones eternally suffer there.

---

* The Indians believe in a type of personification of the soul in the other world.

On the contrary, others believe that the bridge, across which the souls must pass, stretches over the deep waters of death. The good cross over cheerfully and arrive in the country of felicity where they experience all variety of eternal pleasures; the ill-doers, on the other hand, fall into the water where they sink up to the neck, and in which position they remain forever. They can see the country of felicity, and are witnesses to all those delights and pleasures, but they are not able to escape the water and partake of these pleasures.

Again, others believe the soul must cross a wild torrent in a dugout. The saved, who retain little weight, easily and speedily gain the far bank and enter into the country of felicity. The damned, on the contrary, who are overwhelmed by the weight of their iniquities, resemble weak old men; they become weary in their dugouts which slip away from them, leaving them to tumble into the water; they are then changed for evermore into frightful toads.

The peoples of the north who suffer greatly from the cold, believe that the country of felicity, in addition to the advantages already mentioned, includes the joy of an eternal summer, and that the country of the damned, on the other hand, is extremely cold, arid and covered in snow. In this country, the evil ones are only able to kill enough game necessary to sustain a miserable way of life after a most fatiguing and tedious hunt.

North America Indians do not just believe in the existence of a Great Spirit, which they also call the Good Spirit, and which they imagine lives in the air; they believe also in a wicked spirit that resides in the interior of the Earth and enjoys great power. Their sacrifices are offered now to one, and now to the other. They believe also in the existence of spirits of an inferior order, charged to protect individuals or places. They offer tobacco to these protective spirits when they arrive at places supposed to be under their guardianship.[87] I have had opportunity to see a number of these honoured places during my trips on Lake Superior. Thus, one encounters on the shore of this lake, the majestic walls and enormous bluffs of rock that represent by far, the most varied forms and imposing aspect. These prodigious boulder masses are the object of a special cult. When an Indian approaches nearby, he lights his pipe, throws a piece of tobacco into the water, and continues his route in solemn silence. It often happens that when an Indian approaches he takes a long detour, climbing to the summit of the cliffs, where he deposits, as an offering, a piece of tobacco; then, full of confidence in the protection of the protective spirit of this quarter, he ascends in his boat, regardless of the threat of storm, and continues peace-fully on his course.[88]

Indians of a tribe that lives towards the Mississippi, spend one day in the year engaged in certain hideous ceremonies which resemble the reli-gious practices of some oriental peoples in India. An English traveller who spent the summer of 1832 with these Indians stated the following.[89]

In the middle of the village where he dwelled, he noticed a circular grounds of approximately one hundred and fifty feet in diameter; at the extremity they had erected a great hut for sacrifices, some seventy to eighty feet in diameter. The morning of the day on which ceremonies commence, an Indian appears dressed as an ancient, representing the first man. This Indian is painted in red; his clothes consist of four white wolf skins. Two raven feathers adorn his hair, and he holds in his right hand a pipe of extraordinary size; he slowly approaches the village, which eventually he enters after a number of ceremonies. He then walks from lodge to lodge, where he asks everyone for a knife or another sharp instrument, remarking that these tools will serve to form the great raft (the ark). At the end of the ceremony, these implements are thrown into the water as an offering.

The following morning, they retire to the sacrificial lodge, a circular enclosure adorned with the skulls of men and buffalo. A crowd of young Indians follow him, in order to put him through painful ordeals. They are almost entirely naked and painted in a terrible manner. They sleep at the sides of the hut and wait for the master of ceremonies who soon appears. His body is painted in yellow; he wears a yellow belt and his hair is styled in white. The Headman then offers him his great pipe and leaves, only to reappear after the annual feast.

The master of ceremonies remains in the lodge four days and four nights without drinking or eating, and during this time, one hears shouts and the most terrible groans. The young Indians who stay with him in the lodge also remain four days and nights without food or drink.

During the first three days, the Indians who remain outside of the lodge perform different dances, but not those who are within. These dancers wear strange outfits, and are painted in a frightful manner. The evening of the third day, dressed again as a man from the distant past, he runs here and there but steadily approaches the village. As soon as the Indians notice him they appear to be struck by a great fear and thrown into a deep stupor. He finally enters the village, and runs furiously from one hut to the other. He is entirely naked and painted in black; in his right hand he is armed with a white baton. This man represents the evil spirit. The master of ceremonies then approaches him with his great pipe, in which he places great trust, and quickly he directs it towards him. The inhabitants of the village gather round the master of ceremonies, who, with his pipe, protects them against attack from the evil spirit. They finish by wresting the white baton out of the hands of the evil spirit, who now takes to flight.

On the fourth day begin penances that make one shiver with horror. One of the young Indians, exhausted by hunger and thirst, walks to the middle of the lodge, kneels, bows his head and awaits his torturers. The latter enter and with their fingernails, open the skin high on his back and on the two shoulders, to a width of approximately a thumb and half, and they run under the skin a blunted peg of iron from one opening to the other. By means of this iron one secures a baton of wood, the thickness of a thumb, in such a manner that the ends of the baton appear on each side. A cord is attached to each end, and the miserable soul is raised up in the air by cords attached to the batons that cross his shoulders.

This is still not all; in the same manner, they place under the skin, pieces of wood so that they are over and under the elbow, and also on his legs, over and under the knee. And to these batons they hang his arrows, bow, shield, lance, and even the horns and skulls of buffaloes. Then they again hoist the cords until the miserable Indian is raised to a height of six or seven feet off the ground. He remains thus suspended for a long time, bathed in his blood, and emanating a lamentable sound to the Great Spirit to grant him a long life and continuous good hunting. All the other young Indians who have entered the sacrificial lodge are tortured in the same manner, and each remains in this terrible state, until he begins to fear for his life. He is then detached, and usually he falls unconscious to the ground. They are taken down, one after the other; but they are not yet at the end of their ordeal. After they have regained some of their strength, they are conducted to the circle in the sacrificial lodge where they must drag after them all that is attached to the batons. Here there are found more than a hundred young people holding hands, and running around on all fours. Outside of the circle are found the bloody victims of these superstitions. The batons are still in their shoulders, in their arms and in their legs, with all that is suspended from them. Each has beside him two strong Indians who drag him after them, by holding him by a belt of leather that he wears around the kidneys, and they run around with him until the pain and the loss of blood weakens him to such a point that he falls unconscious.

His two companions do not stop their running but keep dragging him over the ground until he no longer shows signs of life. They then detach him and let him lie down. When he revives and returns to consciousness, he crawls without help back to his lodge. An Indian who survives these frightful ceremonies, or rather these atrocities, is always considered to be one of the first of the tribe.[90]

Some Indian tribes of the north, including the Ojibwa, have offered, even in recent times, human sacrifices. An old Canadian who has lived for over fifty years in this region, has told me often that he knew an Indian woman whose son became the last victim of this kind. Some Indians had convened in the forest and held council to find a victim. They finally chose the party to annihilate, the spouse of the Indian in question. They first went to seek his wife, and told her that they had chosen her husband to offer in sacrifice. This women did not dare offer any opposition, because she feared the revenge of these Indians; but she gave them her son to destroy rather than her husband, whose life was indispensable to their subsistence. The Indians consented and went in search of the young man. He came along without knowing why he was being sent for. When he presented himself he was informed of his destiny, and they appealed to him to submit with courage; then he was killed and offered in sacrifice. After chants and other ritual ceremonies, they prepared the meal of sacrifice and the victim was consumed.[91]

The Indians today appear to be far removed from such barbarity, owing to their continuing intercourse with the whites. Religious customs of the Ojibwa and those of most other tribes of the north, now consist of some chants and dances that they engage in from time to time. Those who wish to share in this gather in the evening around a fire in a lodge and, one after the other, sing at the top of their voices. After the chants, they talk for a long time in a monotone, so rapidly that it would be impossible to comprehend them if one did not know in advance what they were talking about. During the chants, they beat continually on a great drum which, in the still of the night, one can hear up to a distance of two or three miles away. They make these resounding chants and cries until midnight; they resume them three evenings running, and on the fourth day, they reunite for the dance. To this end they construct a very long and narrow lodge with branches of trees or from birch bark. They leap about furiously for the whole day throughout the length of this lodge. When the first tire, others take their place. They are accompanied by the sound of several drums, while those that do not dance sit along the sides of the lodge, where they sing and shout to a such an extent that their voices carry almost as far as the sound of the drums. After the dance, the feast of sacrifice begins; and when they have no other resources, they often kill a few of their dogs for this meal.

Some tribes have another kind of religious dance. Of an evening they unite in a large, especially constructed lodge. A woman and a young girl initiate the dance. Then a middle-aged man comes, wearing a cap and a coat of animal skin; this man yells and makes great leaps up and down the course of the lodge. Then a young man appears in the lodge who antagonizes the first, and struggles with him, as if he wanted to overcome him. The older man then seizes a clacker with which he makes a dreadful noise; the young man follows his example, and both begin to run about the lodge shouting with all their might. After maintaining this mêlée for a considerable time, they rest, and another rises and addresses the evil spirit, speaking words by which he seeks to pacify him and makes an appeal to him to take pity upon them by refraining from doing harm to them. The Indian who makes this speech speaks so loudly and shakes so much that sweat pours in a torrent from his face. He then removes with one of his companions to the platform of the lodge while the drums beat strongly. The other Indians remain seated at the sides of the lodge, where they smoke continuously.

These frenzies last all night. The following morning, all the participants are invited to the sacrificial feast, and feed upon boiled dogs. They then distribute to the assembled, a soup in small shells of birch bark.[92]

The North American Indians also keep many types of large and small idols; the larger ones are placed in their villages, or before particular lodges, and consist of great poles at the top of which is a human face. To these poles they attach rags, ribbons and coloured feathers. They keep smaller idols in their lodges, or they often carry them around with them. These are small statues of three to four thumbs length, which represent, in a certain sense, a human being. However, they maintain no temples for idols, and do not offer sacrifices to their idols, which they look upon only as figures of their protective spirits.[93]

Indians sacrifice more often to the wicked spirit than to the good, as they believe that the wicked spirit, independent of the good, can do them harm; they consequently seek to appease it by many sacrifices and to curry its favour.

The Indians still adhere to a particular cult of certain animals and even of some serpents. They never kill these animals. They honour, for example, the rattlesnake, often addressing it in speech and calling it their grandfather. A traveller relates the custom followed by Indians who live in the southern part of the Michigan country. "One day," he stated, "I went with an Indian into the forest, where I suddenly observed in my path a rattlesnake. I took up position to kill it when the Indian restrained me by telling me that the rattlesnake was the grandfather of all Indians, and that it preserved them against misfortune, by always warning them with the noise that it makes, to look around them and maintain their guard. If we were to kill one of these snakes, he told me, others would not fail to soon learn of it, and would rise against us and annihilate us. When I told him that the white men killed all the rattlesnakes which they encounter, he then asked me if the whites had ever been bitten by these serpents, to which I replied affirmatively. 'There is no surprise in that,' replied the savage. 'You have declared war on them, and they have become your constant enemies. Do not do the same thing here in our country; we are good friends with them, and we never do harm to each other.'"[94]

The same superstition is found among the Indians of the north. A white man who travelled among these Indians one day wished to empty his gun on a rattlesnake encountered in his path; but the Indians firmly appealed to him to do nothing, not to give offence and allow the snake to live. The Indians then removed themselves a certain distance and made a circle around the snake. One after the other they addressed it with words, always bestowing on it the title "grandfather." At the same time, they lit their pipes and blew the smoke towards the snake. These ceremonies lasted approximately a half hour and would have carried on longer still, if the snake, annoyed by these honours, had not moved off. The Indians followed it respectfully, and implored it to continue to protect them along with their families at home in their lodges. One of these Indians prayed to it, among other things, not to take offence at the lack of respect shown to it by this foreigner, and not to forget that this senseless one would have killed him if the Indians had not interceded for his life.

Dreams are also the object of superstition among all North American Indians. They debate passionately among themselves about the meaning of dreams, and often their entire life and actions are ruled by dreams.[95] When they have gone some time without an important dream, they fast for several days to bring on a new one.[96]

Besides this kind of fast, Indians have again what they call the fast of destiny, by which they obtain, through dreams, knowledge of what they believe the future will hold. This fast is very difficult. When a young Indian boy or girl reaches the tenth or twelfth year, the parents or relatives urge it to undertake this fast. This practice is, however, less common for girls than for boys. The young Indian removes himself to the forest and builds a small hut with branches in which he remains, without drinking or eating, for as long a time as he can endure it. He fasts thus for six or seven days without the slightest food. This fast is undertaken for the purpose of obtaining singular and important dreams. One may well imagine that by such violent means the Indians do not fail to induce extraordinary dreams. According to these dreams, young Indians conjure up in their imagination, or with the help of their relations, a particular view of destiny that will govern their life, and they firmly believe that what they have dreamt will come about quickly.[97]

One notes, for example, a young Indian girl who, at the age of twelve years, undertook the fast of destiny and endured it for ten entire days. During this time she dreamt that a man would present himself before her and give her two crutches, saying, "I give you these two crutches in order that you would walk, and I will render your hair white as the snow." She explained her dream in a favourable manner and held it in such confidence, that when she found herself in the most imminent danger, she always remained without fear, persuaded that she was, as foretold, destined to live to an advanced age since she was to walk with crutches, and have white hair.

An Ojibwa Indian residing at Fond du Lac dreamt in his fast of a destiny in which it so happened that he would kill five persons in the course of his life. He believed so firmly in the necessity of accomplishing the facts of this dream that when he became a man, he sought occasions to help fulfill his destiny. He had already killed three Indians at various times, and now sought once again for another opportunity, which he was not long in finding. A fur trader offended him; the miserable savage immediately grasped a large knife and killed the Canadian in cold blood. A few other Canadians, having seized the murderer, questioned him. The latter confessed his earlier murders as well, and how they were undertaken with respect to his dream, adding that for him to fulfill his destiny, he had still to murder one more person. When the Canadians heard the words of this savage, they put him to death to punish him for his actions and to prevent at least the last murder that he believed he was obliged to commit.[98]

10

On
Religion
(Sequel)

NDIANS ARE, AS all savage peoples, full of superstition. This natural disposition is exploited cleverly by some among them who find the means of profiting from this in order to live well. One encounters in all Indian tribes a number of jugglers and charlatans, able to pass for luminaries or who are possessed by the Devil, who use their prestige to persuade other Indians that they possess scientific knowledge and supernatural virtue, and that they are able to exert a certain influence on evil spirits.[99]

These charlatans live very comfortably, because they take care to charge their superstitious and simple compatriots well for their deceptions. For example, when during the summer rain ceases to fall for an extended time, Indians who are dependent upon agriculture seek out one of their magicians and pray him to make it rain. He sets about immediately to grant their prayer on the express condition that they pay him in advance. The women (who, as stated, form the cultivator class) immediately go on a quest throughout the village. This quest is for tobacco, pieces of glass, silver buckles, nose and finger rings, garments, foodstuffs, etc. The fruit of this collection, which is often quite considerable, is then put into the hands of the impostor, who immediately commences his operations. Sometimes it happens that rain falls shortly after these chicaneries, and the juggler is then considered to be one of the most distinguished men of the tribe.

But it often happens that, in spite all his efforts, the drought continues. In this case, he always has an excuse and an escape route prepared. Shamelessly, he will often tell them that one of the main reasons for the lack of success of his actions, is that he had not been sufficiently fortified to repel the winds that were hindering the rain, which is to say that he has not been paid sufficiently, and the Indians are naïve enough to undertake a second collection, more abundant than the first, so as to better arm their magician.

A traveller related the following anecdote of an old Indian juggler, highly celebrated for the knowledge in his possession. In 1799, the drought was so excessive in some parts of North America that all crops were threatened with total failure. During this crisis, the women went to find the old juggler and begged him earnestly to make rain. They paid him very well, and he began his incantations, but after much useless effort, he was obliged to renounce all hope of success. The women undertook a new collection, richer than the first, and the magician made a second attempt. He went to a small birch-bark hut made with a small opening facing towards the north and another towards the south; then he faced the north and through the opening murmured some unintelligible words; he closed this opening, and turned to the southern one, murmured anew some words, after which he closed it as well. Some time later, he could be heard to cry, "Go! The rain will not be delayed for long!"

A few Indians happened to pass close by to this spot in a fishing boat. The juggler, having heard the hum of the fishermen's oars from his hut, asked what it was. Somebody told him that it was the men going to the fishery. "Tell them," the juggler shouted from his hut, "that they should return to their homes; one does not take fish during a time of rain." The fishermen did not continue their expedition, and yelled to the juggler, "Father, give us rain; we ask no more than to feel the rain, and so we return empty-handed to our homes!"

The traveller who reported this saw it with his own eyes and heard it clearly. He then departed and retired to a neighbouring village, where he told the chief about what he had seen and heard. He added that he was quite certain that the juggler, with all his craft, would not be able to bring a single drop of rain, because the weather was too fine. The chief replied to him that he had known this man for a long time, and that he himself was convinced that time would not fail to fulfill his prediction. This was indeed the case, in this instance. Although the atmosphere had remained clear all day, clouds developed rapidly, and before long a heavy rain fell for several hours.

These Indian jugglers also interpret oracles and claim to know what lies ahead as well as events that will happen far into the future. We shall quote two examples, one from distant times, and the other more recent. In 1764, a year after the war waged between England and France in Canada, and during which the two powers had rivalled each other to win over the Indians, the English General Johnson sent to the Indians bordering Lake Superior news of the peace signed between England and France, and which committed them also to the alliance. At this news, the Indians assembled, and sent for one of their most famous magicians to consult the oracle on what they should do. The juggler came, and they immediately prepared for him a lodge of animal skins. He chose the night for his incantations. The Indians lit several fires around his lodge. But he had scarcely entered it when he began to stagger and to lean in all directions, and one could distinguish all sorts of different voices in this hut where the juggler was alone. All of a sudden, these voices ceased being heard and were followed by a total silence which lasted but a few seconds. Shortly after, one could hear, from time to time, various new voices which spoke in turn; but the Indians who were outside did not appear very satisfied, and said that these voices were those of the spirits of deception. Finally, a small, weak voice could be heard, and hardly had it registered on the ears of the Indians when there resounded a general shout of joy, because, they said, the Master Spirit, who always speaks the truth, had arrived in the magician's hut. They then began a happy chanting, which lasted for a half hour. When the chants ceased, one could discern the voice of the juggler, who shouted to the Indians that the Master Spirit was in his lodge, and was disposed to reply to all concerns addressed to him.

The local chief was invited to present his questions. He then took a great quantity of tobacco and offered it to the Spirit by passing it into the hut through a small opening close to the ground. Then he asked the oracle if the English were disposed to make war on the Indians, and if their garrison was in the fortress at Niagara. Immediately, the hut of this skilled impostor started to shake in such a way that the English witnesses to this scene believed that it would fall over. According to the juggler, it was a sign that the spirit had left the hut to fly to Niagara (a distance of more than three hundred leagues), in order to take up a position in which to give a precise reply to the question. A general silence followed for a time, the juggler having given the spirit approximately a quarter of an hour to go and return. After waiting for a quarter of an hour, they heard an extraordinary and quite unintelligible voice. It was, the Indians believed, the spirit of the oracle revealing to the juggler what it had seen at Niagara. The impostor then raised his voice and told the Indians that the Master Spirit told him it had seen very few English soldiers at Niagara, but that between Niagara and Montreal (the capital of Canada), it had seen on the Saint Lawrence River a numberless array of boats of English troops ascending the river and who had been dispatched to make war on the Indians. The chief addressed it again with several other questions; he asked, among others, if the English General who had asked for their alliance, would receive them with benevolence, in circumstances where they would go to meet him in their boats. The juggler, on behalf of the spirit of the oracle, replied immediately and without wavering, that the general would refill all the canoes of those Indians who would come down to him with woollen blankets, pots, guns, powder, lead, and casks of brandy. The Indians, on hearing these words, all shouted as one, "I will go, I will go!"

After these questions relating to the general interest, the oracle also allowed a few individuals to put questions concerning their personal situations, and the adroit impostor had the wit to provide replies about the manner in which they might adjust to future events.

At Fond du Lac in 1826, someone witnessed a new example of oracles interpreted by an Indian juggler, by means of a spirit that he claimed to have summoned to his lodge. In the said year (as will be related at greater length), several distinguished officials of the republic, came to Lake Superior in order to negotiate with the Indians.[100] One day, these envoys were invited by the Indians to come and witness the feast of their oracle. They appeared at the place indicated, and found a small hut that had no openings except in the roof and the rest of which appeared very well sealed. All the Indians were seated on the ground, when one of them got up and climbed to the top of the hut, sat down and began to murmur unintelligible words in a very low tone. He raised his voice, little by little, until finally he was shouting with all his might; and then his voice subsided again, by degrees, until it reached the lowest tones and then faded away entirely. This was an invocation to the Great Spirit, begging it to send him a few devils and to submit them to his power. Then he began to sing through the opening in the hut, pronouncing certain words again; the hut trembled violently and the sound of something falling was heard. The Indians sitting about said that it was the sign of the arrival of a spirit. This trembling and this falling sound were repeated fifteen times. The poor juggler was thus surrounded in his hut by fifteen devils. He now seemed to have had enough, because he announced definitively that he was now ready to reply to all questions addressed to him.

The envoys asked him what the President of the United States was undertaking at this time. The hut wobbled immediately, and the Indians explained to foreigners that the magician had sent an evil spirit to the house of the President to see what he was doing. This event was followed by a general silence. But soon a violent tremble shook the hut once again. The evil spirit had returned from Washington and announced that the President was not doing anything but that he was quite at ease about the nature of the negotiations underway at Fond du Lac, and that he had around him several persons all occupied with the documents. This message was satisfactory to the envoys, who returned to their tent.[101]

The following anecdote left by a fur trader will serve to prove how strongly rooted is the belief of the Indians in the supernatural powers of their jugglers. He was named Anderson, and he was known among the Indians for his honesty and was well liked.[102] This brave man frequently tried to convince the Indians of the deceptions that allowed their crafty jugglers to live so lavishly and upon which their credibility depended, but all his efforts were useless and the Indians remained unshaken in their beliefs.

Finally, this honest man made a resolution to prove to them, by a suitable test of an impeccable nature, that these impostors, with all their art, possessed no power. Therefore, he proposed to the Indians that they summon, on two different days, a pair of their most famous jugglers, and grant them full power to inflict upon him, by means of their craft, all the pain that they could induce, provided that this was done publicly in the presence of all the local residents.

The Indians, who liked this honest merchant, feared for his life and made all effort to discourage him in this project, but the former persevered, in the hope that the Indians would thus recognize the proof that their jugglers were complete impostors.

The day was fixed; all the Indians convened at the fur trader's place, and one of the most respected of their magicians was introduced. He approached the trader and told him, with a most assured air, that he considered himself to be an ideal candidate for a duel of this type since he possessed the utmost skill, but that he would never want to use it to inflict pain upon him. Anderson urged him to induce any such experience upon his person, but the wary impostor replied that he liked him too much, because of his goodness and his honesty, and that his heart did not permit him to cause him to perish, that he had never exerted his art against any but the evil ones who did not deserve to dwell on the Earth, and that the Great Spirit forbade him to do harm to such a brave man.

The Indians were quite satisfied with the impostor's reply and it only increased their regard for him, since apart from the fact that they believed all the more in his supernatural powers, they had also been given a vivid demonstration of his uprightness and conscientiousness.

The next day the trader called upon another of these tricksters to come. This was the most famous of his tribe. His reputation was spread far and wide among the Indians, and he was greatly feared, not only because of the supernatural power that he was supposed to possess, but also because of his wickedness.

The Indians renewed their efforts to divert this honest one away from the unavoidable and evident danger to which they believed his life was now exposed through his challenge to the magical powers of this man. But the trader remained intransigent, for he was quite convinced of fakery; he was content to establish certain conditions, that the magician would, for example, stay at a certain distance and that he would remain unarmed. The impostor accepted these conditions without hesitation and disdainfully asserted that even if he removed himself to a distance of one hundred miles, he would not escape his power.

The reward promised to the juggler was brought and placed near him. He then began his rituals. He was dressed and painted in such a terrible fashion that the sight alone would have been enough to turn a timid man superstitious. Anderson maintained himself without fear at some remove. The magician exhausted all his skill and conjurings, but to no effect. The fur trader shouted at him from time to time not to hold back but to overwhelm him with all his magical power. The magician then started to make the most frightening gestures in order to throw fear into the soul of the trader, and all eyes of his assistants were fixed on him, in order to witness the magical power of a man so feared. But Anderson remained tranquil.

The impostor saw in time that all his skill did not make the slightest impression on the good trader, and he searched for an excuse, such as attributing the impotence of his rituals and imprecations to the grandeur of the day itself, which justified him entirely in the eyes of the superstitious savages, and saved his reputation. It was said that the great quantity of salt which this man consumed with his meal had neutralized the effects of the invincible powers he had directed against him, as Indians eat only a little salt, or none at all, and it is this which allows his invincible power to take effect when exercised; but this Englishman had eaten so much salty meat and added so much salt into his other dishes, that the magic was without force against it.

Although clever, this ridiculous excuse was very favourably received by the Indians, so that in spite of his failed efforts, they continued to believe as firmly as before in his supernatural powers.[103]

Warfare

12

Warfare
of the
North American Indians

*T*HE MODERN INDIANS are not nearly as warlike as their fathers. From their earliest years, children were raised for warfare by the older Indians, and they were trained to look at victory over an enemy or the taking of a trophy, as the highest forms of glory and as the finest achievements in life. But today there are only a very few warring tribes; those that have frequent dealings with the whites no longer make war.

Arms of the ancient Indians, prior to the arrival of Europeans in their lands, consisted of a great strong bow with arrows, to which were attached at the tip sharp stones, pointed bone, or pieces of the copper which one finds abundantly in North America. They have quivers and shields of skin made from buffalo, javelins that they launch against an enemy with the greatest dexterity, and long lances made in the same manner as arrows. In addition, they have a suitable axe made with a sharp stone or a piece of copper, and they carry at the waist a short club which serves to crack the skull of their wounded enemies. Some Indians to the North, who have little contact with the whites, still continue to make use of these weapons of war today, and only very rarely resort to the use of firearms. But the other tribes carry guns and buy their javelins, lances and axes from fur traders, who obtain them from the workshops of the civilized world. They also have daggers, or smaller knives worn at the belt. They carry the sabre and the sword only when they serve as auxiliaries to white troops. Of all their ancient arms, they have maintained only the club, which always serves the same purpose.

We have already stated that one no longer sees standing armies among the Indians, but after having held a war council, and having conducted their dances, they now do little more than send small bands to effect murder and devastation in the territory of their enemy and then they retreat immediately.

Dances constitute an essential part of Indian warfare. Before marching against the enemy, the warriors convene at an open place, and to the sound of the drum dance around a tree or a post that they have raised. At intervals in these dances, the older warriors tell about their feats of war in order to impassion the young warriors and to make them strive for the same glory. In these glorious accounts, the Indians care little if they excite the jealousy of a rival. Thus, one day at a war dance it passed that an Indian spoke with over-great emphasis on his battle achievements, his rendering of which, however, brought disgrace upon another Indian, so much so that he approached him and challenged him to a combat which would immediately put an end to his boastfulness and his life.

North American Indian war dances have different names. The first is the dance of recruitment. This dance is made around a pole painted in red. It is initiated by the older warriors, who invite the younger Indians to gather with them. Whoever then advances into their circle and dances with them is considered to have been recruited and to have made a commitment to march with them against the enemy. The second is the war dance proper, which takes the form of an account of the actions of a notable Indian warrior, and this is only performed by a senior warrior-in-arms. The dancer approaches, first leaping very slightly, and stops in the middle of the dance circle. He then makes different leaps and movements that represent actions against the enemy. He then glides gently here and there, stopping from time to time, then suddenly rushes to a certain spot, making all the gestures of a man who is fighting and who kills his enemy, seizing one of the assistants, as if he wanted to make him a prisoner. After this demonstration, he stands upright in the centre of the circle and gives an account of his exploits.

Another type of war dance is made around several poles formed in a circle and defining on the outside the form of a human figure. Dancers are almost entirely naked, and hold in one hand a pumpkin filled with small stones, and in the other the branch of a tree; they jump around making the strangest gestures and the most frightful din around these poles, until their strength is entirely exhausted.

When an Indian war party returns home after a successful expedition, they conduct a graceful dance attended by the women who add their chants in recognition of the return of their husbands.

After the dance, the Indian warriors begin their march, which is always started with a war chant. This chant contains a farewell of the warriors to their women, to their children, and to their relatives, all of whom they are leaving at home, and also an expression of regret for the loss of the happiness and honour of their company during the march against the enemy.

During their march, they observe a host of ceremonies, which are, for the young warriors, tedious above all else. On the first three occasions that a young man takes part in a mass march against the enemy, he must have his face painted black and he must always walk behind an older warrior, following exactly in his footsteps. During the entire march, he is forbidden to scratch his head, which is not a small deprivation for Indians becoming ever grimier.

The warriors, in order to harden themselves, fast during their march to such a point that when they arrive in enemy country they are more exhausted by the lack of food than by the trip. During the whole march they never rest in the shade, no matter how intense the sun.

Indians become extremely cautious when they begin to approach enemy territory. To render pursuit by the enemy more difficult, in case of retreat, they make all kinds of detours, advances and counter-advances so as to deceive them about their course. Often, they attach hooves of a buffalo or claws of a bear to their feet, so as to make their tracks appear to be those of a buffalo or a bear.

When they enter into enemy country and discover a troop of their adversaries, the chief gives a signal, and combat begins. The Indians then disperse instantly, placing themselves behind trees, and from tree to tree, pursue their enemies, who do the same. At the same time they give out cries and the most hideous screams. The nimblest achieves victory over his adversary. When a man falls dead or wounded, his enemy falls upon him and removes the skin from his scalp, for scalps represent the highest symbol of victory, and the most precious booty an Indian warrior can obtain. Thus they continue, back and forth, in the midst of this continuing chaos with their curdling war cries, until one of the two parties is entirely crushed or routed. Flight rarely saves them, however, for the victors do not fail to pursue them, and only very swift and tireless runners escape death.

The custom of removing the scalps of conquered enemies is so widespread among the North American Indians that one can not cite a single tribe that does not practise it. These are their trophies and he who can display the greatest number of scalps is looked upon as the most illustrious warrior. During a battle they think of nothing else than of the taking of these trophies, and they will even expose themselves to extreme dangers in order to obtain them rather than kill the enemy. To this end they carry very sharp knives. When an Indian falls, his adversary descends upon him, places a foot on the throat, seizes the hair of his enemy with one hand,

and pulls it in a manner which extends the skin as much as possible; in the other he takes his knife with which he traces a circle on the cranium, and removes the skin. Sometimes the prostrate enemy is only wounded, and regains consciousness in the midst of his adversary's imposition of this barbarous operation. When finished, if he has time, the latter again strikes his enemy on the head with his club. If danger is too imminent, he leaves his enemy there and goes and seeks refuge behind a tree. It is not rare for a mutilated Indian of this sort to recover and still live a long time. There are several in this region who lost their scalps many years ago.

After the warriors have returned home, they dry these scalps, paint them with various colours, and retain them as their most precious treasures. Sometimes, they suspend them from long poles, and carry them everywhere in triumph.

Sometimes young warriors, avid for glory, enter into enemy territory alone, or in pairs, in order to kill an individual and take his scalp. Hence, a few years ago two young Indians went into the lands of an enemy tribe. Arriving in the locale of one of their villages, they hid themselves so well that for over four months they lay in waiting for their enemies, killing over twenty at different times, and taking their scalps, without ever being captured or discovered, so relentless were they in covering their tracks. When one day a considerable force came in pursuit of them, the two stalwart youths took refuge in the nearby mountains and, making a great circle, returned and came up behind those following them, killed a large number of those at the rear, and then gleefully made their escape. They continued to pester their enemies for a long time, until they had accumulated a great number of those most precious victory trophies.

They then decided to return to their home country, but to crown their enterprise, they decided to take a prisoner with them in order to provide for their compatriots the spectacle of a tortured enemy. This effort did not succeed, however, and it cost them their lives, for as they approached the town, they were discovered, despite all their precautions. The Indians of the settlement gathered on all sides behind their careless enemies, formed themselves into a semicircle, and advanced towards the village in a way such that to escape, the two warriors would have been obliged to pass through their midst or through the village. Other Indians, outside of the town, advanced little by little; they were not long in converging and the two reckless Indians now found themselves in the middle of a circle that increasingly closed in upon them. They hid under the branches of a fallen tree. When they were surrounded, they rushed out giving the war cry, and fell on their enemies; but succumbing to the greater number, they were then bound and led away to torture.

The tortures which Indians were made to undergo, and which their prisoners still sometimes endure today, were very cruel and of the most atrocious barbarity. In each locality, a place was designated for the torture of prisoners. Here, on this island, on a slight rise some hundred paces from the place where the church of the mission now stands, is found a place destined in the past for the torture of Indians.[104] Such places have become quite rare, today. One could see there a great pole, to which the miserable prisoner was escorted. He was divested of all garments; strong cords bound his hands behind his back, and around his neck was twisted a strong length of wild vine, the extremity of which was fixed to the top of pole. He was not attached firmly against this pole; the vine, on the contrary, was eight to ten feet long, and the prisoner could move about a certain amount. His enemies, men and women, held at the ready, torches and small sticks of dry fir branches; they would light them and apply them to all parts of the body of the unfortunate victim of their cruelty.

This is how the notion of the heroic endurance of the Indian warrior has arisen. Far from withdrawing into self despair and pity, he calls out in a loud war chant, runs like a furious animal in the circle in which he moves, and sometimes it happens that he gains a last revenge, by biting an enemy whom he can reach within his path. This continues, and he is burnt until he falls over dead: this is the ordinary manner of torturing a prisoner of distinction. Sometimes he is attached more tightly against the pole, a small fire is lit around it, and the miserable prisoner is roasted by a slow fire, until he expires in the most horrible torment. Heroic Indian endurance in the midst of these tortures, has always been the object of admiration by civilized peoples. Many years ago, an Indian hero was taken captive by his enemies in the Illinois country. In the midst of most terrible tortures, he continued to insult his enemies and overwhelmed them with contempt. In the crowd of his tormentors there was a Canadian whom the prisoner knew. When he saw him, he shouted to him, "Comrade, I am delighted to see you here; now help the Illinois to torture me!"

"And why should I help them?" asked the Canadian.

"It is in order," replied the prisoner "that I have at least the consolation to die at the hand of a man. My great regret is to have never killed a man."

"He has brought down a very great number by his arm," cried one of the assistants. "Have you not killed one Illinois and yet another?"

"Ah! Ah! The Illinois!" cried the half-burned prisoner. "Oh, the Illinois! Oh! I have well disposed of some of the Illinois – but I have never killed a man!" In this way he so keenly insulted his enemies in the midst of his torments, until death finally put an end to his words.

Another Indian warrior was recognized to display even greater heroism during his torture. His enemies built a theatre in order that all the participants could see him well. They stripped him and burned him with torches all over his body in a manner, however, which did not put his life in danger. He sustained this terrible torture without even frowning, as if he had a constitution of iron. Such heroic endurance irritating them all the more, his enemies effected all sorts of atrocities to which he appeared as insensitive as before. One of them approached with a sharp knife, and after having cut all around the skin of his head, pulled it from him. The warrior fell unconscious. His enemies, believing him dead, withdrew and laid him down. It did not take long however, before he regained consciousness, and no longer seeing anyone around, he got up, seized a brand and provoked his surprised enemies into coming back at him. Frightened by this hero's terrible display, none of them dared to approach. They finished, however, by gathering in a large group and descending upon him with brands and red-hot iron bars. He defended himself for a long time against the entire band, keeping them all at a certain distance; the struggle would have lasted longer still, but for his stumbling and falling to the ground in order to avoid a brand thrown at him, whence he was immediately cut to pieces.

I am not able to omit the following. Approximately sixty years ago, Indians in combat against a neighbouring tribe, took one of their enemies prisoner, one famous for his cruelty and love of slaughter; he had for the past thirty years perpetrated all kinds of wrongs against his neighbours, and many had fallen beneath his blows. They called him "Old Skrany," and desired little else than to see him one day fall into their hands, in order that they might have the pleasure of torturing him. They finally came upon him and his arrest was immediate; he was sentenced to be burned over a slow fire. They conducted him, in the midst of savage shouts of triumph, to the place prepared for his ordeal; he was attached to a pole, and a fire was lit close to him. He endured this terrible martyrdom for a long time and without appearing to feel the least emotion, without giving the slightest moan. He finally began to insult his enemies, provoking them to torment him with greater effect, and telling them, with a contemptuous air, that they did not have the capacity to make the heroic suffer and that he wished, in compassion for their inexperience, to show them what it was necessary to do, should they care to release him for a moment, and to place in his hands the red hot gun that was in the fire.

This proposal was so strange that it excited the curiosity of his executioners; they made a circle close in around him and detached him in order to witness the lesson he offered to demonstrate. He indeed showed them what he was made of; when feeling himself free, he seized in his hands the red-hot canon in the fire and struck out with such great fury at those nearest him that he soon cleared a path through the surprised crowd. He raced with speed to the river which flowed nearby, dove from its high banks and plunged into the waves below, coming up on an island located in the middle of the current between two branches of the river; he swam across the other arm of the river, and despite the horde of enemies chasing him and the balls and arrows that rained down around him, he reached a marsh in which he was able to hide until danger had past. He resumed his escape, happily returning to his homeland, wounded and burned, indeed, but triumphant over his enemies for whom he would long remain the terrible "Old Skrany" as he had been for the past thirty years.[105]

When Indians, having achieved a victory, return home with prisoners but have not covered their tracks from their enemies who continue vigorously to pursue them, they kill all the prisoners and take their scalps, after which they disperse, each seeking his salvation in flight.

What has been related to this point concerns wars, or rather, excursions of plunder, which the Indians undertake between themselves. But when Indians make war upon the whites, as when civilized nations engage them for their assistance, their conduct is different. When they find a good opportunity to attack the whites, they usually do so before daybreak, the hour at which, according to Indian opinion, the whites sleep the most deeply. When pursued, they always retreat into a marsh, because they know by experience that regular troops do not function well on such a battlefield.

Among the Indians, the ultimate in the art of war consists in deviously falling upon one's enemies at the moment when they least expect it. They excel admirably in this and have, more than once, subjected the whites to considerable losses. One can cite on this subject the following lines. In a war of the French against the English, General Braddock for the English, in passing through a forest, found himself suddenly attacked by Indians fighting for the French.[106] The Indians were so well hidden that the English scarcely knew from which side the attack originated or the identity of their enemies. The English army was composed of two thousand courageous and well-armed men; but before they could identify the powerful enemy attacking them, or take their measure in order to respond, they were so badly mauled that the small number who managed to escape death found salvation only through quick flight. The Indians counted only three men wounded.[107]

When Indians take prisoners in a combat with the whites, they also torture them in several ways, especially if they are warriors of distinction. The type of torture normally adopted is to burn them over a slow fire, especially attended to by the women in order to please their husbands. Another type of prisoner torture is that inflicted by batons, a torture which often results in death. When they have brought the prisoner to their village, they sink a pole into the ground some distance away, and the men, women and children form in two parallel lines, all of them armed with batons, and the unfortunate prisoner is obliged to run to the pole between the two ranks of Indians who flail away at him without pity. When the prisoner shows great courage and quickly demonstrates his prowess without hesitation, he often happily reaches the pole without having received a single powerful blow, and the Indians save him because of his courage. But misfortune befalls the coward who hesitates and demonstrates his fear before starting his race; he receives frightful and often mortal blows.[108]

In 1782, Heckewelder witnessed a torture of this type that he related in the following manner. One day, fourteen Indian warriors returned with three Englishmen whom they had taken prisoner. When they arrived, the local Indians formed in two ranks in the direction of a pole, and the three prisoners were told that each had to run to the pole in the distance. The youngest of them, a brave and determined man, ran immediately and reached the pole before the Indians were at all prepared for him, with the result that he did not receive a single blow; the intrepidity and the resolution of the young man pleased the barbarians.

The second hesitated for an instant; he ran as a determined man, nevertheless, and gained the pole after having received many blows, but ones delivered with some restraint.

But the third was less brave and looked with anxiety at the raised Indian batons, and he could not bring himself to begin his perilous race. He began to beg them to treat him gently. The unhappy man did not know that he was merely aggravating his enemies the more, and in the end was still obliged to run the course. One shouted at him to run if he wished to spare his life. He therefore started, but was struck so cruelly that it took all of his effort to finish his painful course. If he had fallen before reaching the pole, he would not have failed to have been killed on the spot.[109]

When Indians take a white captive, one famous in war who has made them feel before the effects of his skill and valour, they treat him with atrocious barbarity. One can form some idea from the tortures the valiant Englishman, Simon Butler, was forced to endure.[110] This man, well known to the Indians for his heroism, was captured by the latter during a trip he had undertaken on his own through a deserted region. They rejoiced greatly at such a prize, and subjected him to very terrible torments. These commenced with the painting of his face black, and it was then announced that he would be severely burned. But this was not enough; they tortured him in all sorts of ways during the journey back when they then departed for home. He was set upon a wild horse that no horseman had ever mounted; after turning the horse loose, they engaged in terrible shouting. The animal, frightened by these shouts and by the unaccustomed weight upon its shoulders, ran like the wind through the thickest parts of the forest. One can imagine what the miserable prisoner suffered in this position. The horse rushed in all directions, until exhausted, it returned to the Indian encampment. The Indians left the prisoner on the horse until they reached home. They then took him down and attached him to a pole, where he was left for twenty-four hours, always in the same position. He was then released, but at this time the some six hundred men, women and children formed in two rows and ordered him, exhausted entirely as he was, to run between the two lines. He ran for a time and received severe blows. He then broke from the ranks and made an escape; but a powerful Indian ran after him and brought him down with a blow from his club. There, overwhelmed, he might have been killed had he not been spared in order to endure even greater tortures. With this in view, he was allowed to live.

The unfortunate prisoner was then led from village to village in order to be outraged everywhere by all the worst acts that his barbarous enemies were able to devise. During these terrible visitations, he had to endure the running of the gauntlet thirteen times. He often tried to make his escape, but always in vain. Once he was on the point of fleeing from his pursuers when, unfortunately, he was met and retaken by some other Indians who returned him to the village.

The barbarians finally joined in a group to burn him, as they had told him they would a long time before. As they conducted him to the torture ground, they passed close to the cabin of an Englishman who had lived amongst them for many years, and who had adopted all of their barbarous customs. He was a childhood friend of the prisoner, whom he did not immediately recognize, but did so shortly thereafter. As he passed with the Indians close to the cabin of this Englishman, the latter, wishing to take part in the torture of the prisoner, set upon him, overcame him and began to strike him with fury. The prisoner, revealing himself, sought to calm his rage. Upon recognising him, he promised to save him, if at all possible. He turned to the Indians and persuaded them to turn the prisoner over to him. He led him to his cabin and fed and dressed him; and in a short time the wretched man began to heal. But his cruel enemies soon regretted the loss of the pleasure of their barbaric games; five days later, they requested their prisoner back in order to burn him, and they took him to a distant village. They had already made all preparations for the torture of the unfortunate man when the Indian agent at Detroit, who happened to be in this village, was informed of this inhuman, savage project. He needed to exercise all of his influence to obtain the release of their captive. He finally obtained him and took him to Detroit, where he soon recovered, and where he remained after his perilous thirty-day episode in the forests.

White women and children who fall into the hands of he Indians are much better dealt with; the children are usually adopted by Indians who have lost a son in combat.

The history of North America has preserved for us the admirable example of an heroic Englishwoman whom the Indians took prisoner along with her twelve-year-old son. One day, during one of their excursions, ten savages arrived in the locale where this woman lived. After committing several murders, they continued on their course, taking with them the Englishwoman and her son. The habitation of these Indians was about three hundred miles away. The poor woman was terrified of such a punishing trip and, above all, lamented becoming the slave of these barbarians. She sought in vain to secretly escape. On the second night of their journey, she conceived a plan, the execution of which would have done honour to the bravest hero. She felt the cords, with which the savages had secured her hands behind her back, had loosened somewhat, and she had hope of undoing them. When all the Indians were given over to a deep sleep, she was able, with much effort, to free her hands of the bonds. She then awoke her son, and told him to go directly and silently where she directed him. With the greatest precaution, she removed all the arms which the Indians had beside them, seized an axe and gave another to her son, and instructed him to follow her example. This heroine then delivered a deathblow to one Indian after another, and after almost all had perished, the quaking child also wished to try and deliver a blow to one of them; but lacking the force necessary, he only awoke him by the weak blow he delivered. The woman, quick as lightning, rushed upon him and split the head of the savage, before he had time to rise. She rapidly dispatched some others, with the exception of a woman who accompanied the ten Indians. This woman awoke, and seeing what had transpired, quickly escaped. The heroine then scalped the dead Indians, in the custom of the warriors, and returned triumphantly to her home. She related what had happened, but nobody would believe her until she displayed the trophies that she had gathered from her victory. This extraordinary event is recorded in the annals of North American Indian history and may serve here as proof of the atrocities which are often committed in the Indian country and which we deplore with all our soul.[111]

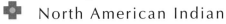

12

Forms of Government Among the North American Indian

*A*GREAT DIFFERENCE MAY be noticed with respect to the form of Indian governments in the present from those that formerly prevailed. The Indians of our day compose a people without importance, confined to the wildest regions of the country, living on the edges of lakes, and dispersed in the immense continental forests. They have no cities, nor even their great former villages, where they gathered in the several thousands. They are no longer lords of the country, but rather very impoverished neighbours whom the government continually drives before them, until finally they will all, in fact, be absorbed by civilized states.

At the time of the arrival of the first English people in North America, the Indians were much more numerous and lived in a less dispersed fashion. They also had chiefs who reigned over them with much more authority and who maintained their unity. Their form of government was monarchical, that is to say, each tribe (and tribes were more numerous than at present) had a king or a supreme chief, who had under him several other chiefs who governed in the different villages. In general, these kings governed for life, but their sons did not always succeed them, and after the death of their chief, especially in time of war, the Indians often elected a king who was an experienced and courageous warrior, without taking into account his lineage. It has been recounted that some head chiefs, through their extraordinary natural talent, increased their supreme authority over a great number of other tribes, their chiefs acknowledging him as dependants. Powhatan, for example, commanded thirty different peoples whose chiefs would pay him tribute. It was similar with his successor, Opechankanow.

The natural talent that raised an Indian to supreme command, served also to sustain him there and insured him of increased power and authority, enhancing his valour. Eloquence in advice, wisdom in difficult decisions, intrepidity, courage, valour, human strength, these were all qualities that raised a man to the first rank in the eyes of the Indians.

They had no other law than some ancient customs; the decisions and orders of the sovereign, upon whose wisdom they relied, constituted their laws in peace-time, just as his reputation for heroism and experience in war were the sole rules governing their conduct during these enterprises.

Indians of today have, indeed, many chiefs; but most of the time these chiefs rule only in a specific locale, are independent of any other, and enjoy only the slightest influence over others. There is not presently in North America a single Indian chief whose authority is decisive throughout his entire tribe; even less does one find an Indian king who extends his supremacy, as formerly, over several tribes.

The foundations of Indian government rest today, as before, on meetings that are convened quite often. At the opening of these meetings, a number of ceremonies were observed, a great number of which are still in use today. It falls to the chiefs to summon a council. They send some of the young out to different communities and invite all the men to attend on the day indicated. The Indians are charged to invite the councilmen of their vicinity who usually bring along a great quantity of tobacco, which is then shared among those invited. In addition, they bring to the chief of each locality a small assortment of shells threaded on a cord of silk. These shells are of different colours (red, green, white, or black), according to whether the object of the deliberation concerns war or peace, sad or joyful circumstances.

When neighbouring tribes are summoned to a meeting, the envoys of the foreign chiefs bring shell strings and tobacco, the pipes for which are called peace pipes or calumets.* The chief then summons his council, in order to learn what course should be adopted. If one is inclined to acknowledge and to participate in this meeting of allies, he fills and lights the calumet, and all the dignitaries and warriors, one after the other, take a few puffs of smoke. When the council adopts a contrary view, a dissenting member does not touch the peace pipe, and returns it with the shells, which indicates to that neighbouring tribe that it is perceived as an enemy.

When the lodge of the chief is spacious enough, all those who have come to the council gather there. More often, however, they assemble out in the open, if time permits, or in a large lodge erected deliberately for the purpose. They always gather around a great fire; sometimes several are

---

* The calumet is a great pipe of black or red stone, inlaid usually with tin; it is very well fashioned, and is attached to a large, long stem, covered with all kinds of ornaments.

lit, around which they sit or sleep. Here and there are placed large piles of tobacco from which each may fill his pipe and smoke in silence.

The attention and the serious reflection which they bring to their councils is rather remarkable. They gather for quite a long time, but maintain silence. This silence is finally broken by the chief or by an orator of the tribe, who reveals the subject for the meeting. It always concerns the interest of the entire tribe, or at least of a considerable portion thereof, such as, for instance, when great offences have been received on the part of a neighbouring tribe, repeated murders, breaches in the right of hunting or of other ancient rights sanctioned by custom. He then asks them for their determination; for example, do they wish to take up arms immediately, or to send deputies to ask for satisfaction, etc.

In ending his speech, the chief or the orator prays his listeners to deliberate among themselves and to then make known their opinion.

After this speech, they reflect upon the course to be taken, and after long thought and deliberation, a new speaker arises and, in a low voice, makes known the opinion of members of the council. Several others may speak after him, but these would never be any except those who by their age and experience, or by their courage and great achievements in war, enjoy a well-deserved reputation. The attention that Indians give to orators at meetings has always been an object of interest to white folk. Over the duration of a speech, nobody moves from his place, nor do they fail to hear a single word, although from time to time there will be a long and deep exclamation – "Oh! Oh!" – which in the language of the Indians is a sign of approval.[112]

The following story contains an example of the attentiveness and of the transfixed nature of Indians in council. Many years ago, the commander of the fort at Detroit summoned a council of the Ojibwas to assist in the cross examination of two Indians of this tribe who had been accused of several murders. As there were many more Indians in the vicinity of Detroit than there are today, a great number came to the council. The two murderers were brought, questioned and convicted. After the commander had pronounced the death sentence, one of them suddenly rushed about with a great knife which he had concealed, and cleared a passage out of the hall of the council. A great uproar was heard; the guards who were outside the house came to attention and fell upon the murderer who was attempting to escape, and killed him at their feet. All of this caused an awful din in the Council House as outside; but all the chiefs and warriors who were at the

Council did not move from their spots, and did not even look around, all remaining immobile, smoking their pipes, as if their business had not even been disturbed.

The violation of the sacred laws acknowledged by Indians in council meetings is very severely punished in the young man who forgets them, sometimes even by death. It so happened, one day, that a respected chief, interrupted in his speech by a question addressed to him by a young warrior in his care, suddenly stopped, cold-bloodedly took the axe suspended from his belt, and split the head of the young man. He then gave a sign to his people to remove the corpse, and continued his speech, as if nothing had happened.

Since previous to the arrival of Europeans, and for a long time afterwards, handwriting was unknown to the Indians, the ancient inhabitants of this country invented an ingenious means for recording all that was said in a meeting. The orator from time to time pauses; the chief of the party to whom the discourse was addressed holds some small batons, and each time that the orator pauses, he passes one of them to one of his counsellors, signifying that this man was being charged to retain this point of the speech. At the pause that followed, another counsellor received a small baton, and thus it continued until the end of the speech. These counsellors were known for their attentiveness and their thoughtfulness, and for that quality of mind capable of recalling perfectly those portions of the speeches they had committed to memory. Some lengthy speeches were able to be preserved just as well as if by stenographers. When, therefore, the party to whom the discourse was addressed came to deliberate upon it, he had the help of these men in recalling all points of the speech and was able to order his thoughts carefully in preparing his reply.

In most tribes, the executive power is in the hands of the chief, and often he takes on, one after the other, the role of judge and executioner, because he does not want to give over to another the pleasure of killing the man. This usually happens only in the case of public offenders or criminals from an alien tribe who have been taken and immediately condemned and to be executed by the chief. As for private crimes, such as murders committed by Indians among themselves, they are punished among themselves, and the chief does not interfere. The relatives of one who has perished, kill the murderer when they discover him, and when they do not find him, they take their revenge on his parents or kin and sometimes kill three or four persons, before their lust for revenge is appeased.

Formerly in North America, there were several tribes in the east about whom contemporary historians have reported that, known fugitives, even those of little importance, might still be punished with death. One day, a French missionary in Canada saw an Indian give a blow of his club to a woman and he appeared ready to then kill her. The missionary immediately ran to save the woman and asked the Indian why he would attack her so pitilessly; he replied to him: "She is my sister, but she has fled and deserves death." Only with much effort was the missionary able to save the life of this poor Indian woman.

The North American Indians do not fall under the laws of the government of this country; however, they are treated in accordance with these laws when they have been found guilty of the murder of a white person; in such a case, the whites attempt to seize the murderer and deliver him to the closest criminal court, which then condemns him to hang. The Indians find that entirely just and never oppose the extradition of the murderer of a white.[113] One day, an Indian killed an Englishman; he was taken and given over to the Justice of the Peace. The English invited their Indian neighbours to come and assist in the cross examination of the murderer in order to be convinced that he was a scoundrel deserving of death. The Indians, full of confidence in the justice of the laws of the whites, preferred not to appear, and sent to the criminal court the following short message: "Comrades, we know that N. who has killed one of you, is a wicked man, and we are not concerned in the slightest about this; judge him according to your laws, and hang him, in order that he no longer returns among us."

Here is another example of a negotiation of the whites with the Indians. It occurred at Fond du Lac, in the month of August, 1826; the Government of the United States had invited all the chiefs and great warriors of the Ojibwa tribe to come there and had advertised the day of the meeting. A great number of the principal Indians of this large tribe gathered there at the request of the government. The Governor of Detroit attended with many officials, officers and soldiers, along with a considerable number of Canadians who manned the boats. The object of this gathering was to reduce the continuing hostilities between the Ojibwas and the Sioux, as well as the barbaric atrocities continually being inflicted by the warriors. The government tried, less by threats than with good words and gifts, to induce the Ojibwas to adopt more peaceful intentions. It is difficult to say what success these humane overtures of the government had, or their assuredly dignified speeches, but it is not less certain that these barbarous savages were not long in recommencing their hostilities, which still continue today.

There is a great difference between meetings of the Indians convened by the whites, and those that are exclusively Indian conferences.

When the designated time drew near, one would see large troops of Indians coming in all day, with more than three thousand arriving. When one of these bands entered, it performed a drum dance. Without doubt, this dance was performed to amuse and gain the attention of the whites, who looked upon them with curiosity. Also in attendance were crowds of women and children, since the government promised to give presents to all Indians who appeared. On the second of August, towards noon, the negotiations began. The Indians all seated themselves on the ground in a semicircle, and the two commissioners of the government sat at some distance at a table. The two parties smoked the calumet in sign of friendship, and the governor addressed a speech to the Indians, by means of an interpreter, in which he outlined to them the subject of the meeting and the different points on which they would have to deliberate in order to reply. Nobody spoke a word after him, but the reply to the different articles was to be given the next day in order to leave the Indians time to deliberate among themselves.

The following day, at eleven o'clock, three cannon shots gave the sign for the opening of the council. The calumet pipe was passed again from mouth in mouth, after which several chiefs rose one after the other to give their observations on the articles which had been submitted to them.

At one hour after noon, the session was suspended for three hours, and then the negotiations were resumed again until sundown. The next meeting was set for the fifth of August. The fourth was employed by the commissioners to write down all that had been dealt with up to that point.

On the fifth, the session was opened for ten hours, with customary ceremonies. There were speeches made and explanations given on details of the negotiations. The Indians gave their consent, and the principal chiefs signed the original document, which is to say that each man marked with a feather, a cross next to his name that one of the commissioners had written for him.

Then they gathered in the whole once again, and the commissioners had distributed to the assembled, medals of silver with an effigy and inscription of the President of the United States, John Quincy Adams. All the principal chiefs of the Ojibwa received one in sign of friendship.

The time of the last meeting was then announced, to which all women and children were invited to receive the presents promised by the government, awaited with such impatience. The sun finally rose upon that happy day. The Indians, especially the women and children, waited restlessly for the signal for the meeting. The cannon finally resounded and a multitude of men, women, children and dogs rushed forward. All received valuable gifts; from the child in the cradle to the elderly man, there were none who returned unhappy, taking away beautiful items, many of which were unknown to them. These presents consisted of large knives for the men and smaller knives for the women and children. There was tobacco for the men, and for the women, a collarette and a coloured headscarf; cloth for spats and outfits for men, women and infants, as well as blankets or cases of wool; finally, for the men, powder and lead, gunflints and hooks; for the women and children, ribbons and rings, all of these things in great quantity.

During the visit of the Indians, they were given each day a pound of pork and a pound of flour for each head. The Indians appreciated the bounty and generosity of the government, and recognized that they had never been so well off. They spoke and rejoiced all the more when the commissioners announced, when preparing to take their leave, that each Indian would receive as much pork and flour as he could carry. All the men appeared with straps, with the help of which they are accustomed to carry great loads on their backs, and one can well imagine that, in this circumstance, they did not spare their shoulders. On the ninth of August, the commissioners disembarked in light, birch-bark canoes and the Indians did not delay in returning to their homes.[114]

Diseases and Cures

13

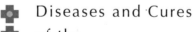

Diseases and Cures
of the
North American Indians

*T*HERE ARE, AMONG the whites, many diseases unknown to the Indians, above all those that are produced by easy living, incontinence and dissolute practices. One encounters among Indians very few men who are disabled or deformed. There is, however, to the northwest of this continent a small Indian tribe whose national symbol is a flattened head. Women of this tribe have the custom of pressuring the skulls of their children when they are first born, in a manner such as to render it as flat as possible; hence, the one with the flattest head is considered the most fair.[115]

On the whole, one does not find general deformities among the other tribes in North America. The Indians are generally well formed peoples, and the Indian women do not adopt senseless fashions which damage their health such as narrowed clothing, small shoes, and tight corsets; they are content with the strong constitutions which Providence has given them, and they think only of maintaining it, such as it is.

There are sicknesses that the Indians have experienced only since the arrival of the whites in their country, and these sicknesses have often ravaged them terribly, as they did not have customary treatments against them. It has been many years since the small pox desolated the North American Indians in such a terrible manner that in many tribes it carried off half of the population. A merchant warehouse in Charleston, South Carolina, was the source of this disease and from there it had spread among the Cherokee Indians by the way of the goods which they had bought, and by way of the Cherokee it spread to a host of other tribes.[116] At first, it made only slow progress, and Indian doctors had time to observe this singular sickness, which was unknown to them until then, and to test out all kinds of remedies. The first which they tried, seeing that the invalids suffered greatly from heat, was to make them come out of their lodges, and make them lie down on the ground, leaving them there in the fresh air, even during the night, thinking that the freshness of the dew would soothe the inflammation being experienced. One may imagine that all their patients died in short order.

They then tried another course. When the invalid was at the height of the sweat, they exposed his chest, upon which they spread ice water, accompanied by all sorts of chants, grimaces and conjuring. When they became convinced that this remedy was also to no effect, all the doctors and magicians of the Cherokee tribe convened and held a great medical council. After much debate, the final decision which these respected practitioners unanimously adopted was worthy of the membership of this council. It was agreed that they should employ all methods to bring the patient to the height of his perspiration and then they would quickly plunge him into a current of water. These unfortunate patients all died quite suddenly in the hands of their uninformed doctors.

The Indian charlatans were thus found in a state of great embarrassment, recognizing that they did not have any understanding of cures for this terrible sickness. They abandoned the sick to their lot. A great number killed themselves, by hurling themselves into fire or water; others stabbed themselves with their knives, or slit their throats and died bathed in their own blood. A great number killed themselves after they were already healed, for the sickness had so disfigured them that they were mortified at living any longer. Among these last mentioned was a renowned old warrior. His relatives soon suspected his intentions, and they carefully watched all his movements, concealing all sharp instruments of any kind. This served only to irritate him further, and he sought another way to implement his destructive plan. With great vigour, he ran and drove his head against a hard surface so that he fell unconscious; when he regained his wits, he lay down as if resting. His kin left him alone, believing, indeed, that he was sleeping. But when he saw there was no longer anybody in the lodge, he searched in all corners, finding nothing but a grubbing axe. He took it, placed the handle firmly in the ground, and put the other end in his mouth, and fell upon in with all his power in such a manner that the shaft moved up into his throat and suffocated him.

In general, suicide is rare among the Indians. They will, however, blow their brains out, hang themselves or take poison. Acute mortification or sickness are the ordinary causes of suicide.

Illness among Indians generally flows out of their miserable and unregulated living conditions. Often they have to suffer hunger and feed upon decayed matter, detrimental to their health, but when they do have a successful hunt, they eat without restraint, such that they can no longer walk or stand upright. They give themselves over to drink, as well, so that they often go for almost a week in a state of continual drunkenness.

Added to this, they go hunting in winter and summer. Hunting, as they undertake it, is very fatiguing. They sometimes go for days on end, and sleep here or there or wherever the night finds them. Even during the winter, they usually sleep in the open air, on frozen ground, and this, after having perspired all day, still in their clothing impregnated with sweat. It is true that they usually make a fire when they camp, but it is also true that they sleep on the cold ground, and that they do not usually cover themselves with more than single, often very light, blanket. A great number of them, in truth, do not lose their endurance from this, but it is also true that many soon become worn down by this type of life. One sees many Indians subject to the vomiting of blood and to all sorts of body ailments, well before the advent of old age. Consumption is widespread among them.

One counts few Indian men who reach old age, especially among those who are in closer proximity to the whites and have more frequent interchanges with them. The women live for a longer time than do the men because their way of life is less disorderly and subject to less fatigue.

One finds among all Indian tribes a numerous body of medical practitioners who claim to possess a wide knowledge and understanding of how to heal all types of sickness. In fact, most of these peoples are impostors and charlatans, just as one finds amongst civilized peoples: those who impose themselves, by their chatter, upon credulous and ignorant people alike, and upon whose dependence they live well. However, it is necessary to confess, because experience demonstrates it, that there are among the Indian physicians, men who possess a great natural skill in the curing of invalids, and who, from long experience, have come to understand the powers of certain roots, plants and barks. The fruit of this experience is transmitted from father to son, and increases with the addition of new knowledge. With the help of these simple tools for recovery, some Indian physicians have produced cures of an extraordinary nature. They are adept especially in the curing of injuries.[117]

A few years ago, a learned Englishman who has spent much time amongst the Indians, related that, in terms of curing new injuries such as bruises, cuts, and gunshot wounds, he had met an old Indian, experienced in the ways of the finest surgeons of the civilized world, who still preferred the Indian remedies, which were simpler, less painful and fostered a faster recovery.

Indians have excellent and infallible antidotes for poison from snake-bites from venomous serpents, as well as against poisons that have been swallowed. To heal snakebite, surgeons often slice into the living flesh, causing much suffering. The Indians, on the contrary, who in their trips through the forests are often exposed to this danger, never cut into the flesh, and heal perfectly in a few days, even from the most harmful bites. When they travel, they take care to always carry with them, staunch remedies against snakebite. When an Indian is bitten by a snake, he places a portion of his remedy in his mouth, chews it, swallows a portion, and spreads the remainder on the injury. He immediately feels terrible pains caused by the struggle between the poison and the antidote. But soon the poison is repelled in its effects, by the same manner in which it had entered, and at the end of two days the Indian, perfectly cured, is able to continue on his way.

The reputation of a man skilled in the art of healing injuries spreads far and wide, and the Indians often make long journeys, exposing themselves to even greater danger en route, to put themselves in the care of a famed surgeon, and their faith is rarely misplaced. At the beginning of the war of the North American English colonial revolution, an Indian chief was wounded very seriously by one of his compatriots for having taken the part of the colonists. The chief then took a long trip with some of these colonists. He continued his course, although with each breath blood issued from the injury that the enemy ball had made in his chest. He went eighty miles in this sad condition before arriving at another town. The English wished to have him treated by one of their surgeons, but the Indian refused to lie down: he stated that fifty miles on there was to be found a famous Indian surgeon who would heal him in a short time, if he was only fortunate enough to get there. He thus continued his tedious travels and luckily arrived at the home of the medicine man, who indeed did heal him completely in a very short time. Ten years after, this chief came to Detroit, where he met one of the Englishmen who was present when he had been injured.

At Sault Ste. Marie, at the head of Lake Superior, a violent struggle ensued between two Indians; one of them took his axe and gave the other a terrible blow in the side, one in which he sank the axe so deeply into his body that he was unable to withdraw it, and he then took to flight. Nobody was present at the fight, with the result that the wounded Indian remained for a long time bathed in his own blood. When he was found, the axe was pulled out of his wound, and he was carried, as if dead, to the nearby military fort. Soon a few Indians arrived, among them one of their surgeons. When the latter noticed that the wounded man was still breathing, he ran to seek his container of remedies. He drew out a white substance, dissolved it in a bit of water, and attempted to make the injured man swallow it. But his mouth and eyes remained closed, and he seemed dead. The Indian opened his mouth with the help of a piece of wood and made him swallow his medicine. A short time later, the patient began to open his eyes. The physician employed still other remedies, and the injured man regained consciousness. They carried him to his lodge, where the Indian physician treated him steadily and with the greatest care. On the sixth day the Indian appeared ready to walk, and by the end of a month he was perfectly healed, except for coughing bouts that afflicted him from time to time. Twenty years later he was still alive.

A white man from Maine who lived in the vicinity of an Indian village, received a leg injury which he received very suddenly when out walking. He consulted all the physicians and surgeons of his acquaintance; they all worked together in seeking a cure, but they were not at all successful. Finally, an Indian came to visit him, and offered, in friendship, to heal his injury. The offer was accepted and the Indian proceeded in ways so effective, although simple, that at the end of seven days his patient could go about everywhere.

When Indian physicians treat the whites, they use only their own remedies, without ceremony. But when they have to deal with Indians, they first perform a number of ceremonies, such as chants, dances, sacrifices and invocations and, as usual, these are also impostors; they do not fail to tell their patients that these ceremonies will contribute more to their cure than the remedies. They usually attribute sicknesses to wicked spirits, or to the ill will of a magician, and give to understand that these need first to be suitably acknowledged (which is to say, well paid) in order to achieve the state of mind in which to seek out the locale of the evil spirits or that of positive forces. After having received payment, they begin to demonstrate their art by singing, shouting, and by jumping around the patient, until they are quite exhausted. Then they rest and wait awhile, until they can discern the effect of their art. If the invalid becomes cured, it is claimed that the artifice of the charlatan has healed him. If no change is noticed in the state of the patient, the juggler resumes his noisy ceremonies until the invalid feels some improvement, or until the impostor finds some way to explain the resistance of the evil spirit. If the ill person should die, then the simple explanation given by the impostor is that the devil, pursued by the medicines within the body of the invalid, delivered him the death blow in order to escape.

When someone is very sick, Indian physicians often say that his soul is in flight. They then take a small canister designed for this circumstance, around which they run for some time until senseless. If the soul returns to the canister, they carry it to the patient and blow it into his mouth. If the invalid dies despite this, it then becomes necessary to find a pretext to explain why the soul can not be regained a second time.

Mortuary Customs

14

Mortuary Customs
of the
North American Indians

*T*HE FIRST THING that Indians do upon the death of one of their people, be it a man, woman or child, is to fire two or three gunshots from the lodge of the deceased, in order to announce the death to the neighbours.

The Indians of this country generally have the habit of burying their dead only a few hours after their passing. Often they do not wait for even two hours, and proceed to burial as soon as the invalid has closed his eyes. One can imagine how many people who appear to be dead have been buried alive as a result of this barbaric custom. Some Indians have proof of this, but they still cling to their customs, for neither these sad instances nor representations from the whites have been able to divert them from this practice.

A few years ago, on the northern coast of Lake Superior, an Indian, apparently dead, was buried quickly by his relatives, according to this custom. When all the ceremonies were over and the burial was finished, each returned to his lodge. The widow of the deceased remained alone at the tomb, shedding her tears and wailing. Suddenly, she heard a slight noise in the tomb; frightened, she rose and ran to the village to spread this news. The Indians hurried back and dug away the earth and found the one they had buried was alive. That still did not prevent them from hurriedly burying the next dead man that came to close his eyes. The Christian religion is alone strong enough to abolish this cruel and absurd custom.

All North American Indians show great respect for their dead. When one of them has been killed in combat, his compatriots take all possible care to guard his body, in order to prevent his enemies from scalping him, thus insuring him an honourable burial. When an Indian passes the winter with his family, far from their homeland, and should he come to die, it happens often that his relatives burn the corpse and preserve the ashes, which they take with them upon their return home.

Indians do not make coffins in which to enclose their dead, but they are in the habit of furnishing the interior of the grave with tree bark, and when the body has been lowered, they cover it with additional bark, in order that the corpse does not come into direct contact with the ground. Only those Indians who live in the vicinity of the whites put their dead in coffins, which they receive as gifts.

Some tribes of the north are in the habit of putting their dead into a kind of coffin made from tree trunks. But instead of depositing these coffins in the ground, they construct a scaffolding eight to ten feet high, on which they place the coffin and where they leave the corpse to decay. They state that being able to view the dead thus, consoles them to their loss. For this reason, they place this scaffolding close to their homes, without concern for the horrible odour which the putrefaction of the corpse always produces for a considerable time, in order not to be deprived of the consolation given to them by the remains of the friend they have lost.

Indians do not, in general, perform many ceremonies at their funerals; they prolong it, however, and attend it with many chants, when it is being held for renowned personalities, such as chiefs or famous warriors.

This is their regular mode of burial practice. When a man dies, they wrap his body in a white sheet or in a blanket of wool, and place it on the ground by the side of the hut. Then all the relatives and friends of the deceased, after having painted their faces in black, sit on the ground facing the body, light their pipes, bow their heads, and remain immobile, without saying a word. When the moment has come to leave for the burial ground, the parents and relatives approach and unveil the corpse, address him with words which are interrupted by tears and cries of sadness, say goodbye to him, embrace him in their arms and give him a last kiss.

When the deceased is a married man, his widow cuts a few locks from his hair, which, after having preserved them for a year, she has to burn. Usually, the local chief addresses a short eulogy to the dead in which he wishes him a happy voyage, and in an animated way, demonstrates the courage he must have against the dangers that he will meet. In one of these funeral speeches, I one day heard an Ojibwa chief address the deceased by way of the singular passage which follows:

> I have killed in different battles many men of the Sioux tribe. I yield them to you, that they may be your slaves; they can render you great service in your long travels, and when tired of your voyaging of an evening, you may lie down and they will provide for you from the woods nearby, attend your fire, and undertake many other services for you.

After the funeral speech, a number of men conduct the covered body to the tomb. If they have a coffin, they place the covered corpse within, along with the various presents which they have given him for his journey, carry the coffin to the grave which they have dug, and lower it without further ceremony. When they have no coffin, they place the body in the grave wrapped in a cover, put the presents beside him, cover him with tree bark, and then pile him over with earth. The funeral over, they then sink a pole over the spot where the head of the deceased rests, on top of which there is the rough figure of an animal or a bird. Each Indian family bears the name of an animal, and it is this animal that has been reproduced at the top of the pole.

Indians maintain a great respect for their graveyards and protect them with great care from any desecration. They also establish around their graves strong enclosures made from tree limbs and these are often renewed.

Some Indian tribes are in the habit of lighting a small fire every evening at the grave, which they maintain until midnight. They do this for at least four nights running, and sometimes longer.

The tradition of leaving diverse presents with the departed in their grave, is generally known among all Indians of North America. It is an extension of their belief that the souls of the dead are considered still to be persons who have yet to make a lengthy journey before arriving in the fair land of peace where they will find an abundance of good and wonderful things; during this voyage, they will still have need of all the things to which they became accustomed in this life. For this reason they are given arms, a gun, tobacco, provisions, etc.[118]

Some tribes have the custom of dressing the deceased, especially when it is a chief or an Indian of distinction, with all of his more beautiful ornaments; they state that an Indian who presents himself at the entrance to the land of happiness impoverished and without ornamentation is not admitted, and is obliged to return to the Earth or to wander in eternal misery.

Besides the provisions that they place next to the dead in his grave, they also leave, from time to time, fresh provisions above the grave; these are consumed during the night by dogs or hungry wolves; but Indians believe that souls, when they lack food, return to seek it at their tomb.

It is the habit of all Indians to cry for the dead, but the mode of this practice varies with different tribes. Among the ancient Canadians it was the custom for the relatives of the deceased to commence immediately upon the death, their cries and terrible groans. Sometimes one stopped and paid other persons to mourn the death and cry for his loss. Their mourning lasted for a year, during which they performed the most disagreeable ceremonies. The parents and kin had to crop their hair very short and paint their faces in black. They were not to look anyone in the face, appear in public, or eat anything hot, not even approach the fire to heat it. That did not last, indeed, for all of the mourning year, but always for a considerable time. Today the Indians of Canada have amalgamated considerably, and are all converts to the Christian religion.

Among the modern Indians of North America, it is customary that the parents of the deceased, paint their faces in black, and that they so appear everywhere during mourning, which lasts for a year, without ever washing, cutting, or combing their hair, and by wearing only their oldest outfits.

Women of the Ojibwas, as well as those of several other, more northern, tribes, are in the habit when they lose one of their children, to make a doll which they bind in a small cradle made deliberately for this purpose, and carry it everywhere with them for a year, as they would have carried the child which they lost.

When an Indian woman comes to lose her husband, it is traditional that she wraps his more beautiful garments in a piece of fabric, to which she attaches the ornaments of her dead husband, such as his finger rings, nose rings, etc. She always keeps this roll close by her, which is the mark of her widowhood, and she has to carry it with her everywhere she goes. A year passes, sometimes even longer, until the parents of the deceased take the roll, and then she is allowed to remarry.

It transpired once that the parents of the deceased allowed the widow to carry the roll for several years. She was so irritated and had become so impoverished in her daily living that she was on the verge of opening the roll for what it contained. She did not, however, dare to infringe upon the requirements of her widowhood. She approached different persons to appeal to the parents of her dead husband to clear her of her status as a widow, until finally it was granted and she was delivered from this stern mourning.

Besides this roll, the widow constantly carries at her side, for a year, a wooden bowl in which she puts, at each meal, the best pieces; and any stranger or neighbour who comes to her lodge is presented with this bowl and comes to savour those choice morsels with pleasure, since it is said that these represent the spirit of her late husband who thereby takes part in this meal.

Almost all North American Indians, from time to time, hold funeral feasts on the graves of their ancestors and departed friends; at such they sing and dance to the sound of the drum. They contend that the spirits of the dead witness this and greatly rejoice during these feasts celebrated in their honour by their friends and kin.[119]

As Indians passionately adore their children, one can easily imagine the extent of the sadness of those parents who come to lose one. It is not rare to see their chagrin render them sick, even unto death.

A traveller gave an eyewitness account as follows. During the time that he spent with the Sioux Indians, there died in his locale a small boy of four years. His father and mother were thrust into the most awful sorrow. That of the father, especially, approached desperation. He often seized an arrow or a sharp stone and tore away at his body. Finally, he was attacked and carried away by an awful disease. What was more startling in this circumstance was that the mother of the child, who until then had continually cried and wailed and did not appear to be less desperate than the father, after the death of the latter, regained her smile and recovered little by little her serenity and gaiety.

The stranger was surprised to see this woman, who had to join the loss of her husband to that of her son, so resigned and so tranquil, and he could not understand the cause of this sudden and profound change. When he asked her about this, he received a singular reply:

> When my son died, he was only a weak child, incapable of obtaining his subsistence in the country of the Spirits; also, my husband and I, we were in an awful state of grief, recognizing the miserable position in which our small, pauper child had been left in that country. But when I saw his father, who liked him so much and who was an excellent hunter, go to rejoin him, my pain was changed to joy, because now I am certain that my dear child is happy. I have now but one desire, which is to find myself soon in their company.[120]

Such are the impressions made upon the Indians by ideas that they have formed of the after life.

Notes

Editor's Introduction

1. See Blied, *Austrian Aid to American Catholics*, 19–29, 78 f.; for brief biographical sketches of the main participants in the general movement, see Ceglar, *Works of Bishop Frederic Baraga*, vol. 1, 289–309. In time, Baraga came to rely more heavily on the financial support of the *Propagation de la Foi*. See Baraga to PFAP. March 2, 1860. Original in PFAP. Copy in BBC-A 505.F.

2. See Buley, *Old Northwest*, vol. 1, vii, 62–64.

3. Knopf, "Introduction," *Anthony Wayne*, 3.

4. Ibid., 1–10; Prucha, *American Indian Policy*, 41–49.

5. Washburn, *American Indian and the United States*, vol. 4, 2295 f., and see Harmon, *Sixty Years of Indian Affairs*, 36–37. See also Prucha, *American Indian Treaties*, 92–95; and Horsman, "British Indian Department and the Resistance to General Anthony Wayne, 1793–1795."

6. Prucha, *American Indian Treaties*, 92; and see Allan, *British Indian Department*, 46–58.

7. Prucha, *American Indian Treaties*, chaps. 5 and 7.

8. Ibid., Appendix B.

9. Cruikshank, "The 'Chesapeake Crisis' as It Affected Upper Canada."

10. See Sugden, "Early Pan-Indianism." See also Edmunds, "Tecumseh's Native Allies: Warriors Who Fought for the Crown."

11. Letter from the Principal Inhabitants of Prairie du Chien to Captain Roberts, Feb. 10, 1813, in Wood, *Select British Documents*, vol. 3, part 1, 252–53.

12. See Sugden, *Tecumseh*, chap. 29; Jones, *To the Webster-Ashburton Treaty*, 11 f.

13. See Horan, *McKenney-Hall Portrait Gallery of American Indians*, 31–37; Prucha, *American Indian Policy*, 43–50; Prucha, *Documents on United States Indian Policy*, 14–16. On the intimacy of Astor with the Northwest Company of Montreal, see Ronda, *Astoria and Empire*, 46–49, 55–64; Haeger, *John Jacob Astor*, chaps. 4–6.

14. For a critical biography of Astor, see Haeger, *John Jacob Astor*. On Crooks, see Prucha, "Army Sutlers and the American Fur Company."

15. On the steady stream of complaints from Major Mathew Irwin to McKenney, see *Biography of Major Irwin*.

16. Brown, *Historical Geography of the United States*, 270–72.

17. See Abel, "History of Events," 378 f.; Horan, *McKenney-Hall Portrait Gallery*, 99–104.

18. Horan, *McKenney-Hall Portrait Gallery*, 79–80; 96–97. On McKenney's views, see Viola, *Thomas L. McKenney*, chap. 11.

19 Such a clause was included in the 1842 Treaty of La Pointe. On the experience of the Potawatomis following the Blackhawk War of 1832, see Edmunds, *Potawatomis*, chap. 10. On the experience of the Chippewa of the Upper Great Lakes after 1814, see Prucha, *American Indian Treaties*, 196–201, and Danziger, *Chippewas of Lake Superior*, chap. 5.

20 For Jackson's important speeches on the question of treaties and removal, along with those of his major opponent on these matters, Senator Theodore Frelinghuysen, see Prucha, *Documents on United States Indian Policy*, 47–52, 71–72.

21 In Michigan, the Detroit Treaty of 1855, signed with the Ottawas and Chippewas, modified the strict policy of removal, which had been in place as a result of the 1836 Treaty. See Washburn, *American Indian and the United States*, vol. 4, 2510 f. See also Danziger, "They Would Not Be Moved: The Chippewa Treaty of 1854."

22 Gregorich, *Apostle of the Chippewas*, 30, 43–46. Conflicts between Catholics and Protestants over the Grand River missions, including correspondence on questions of removal, are contained in the Notre Dame University Archives. See UNDA, Frederic Baraga Papers, 1809–1908. Microfilm. MBAR-3. Records from the National Archives. Department of Interior. Office of Indian Affairs. Incoming Correspondence, Grand River Missions. 1825–1840.

23 Horan, *McKenney-Hall Portrait Gallery*, 36. See Morse, *Report to the Secretary of War on Indian Affairs*.

24 John Johnston to his sister, Sault Ste. Marie, 25 July 1833, in "Letters on the Fur Trade," 140.

25 Berkhofer, *Salvation and the Savage*, 102.

26 See Schultz, *Indian Canaan*.

27 Morner, *Expulsion of the Jesuits from Latin America*, 11–13. And see Hollis, *History of the Jesuits*, 79–82, 137–39.

28 Verwyst, *Life and Labours of Rt. Rev. Frederic Baraga*, 209–11. And see Stevens, "Catholic and Protestant Missionaries among Wisconsin Indians: The Territorial Period."

29 See the narratives comprising "Shadows at La Pointe," in Vizenor, *People Named the Chippewa*, 37–55.

30 Harold Hickerson, "The Genesis of a Trading Post Band: The Pembina Chippewa," *Ethnohistory* 3 (1956): 289–345. The *Narrative* of John Tanner (1830) is a rich source for the westward expansion of the Algonkians of Lake Superior in the period after 1790. See Tanner, *Narrative of the Captivity and Adventures of John Tanner*; and see Peers, *Ojibwa of Western Canada*, 31–34. Alexander Henry the Younger is informative on the development of trade in the middle Red River Valley, at Pembina and elsewhere. See Coues, *Manuscript Journals of Alexander Henry and David Thompson*, vol. 1, 60–61. See also Ray, *Indians and the Fur Trade*.

31 Hickerson has left a fascinating picture of the specifics of this process in his editing of a fur trader's journal. See Hickerson, "Journal of Charles Jean Baptiste Chaboillez."

32 See Schoolcraft's comments in Mason, *Schoolcraft's Expedition*, 57–58; see also William T. Boutwell to the Editor, *Missionary Herald*, Aug. 8, 1832, in Mason, *Schoolcraft's Expedition*, 349–50 and Hickerson, "William Boutwell of the American Board and the Pillager Chippewa."

33 Hickerson, *Chippewa and their Neighbours*, 96–119.

34 For an elaboration of the dynamics of this situation, see Hickerson, *Southwestern Chippewa*; and, Hickerson, "The Virginia Deer and Intertribal Buffer Zones in the Upper Mississippi Valley."

35 See Hickerson, "William Boutwell," 4–5; 16–19.

36 On the literature of missions and Native peoples, see Axtell and Ronda, *Indian Missions*; Pagden, *European Encounters with the New World*, 204–12; Berkhofer, *Salvation and the Savage*, 161–80.

37 Freeman, "The Indian Convert: Theme and Variation."

38   Stevens, "Catholic and Protestant Missionaries," 148.

39   The idea was still current in the late nineteenth century and appears in *Appleton's Cyclopedia of American Biography*. See Pilling, *Bibliography of the Algonquian Languages*, 29. The idea was repeated in Hodge, *Handbook of American Indians North of Mexico*, 885. See the introductory comments in Baraga, "A Lecture Delivered by Bishop Baraga, 1863," 99–110. Essential documents concerning Baraga's birth and ancestry are reproduced in Ceglar and Baraga, *Frederic Baraga*, 397–408.

40   Ibid., 404–22; Walling, "Biographical Introduction," in Baraga, *Diary of Bishop Frederic Baraga*, 21–23.

41   For general details on Hofbauer, see Sharrock, "Hofbauer."

42   Attwater, *Penguin Dictionary of Saints*, 41–42.

43   Baraga to Dean Sluga, Aug. 9, 1830. Ceglar and Baraga, *Frederic Baraga*, 545.

44   Attwater, *Penguin Dictionary of Saints*, 88–89; for additional information on Hofbauer, see Artz, "St. Clement Hofbauer – a man of vision"; Hofer, *St. Clement Maria Hofbauer*; and see Walling, "Biographical Introduction," in Baraga, *Diary of Bishop Frederic Baraga*, 23.

45   Baraga's Notebook from Vienna, 1816–1822. July 12, 1817. In Ceglar and Baraga, *Frederic Baraga*, 413–14.

46   Certificate of Completed Law Studies, University of Vienna, Aug. 21, 1821, in ibid., 437; Baraga's Notebook from Vienna, 1816–1822. Dec. 1820, in ibid., 417–18.

47   Verwyst, *Life and Labours of Rt. Rev. Frederic Baraga*, 81.

48   Baraga to his sister, Amalia, May 6, 1819; July 14, 1819, in Ceglar and Baraga, *Frederic Baraga*, 429–32; Lambert, *Shepherd of the Wilderness*, 20–24.

49   Walling, "Biographical Introduction," in Baraga, *Diary of Bishop Frederic Baraga*, 23; Verwyst, *Life and Labours of Rt. Rev. Frederic Baraga*, chaps. 13–14.

50   Ferguson, *Europe in Transition*, 328, 343 f.

51   The publishing history and the nature of the text are reviewed by Knott, in "Introduction" to Thomas à Kempis, *Imitation of Christ*, 22–36.

52   Ferguson, *Europe in Transition*, 328, 349–50, 352–53.

53   March 27, 1860, Baraga, *Diary of Bishop Frederic Baraga*, 165. Gregorich, *Manuscript Biography*, 13–12B; Kotnik, "Bp. Baraga's Copy of Butler's Lives of the Saints."

54   Baraga's Notebook from Vienna, 1816–1822; Jan. 9, 1820, in Ceglar and Baraga, *Frederic Baraga*, 416. This view naturally changed upon reaching America, where there was a practical need to learn English.

55   Baraga's Notebook from Vienna, 1816–1822. Jan. 3, 1821. In ibid., 418.

56   See Beales, *Joseph II*, chap. 14.

57   See Bernard, *Joseph II*, 106–16.

58   O'Brien, *Ideas of Religious Toleration*, 13.

59   See Beales, *Joseph II*, 465 f.; Blanning, *Joseph II*, chap. 4.

60   O'Brien, *Ideas of Religious Toleration*, 31–35.

61   Ibid., 32; on Rautenstrauch, see Bernard, *Jesuits and Jacobins*, 94–96. See also Beales, "Christians and Philosophes."

62   For the role of Jansenism in later-eighteenth-century Austrian church reform, see Beales, *Joseph II*, 460–64; Blanning, *Joseph II*, 40–44; Chadwick, *Popes and European Revolution*, 392–417, and Bernard, *Jesuits and Jacobins*, 12–16.

63   On the general development of "Josephinism," see Bernard, "Origins of Josephinism"; and Bernard, *Jesuits and Jacobins* (1971), chaps. 5 and 6.

64   See his *Wiener Kirchenzeitung* (1784), cited in O'Brien, *Ideas of Religious Toleration*, 33.

65   Ibid.

66   See Walling, "Biographical Introduction," in Baraga, *Diary of Bishop Frederic Baraga*, 22–23; Lefebvre, *Napoleon*, 5th ed., vol. 2, 226–29. Baraga referred to his native Slovenian

tongue as the "Ilyrian language." Baraga to J. G. Shea, cited in Norton, *Catholic Missionary Activities in the Northwest*, 47.

67 In his youth, Baraga was a talented artist. He would not lose his interest in high art and music, but he progressively subjected such ideas to the service of God and the Church. He remained in contact with the great Slovenian artist, Metej Langus. See Gregorich, "Contributions of the Slovenes to the Chippewa and Ottawa Indian Missions," *Michigan History Magazine* 25, no. 2 (1941): 168–87; and see Ceglar and Baraga, *Frederic Baraga*, Appendix III: "A Description of Baraga's Miniatures," 595 f.

68 Rickett, *Brief Survey of Austrian History*, 65; and Blanning, *Joseph II*, 92–101.

69 See particularly, Reinerman, *Austria and the Papacy in the Age of Metternich*, vol. 1, *Between Conflict and Cooperation*; Cujes, *Ninidjanissidog Saiagiinagog*. Publication No. 2. Research Centre for Slovenian Culture, 5; Pozar, "Frederick Baraga and his Book," 30; Gregorich, "Contributions of the Slovenes," 5.

70 Jansenism and so-called "Josephism" and their influence on Habsburg Catholic Church reform is a complex matter. Beales has shown how Josephism had deep roots in the reign of Joseph's mother, the Empress Maria Theresa, and that it owed much to internal Church movements for reform as much as to forces of secular enlightenment. While Baraga does not appear to have had any connections to a religious order, he did attempt to join the Redemptorists early in his career and he clearly shared and retained much of that outlook. The call for a life of personal austerity, service, and devoted pastoral care are aspects of Jansenism that, on the other hand, were not alien to Baraga's outlook. It should be recalled that, in its original form, Jansenism was not hostile to Papal infallibility. Only with the assault on its order by Richelieu did the Port Royal community come to be associated with the Galican Church, hence its eventual appeal to Church reformers in mid-eighteenth century Austria. Joseph II was in no way anti-Catholic as such, but shared in the wish of many of his enlightened advisors to limit the influence of the Papacy and to encourage development of a Church which could be seen to be useful and productive. Hence his assault on those monasteries he saw to be unproductive, in the national sense.

71 Blanning, *Joseph II*, 42.

72 Ibid.

73 Ibid. And see Kotnik, "Bp. Baraga's Copy of Butler's Lives of the Saints," *Ava Maria Koledar* 61 (1974), 2–34; Report of Dean Bartholomew Bozic to the Bishop's Office regarding the Confraternities and Baraga. Feb. 18, 1828, in Ceglar and Baraga, *Frederic Baraga*, 498–99.

74 As with Hofbauer, the life of a pure contemplative was not acceptable to Baraga. Time could be put aside for personal communion, but not to the sacrifice of one's pastoral duties. In the *Diary*, April 13, 1860, 168, we may read: "Great Spiritual misfortune this morning. Instead of 3 rose at 5. 2 hours absolutely lost!" This is the statement of one committed to work in the world.

75 Beales, *Joseph II*, 477–79; Bernard, *Jesuits and Jacobins*, 59–60.

76 Lambert, *Shepherd of the Wilderness*, 27–29; Blanning, *Joseph II*, 44 f.

77 Baraga to Kalan. March 21, 1828, in Ceglar and Baraga, *Frederic Baraga*, 501–2.

78 Baraga, *Diary of Bishop Frederic Baraga*, Sept. 28, 1853, 46; Nov. 9, 1856, 93.

79 On Baraga's discomfort with the exercise of power, see Kotnik, "Bp. Baraga's Copy of Butler's Lives of the Saints," 20–22.

80 Cujes, *Ninidjanissidog Saiagiinagog*, 89; Ceglar, *Works of Bishop Frederic Baraga*, vol. 1, 236–47.

81 Bishop Anthony A. Wolf to Baraga, June 6, 1827, in Ceglar and Baraga, *Frederic Baraga*, 495–96.

82 The earliest important English biography was that of Verwyst, *Life and Labours of Rt. Rev. Frederic Baraga*. The closest student of Baraga's life was Joseph Gregorich; his

multi-volume manuscript on the life of Baraga is held in the archives of the Bishop Baraga Association, Marquette, Michigan. Gregorich also published a short biography, *Apostle of the Chippewas*. Of interest is Rezek's *History of the Diocese of Sault Ste. Marie and Marquette*, vol. 1. Popular biographical treatments are provided in Jamison, *By Cross and Anchor* and by Lambert, *Shepherd of the Wilderness*. See also the "Biographical Introduction" and "Bibliography" in Baraga, *Diary of Bishop Frederic Baraga*. The first biography to appear was in Slovenian: Voncina, *Baraga*. Also appearing in Slovenian was Jaklic, *Irenej Frederik Baraga*.

83 The name "Leopold" was selected to honour both St. Leopold, a medieval Austrian Margrave, and the Emperor's daughter, Leopoldina, who died in 1826 as Empress of Brazil.

84 Cujes, *Ninidjanissidog Saiagiinagog*. Publication No. 2. Research Centre for Slovenian Culture, 5; Beales, *Joseph II*, 477. See the 1828 correspondence between Baraga and his superiors regarding his involvement in the establishment of Sodalities in his parishes in Ceglar and Baraga, *Frederic Baraga*, 500–506.

85 Baraga to the Bishop of Ljubljana, Aug. 10, 1929, in Ceglar and Baraga, *Frederic Baraga*, 524.

86 Baraga to Bishop Fenwick, Cincinnati, Nov. 13, 1929, in ibid., 533; Baraga to Directorate, Leopoldine Society. July 25, 1830, ibid., 543; Baraga to Directorate, Leopoldine Society, Sept. 22, 1830, ibid., 553; Baraga to his Sister, Amalia, Nov. 30, 1830, ibid., 578.

87 Knott, "Introduction" to Thomas à Kempis, *The Imitation of Christ*, 23.

88 Gregorich, *New Catholic Encyclopedia*, vol. 2, 84; Walling, "Biographical Introduction," in Baraga, *Diary of Bishop Frederic Baraga*, 23.

89 On the historical distribution and cultural features of the Ottawas, see Feest and Feest, "Ottawa," in *Handbook of the North American Indians*, vol. 15: *Northeast*, 772–86.

90 Shea, *History of the Catholic Church*, 589 f.; Rezek, *History of the Diocese of Sault Ste. Marie and Marquette*, vol. 1, 141 f.; McGivern, "Baraga," *Dictionary of Canadian Biography*, vol. 9, 31; Baraga, *Diary of Bishop Frederic Baraga*, Feb. 12, 1858, 118, Note 87; April 28, 1860, 170.

91 Communities where such sentiment was strong included L'Arbre Croche, Sault Ste. Marie, Drummond Island, Michilimackinac, L'Anse, La Pointe, Fond du Lac, Grande Portage, Pic, and Michipicoten. See Shea, *Catholic Missions*, chaps. 19 and 20; Verwyst, *Missionary Labours*, and Verwyst, *Life and Labours of Rt. Rev. Frederic Baraga*, chaps. 2–7.

92 Nute, "Introduction" to *Documents Relating to Northwest Missions*, and Antoine Tabeau to J. O. Plessis, Bishop of Quebec, March 27, 1818, at 36–38. See also Lemieux, "Provencher" *Dictionary of Canadian Biography*, vol. 8, 719.

93 On Catholic missionaries active on the Michigan frontier between 1799 and 1830, see Verwyst, *Life and Labours of Rt. Rev. Frederic Baraga*, chaps. 8 and 9. On Assiginack, see Leighton, "Assiginack," *Dictionary of Canadian Biography*, vol. 9, 9–10.

94 See Leighton, "Assiginack," 9–10; and "Reminiscences of Capt. Thomas Gummersall Anderson," in Talman, *Loyalist Narratives from Upper Canada*, 24–28.

95 See Rezek, *History of the Diocese of Sault Ste. Marie and Marquette*, vol. 1, 74–84; Cujes, *Ninidjanissidog Saiagiinagog*, 12, 16–17; Walling, "Biographical Introduction," in Baraga, *Diary of Bishop Frederic Baraga*, 25.

96 As early as 1800, there was an expression of interest by a Protestant, David Bacon, in going to L'Arbre Croche. See John Askin, Letter of Introduction, Sept. 13, 1800, in Quaife, *John Askin Papers*, vol. 2, 525.

97 Foster, "Oberlin Ojibway Mission," 2.

98 See Thomas, *Millennial Impulse in Michigan*; and Cross, *Burned-Over District*.

99 See Baraga's report on his visit to missions for the summer of 1859, submitted to the German Catholic publication in Cincinnati, *Wahrheitsfreund* 22 (1859). This report is also in BBC. A – 668G, and is reproduced in Baraga, *Diary of Bishop Frederic Baraga*,

137–39. See also Thomas, *Millennial Impulse in Michigan*, 60 f. and Lambert, *Shepherd of the Wilderness*, 82. The main study of Strang is Quaife, *Kingdom of St. James*; for a more recent review, see Weeks, "Utopian Kingdom in the American Grain."

100   Baraga to Schoolcraft. July 17, 1833. NA-OIA. M-1-71. 96; Résé to Schoolcraft, Aug. 24, 1836. NA-OIA: M-41, 208–9; Gregorich, *Manuscript Biography*, chap. 13, 13b; chap. 19, 12; Lambert, *Shepherd of the Wilderness*, 157–58.

101   See Berkhofer, *Salvation and the Savage*, 100–106; Prucha, *American Indian Treaties*, 209.

102   See Cass, *Considerations on the Present State of the Indians.*

103   Abel, "History of Events," 288–90.

104   Baraga to Bishop P. Lefevre, July 1, 1842, cited in Stevens, "Catholic and Protestant Missionaries," 141–42.

105   Walling, "Biographical Introduction," in Baraga, *Diary of Bishop Frederic Baraga*, 26.

106   Cass, *Considerations on the Present State*, 6.

107   Blackbird, *Complete History of Ottawa and Chippewa Indians*, 23–29. The official response of the Church to Blackbird's contention that William had been assassinated was that he had died of a chest hemorrhage, traceable to an accident he had previously sustained in America. A letter dated July 13, 1833 was sent from Rome to Rt. Rev. Frederic Résé, Bishop of Detroit, providing the medical explanation. The letter is reproduced in "Notes" in Verwyst, *Life and Labours of Rt. Rev. Frederic Baraga*, 463–64.

108   This was printed as *Otawa Anamie-Masinaigan Wawiyatanong*. Walling, "Biographical Introduction," in Baraga, *Diary of Bishop Frederic Baraga*, 24; Ceglar, *Works of Bishop Frederic Baraga*, vol. 1, 21–25.

109   Assiginack was the uncle of Andrew J. Blackbird (Makatebinessi) and of his brother, the late William Makatebinessi.

110   Blackbird, *Complete History of Ottawa and Chippewa Indians*, 32; and see Leighton, "Assiginack," 9–10.

111   Lambert, *Shepherd of the Wilderness*, 59–60; Leighton, "Assiginack," 9–10; Grant, *Moon of Wintertime*, 78, 84–92. These are just a few of the personalities of the day who may be said to have contributed to development of a Native historical perspective. See MacLeod, "Anishinabeg Point of View."

112   On Baraga's concerns about "Indian removal" and the Grand River Indians in the aftermath of the 1831 Treaty, see Gregorich, *Manuscript Biography*, chap. 13, 11B-13b, and Verwyst, *Life and Labours of Rt. Rev. Frederic Baraga*, 168–70.

113   See Lambert, *Shepherd of the Wilderness*, 126–31; Penny, *North to Lake Superior*, 61–63.

114   See O'Brien, "Lady Antoinette Von Hoeffern."

115   Baraga to Crebassa, June 18, 1843, in Hilger, "Letters and Documents of Bishop Baraga Extant in the Chippewa Country," 296–97.

116   Baraga left an account of one of his excursions on snowshoe in *Wahrheitsfreund*, 23 (1860), 374–75. Also in BBC-A 674G. Printed in Baraga, *Diary of Bishop Frederic Baraga*, 156–58.

117   Walling, "Biographical Introduction," in Baraga, *Diary of Bishop Frederic Baraga*, 25. This is not the only example in the literature. Richard Forbis has written of a similar situation among the Flathead, prior to the arrival among them of the Belgian Jesuit, Pierre de Smet, in the 1840s. Forbis, "Flathead Apostasy."

118   Walling, "Biographical Introduction," in Baraga, *Diary of Bishop Frederic Baraga*, 26; "A Letter from Hon. Peter White," cited in Elliott, "Father Baraga among the Chippewas," 605 f.

119   See Hilger, "Letters and Documents of Bishop Baraga," 299–300.

120   Cujes, *Ninidjanissidog Saiagiinagog*, 33 f.

121   Ibid., 8, 36–41; and see O'Brien, "Father Frank Pierz."

122   Prud'homme, "Our Lady of Dolours," 1–4.

123   Ibid.

124 Collins, "Chronicle of the Roussains and Mamainse"; Walling, "Biographical Introduction," in Baraga, *Diary of Bishop Frederic Baraga*, 26. For this old fur-trade family of
the Fond du Lac area, see *John A. Bardon Papers*. Fur Trade Manuscripts. Minnesota
Historical Society; and Public Archives of Canada, *Report*, 39; Wallace, *Documents Relating to the North West Company*, 221; and Rezek (1906), vol. 1, 70.

125 "Father Frémiot's Report to His Superior in New York" (Fort William, Oct. 18, 1849).
In Arthur, *Thunder Bay District*, 13–16; and see Norton, *Catholic Missionary Activities in the
Northwest*, 72–73.

126 See Ceglar, *Works of Bishop Frederic Baraga*, vol. 1.

127 See ibid., vol. 1, and the bibliography published in Baraga, *Diary of Bishop Frederic
Baraga*, 323–25; Cujes, *Ninidjanissidog Saiagiinagog*, 58 f.; and Pilling, *Bibliography of the
Algonquian Languages*, 24–29.

128 Baraga, *Theoretical and Practical Grammar*, 3.

129 Baraga, *Dictionary of the Otchipwe Language*. For a description of the various later editions, see Pilling, *Bibliography of the Algonquian Languages*, 27–28; and Ceglar, *Works of
Bishop Frederic Baraga*, vol. 1, 157 f.

130 Baraga, *Diary of Bishop Frederic Baraga*, March 2, 1853, 48. The incident has been described on several occasions. See Jamison, *By Cross and Anchor*.

131 On the publishing history and the role of Fr. Albert Lacombe in later editions, see Ceglar, *Works of Bishop Frederic Baraga*, vol. 1, 157–83. The 1992 edition contains a useful
Introduction by John D. Nichols.

132 See Morton, "Bellecourt," *Dictionary of Canadian Biography*, vol. 10, 46–47; Cadieux,
Lettres des Nouvelles Missions du Canada, 67; and Reardon, *George Anthony Belcourt*, chap. 2.
As late as 1859, Baraga does not seem to have seen Belcourt's work. See Ceglar, *Works
of Bishop Frederic Baraga*, vol. 1, 182. On Meeker, see Schultz, *Indian Canaan*, 72.

133 Ibid., 71, 166.

134 Foster, "The Oberlin Ojibway Mission." Frederick Ayer had been at La Pointe as early
as 1831, along with his former classmates from Andover Theological Seminary, William T. Boutwell, and Sherman Hall. See Philip P. Mason's notes 14 and 16 in Mason,
Schoolcraft's Expedition, 98–99. Hickerson has shown just how ill-received this approach
could be on occasion. See Hickerson, "William Boutwell."

135 For recent comments on the current state and vibrancy of Ojibwa in the upper Great
Lakes states, see Treuer, "Introduction" to *Living Our Language*.

136 See Smitek, "Baraga, Schoolcraft and the Beginnings of American Ethnology." In
passing, Baraga did make a contribution to material culture studies of the North
American Indians through his donation of artefacts to the museum of Carniola. See
Kabinet Cudes?; and see "Cabinet of Curiosities."

137 Cass, *Considerations on the Present State*, 6. Alcohol and its influence on Natives on the
frontier and in more recent times has generated a large literature. See Mail and Mc-
Donald, "Native Americans and Alcohol." See also Grant, *Moon of Wintertime*, 57, 110,
138–39. Hickerson's comments on alcohol and its significance in the hard daily life of
trapping are of interest; see Hickerson, "Journal of Charles Jean Baptiste Chaboillez,"
301n39.

138 Baraga, *Diary of Bishop Frederic Baraga*, Nov. 3, 1862, 279.

139 Ibid., 279n157.

140 Frederic Baraga, *Abrégé de l'histoire des indiens*.

141 *Report to the Leopoldine Society*. Dec. 28, 1835, cited in Ceglar, *Works of Bishop Frederic
Baraga*, vol. 1, 201.

142 Baraga, *Geschichte, Character, Sitten und Gebräuche der nord-amerikanischen Indier*.

143 The Slovenian edition was probably prepared by Janes Zeigler, rather than by the
priest Jozef Kek. See Ceglar, *Works of Bishop Frederic Baraga*, vol. 1, 203; but see also
Pozar, "Frederik Baraga and his Book," 37.

144 Ibid., 37; Baraga to his sister, Amalia. April 25, 1837, in Ceglar, *Works of Bishop Frederic Baraga*, vol. 1, 202.

145 For the northeast contact zone, see the extensive bibliographic information provided in Biggar, *Early Fur Trading Companies of New France*, 175–296; and Quinn, *North America from Earliest Discovery*, 569–95; for the Spanish American literature, an introduction is provided in Huddleston, *Origins of the American Indian*.

146 See Lemieux, "Le Jeune."

147 "Lecture Delivered by Bishop Baraga, 1863." This lecture was given in German, rendered into English by Father Zaplotnik in 1917.

148 Ceglar and Baraga, *Frederic Baraga*, 414n61.

149 Baraga to the Bishop of Ljubljana, Aug. 10, 1829, ibid., 524; Baraga to Bishop Fenwick, Cincinnati, Nov. 13, 1829, ibid., 533.

150 A German edition of Carver's *Travels through the Interior Parts of North America* (1778) was published in Hamburg in 1780; Long's *Voyages and Travels* (1790) was also published in German in Hamburg in 1791. See Pozar, "Frederick Baraga and his Book," 63, 68.

151 See Ceglar, *Works of Bishop Frederic Baraga*, vol. 1, 201–2; Pozar, "Frederick Baraga and his Book," 57 f.

152 See ibid., 60 f.

153 A valuable reference to productions of this nature may be found in Freeman, *Guide to Manuscripts Relating to the American Indian*, and also Field, *Essay on Indian Bibliography* (1873).

154 Thatcher's work on Indian biography is now scarce. It continued to appear in print at least as late as 1865. See Field, *Essay on Indian Bibliography*, 891. Information drawn from Adair and Carver also entered Baraga's text. See Pozar, "Frederick Baraga and his Book," 57–70, and Ceglar, *Works of Bishop Frederic Baraga*, vol. 1, 201–2.

155 Ironically, it may have been less rational factors such as "charisma" which led to greater or lesser success on the part of missionaries in seventeenth-century eastern North America. See Conkling, "Legitimacy and Conversion in Social Change."

156 See Verwyst, *Life and Labours of Rt. Rev. Frederic Baraga*, 184 f.

157 See "Cabinet of Curiosities."

158 Cass, "Indians of North America"; Berkhofer, *Salvation and the Savage*, chap. 6.

159 Hickerson, "William Boutwell," 1–29. See also Higham, *Noble, Wretched and Redeemable*, 20–21.

160 See Cass, *Considerations on the Present State*, 3–6.

161 An example of how these various ingredients mixed together into a long-term, if rather contorted, form of cultural survival, is outlined in Mochon, "Stockbridge-Munsee Cultural Adaptations."

162 Baraga, *Chippewa Indians*, 22.

163 Vecsey, *Traditional Ojibwa Religion*, 165–68.

164 Such practices were intimated in Indiana Territory after 1800 when Governor Harrison began to enter into selective negotiations with "any Indian over whom he could exert a temporary influence". See Abel, "History of Events," 266–67. In Canada, the trend towards replacement of traditional Native leadership by new types of Band representatives commenced in 1830 and was well established by the 1870s. See John L. Tobias, "Protection, Civilization, Assimilation." See also the observations on conflicts in leadership made by Fr. Frémiot at Fort William in 1849, in Arthur, *Thunder Bay District*, 13–16.

165 Baraga, *Chippewa Indians*, 22.

166 Baraga, *Chippewa Indians*, 33–35.

167 See Kidder, *Ojibwa Narratives*, 55–60. See also Kohl, *Kitchi-Gami* (1860), 111; Hoffman, *The Midéwiwin*, 221–22; Dewdney, "Ecological Notes on the Ojibwa Shaman-Artist";

Hickerson, *Chippewa and their Neighbours*, 51–63; Vecsey, *Traditional Ojibwa Religion*, 10–11; 109.

168 See Hickerson, "The Feast of the Dead"; MacDonald, "The Ancient Fishery at Sault Ste. Marie"; and MacDonald, *Saulteur-Ojibwa Fishery at Sault Ste. Marie*.

169 Armstrong, "Reminiscences of Life among the Chippewa," part 4, 142.

170 Hoffman, *The Midéwiwin*; Hickerson, *Chippewa and their Neighbours*, chap. 4; Hickerson, "Feast of the Dead," 81–107; Vecsey, *Traditional Ojibwa Religion*; Emerson, "The Mystery of the Pits," and "The Puckasaw Pits and the Religious Alternative"; Dewdney, "Insights on Vision Sites"; MacDonald, "The Sacred Shore."

171 See George Nelson's *Letter-Journal, 1823*, in Brown and Brightman, "Orders of the Dreamed," 34.

172 The English geologist Charles Lyell published his influential *Principles of Geology* in 1830, a work which would do much to inspire the work of Darwin. See also Lyell, *Antiquity of Man* (1863). In Northern Michigan, the work of Douglas Houghton (1809–1845) was rapidly advancing modern geological knowledge before his untimely death by drowning on Lake Superior. Louis Agassiz's treatise, *Lake Superior*, with its remarkable discussion of ancient glacial beach ridges, did not appear until 1850.

173 The origins of this view are discussed in Huddleston, *Origins of the American Indian*, 33 f.

174 Ussher's timescale, promoted in his *Annals of the Old and New Testament* (1650–54), was thereafter recognized, although before his time others had established similar benchmarks through reasoning based on the generations in the Bible. See Eiseley, *Darwin's Century*, 61.

175 See Huddleston, *Origins of the American Indian*, 48 f.

176 His work was published first in the Jesuit-sponsored *Journal de Trevoux*. See William N. Fenton and Elizabeth L. Moore's Introduction to Lafitau, *Customs of the American Indians*, lxxxvii.

177 The post-1830 establishment of the Mormon Church (Church of Jesus Christ of Latter-day Saints) gave a new twist to the "lost tribes of Israel" theory. Others who enjoyed well-tailored explanations of history also kept the notion alive; but such views were clearly moving in a different direction from the course which modern anthropology was following. See Williams, *Fantastic Archaeology*, 31–32; 51–53; 156 f.; and Hallowell, "Beginnings of Anthropology in America," 4–6.

178 Hallowell, "Beginnings of Anthropology in America," 4–8.

179 See, for example, Dixon, *Quest for the Origins of the First Americans*.

180 BBC. M 24-1. Baraga to the Archbishop of Vienna. Sept. 12, 1843.

181 See Wissler, "American Indian and the American Philosophical Society."

182 Cited in Wissler, "American Indian and the American Philosophical Society," 191.

183 Cited in Baraga, *Dictionary of the Otchipwe Language* (1878), "Preface"; see also Smitek, "Baraga, Schoolcraft and the Beginnings of American Ethnology."

184 Heckewelder, *History, Manners, and Customs of the Indian Nations*, 118–27; for a review of Algonkian commentaries, see Goddard, "Description of the Native Languages of North America before Boas," 22–23; 26–28. An earlier review of Algonkian linguistic studies is found in Pilling, *Bibliography of the Algonquian Languages*.

185 Berkhofer, *White Man's Indian*, 3.

186 Axtell has reflected on this question at some length. See Axtell, *Beyond 1492*, chap. 2.

187 See the discussion in Jaenen, *Friend and Foe*, chap. 1.

188 Williams, *Key into the Language of America*, A2.

189 See Dickason, *Myth of the Savage*; Jaenen, *Friend and Foe*, chaps. 4–5; D. B. Smith, *Le Sauvage*.

190 Julius Caesar, *Gallic War*. Book 6, C. 11, 124 f.

191 See LaRoque, "The Métis in English Canadian Literature."

192   See Fenton and Moore's Introduction to Lafitau, *Customs of the American Indians*, lii–liv; Pagden, "The Savage Critic: Some European Images of the Primitive," in *Yearbook of English Studies* 13 (1983), 32–45; Pagden, *European Encounters with the New World*, chap. 4; and Elliott, *Old World and the New*, chap. 2.

193   See Pagden, "Savage Critic", and his *European Encounters with the New World*, chap. 4.

194   Geoffrey Symcox, "The Wild Man's Return: The Enclosed Vision of Rousseau's Discourses," in Dudley and Novak, *Wild Man Within*, 223–48.

195   This was an early message reported from the New World. See Acosta, *Natural and Moral History of the Indies* (1590). See also Huddleston, *Origins of the American Indian*.

196   See Giraud, *Métis in the Canadian West*; Van Kirk, *Many Tender Ties*; Brown, *Strangers in Blood*; Jackson, *Children of the Fur Trade*.

197   Pagden, *European Encounters with the New World*, 117.

198   Sir Alexander Mackenzie, "A General History of the Fur Trade," 67.

199   Eccles, "The Role of the Church in New France," 26–37; 84–85; Saunders, "The Emergence of the Coureur de bois as a Social Type"; Grant, *Moon of Wintertime*, 54–58; Jaenen, *Friend and Foe*, 108–11.

Main Text

1   Researches in the twentieth century have produced evidence that many approaches had been made to the western hemisphere well before Columbus. The 500th anniversary of the Columbus landing spawned many evaluations other than those of the "heroic" variety. A summary of the literature, set out along thematic lines, may be found in Viola and Margolis, *Seeds of Change*.

2   Morison noted that "... this was not necessary. The fable that she actually pawned them for Columbus dates from the seventeenth century." Morison, *Admiral of the Ocean Sea*, 103–104.

3   Columbus has had his supporters ever since, but also detractors. The respected geographer, Carl Sauer, saw Columbus as a man of limited talent and moral fibre. See Pagden, "Foreword," x; but see also Morison, *Admiral of the Ocean Sea*, 6.

4   Morison discusses the composition and nature of the letter, written in the aftermath of a storm of Feb. 4th to 7th, 1493. See Morison, *Admiral of the Ocean Sea*, 320–23. Owing to the storm, Columbus actually entered the Tagus estuary and landed at Lisbon, Portugal (much to his political inconvenience) before departing for Spain on the 13th of March. For the mechanics of the storm and the landing in Portugal, see Morison, *Great Explorers*, 423–35.

5   The early literature on Native origins is reviewed in Huddleston, *Origins of the American Indian*.

6   In making this observation, Baraga shows himself to be in line with that tradition of observation that flowed up from Acosta, through Lafitau and into the early nineteenth century. Ideas linking the Native American tribes to the "lost tribes of Israel" do not seem to have exercised much influence on Baraga. This may partially be attributed to the influence of Heckewelder and others, centred at the American Philosophical Association, who tended to hold the view that North America was peopled via a northwest land bridge. See Huddleston, *Origins of the American Indian*.

7   Much has been learned since Baraga's time about earlier approaches to the continent, particularly by the Norse and English merchants out of Bristol, including the ventures of the Cabot brothers. For summaries see Oleson, *Early Voyages and Northern Approaches*; Quinn, *North America from Earliest Discovery*; Sauer, *Early Spanish Main*, 1–11.

Notes

8   Giovanni da Verrazzano, or Jean de Verrazane (1484–1528). See Wroth, *Voyages of Giovanni da Verrazzano*; Quinn, *North America*, 154–58; and Morison, *Great Explorers*, 129–68.

9   On the failed Carolina colony, see Quinn, *Roanoke Voyages*, and *North America*, 329f.

10 Christopher Newport (d. 1617). See Quinn, *North America*, 437–40 and Andrews, "Christopher Newport of Limehouse, Mariner," 28–41.

11 The Algonkian-speaking Powhatan Indians were encountered by the Virginia colonists. On the historical sources and personalities of the Virginians and Powhatans, see the "Prologue" in Rountree, *Powhatan Indians of Virginia*, 3–16.

12 John Smith (1580–1631). He was born in Willoughby, Lincolnshire. An adventurer, he fought in France and Hungary. Captured by the Turks, he was sold as a slave, but escaped to Russia. He then joined the expedition for the colonization of Virginia in 1607. He was elected president of the colony for the years 1608–09. His published accounts are important early sources.

13 Baraga has drawn upon some of the standard references, here, such as Smith's *Generall Historie of Virginia* (1624) and later summaries such as in Heckewelder. For a review of the Pocahontas legend and history, see Grace Steel Woodward, *Pocahontas*, chap. 5; revision of the legend may be considered in Rountree, *Pocahontas's People*, 37–39; and in Gleach, "Controlled Speculation," 21–42.

14 For a review of the extent and nature of Powhatan's authority, see the Epilogue in Rountree, *Powhatan Indians of Virginia*, 140f.

15 John Rolfe (1585–1622). See Rountree's Prologue in Rountree, *Powhatan Indians of Virginia*, 3–16.

16 Samoset appears in Bradford's *Of Plymouth Plantation* (1650). According to Morison, Samoset was an Algonkian of Maine in the Pemaquid Point area, who befriended local European settlers and fishermen and conveyed land to one John Brown in 1625. He died about 1653. See William Bradford, *Of Plymouth Plantation*, 80.

17 The Algonkian Massasoit has long been associated with the first recorded "thanksgiving" in the Plymouth Colony, as recorded in Edward Winslow's letter to England of Dec. 21, 1621, and reproduced in what has become known as *Mourt's Relation* (1622). Massasoit was in attendance at this "thanksgiving" and was described as "their greatest king." See S. E. Morison in Bradford (1967), 90n8. Massasoit was of the Wampanoag tribe. Speck translated his name roughly as "He Who is Great." Frank G. Speck, *Territorial Subdivisions and Boundaries*, 51–52.

18 The treaty with Massasoit was concluded in 1621. The details are reproduced in Bradford's *Of Plymouth Plantation*. See Bradford, *Of Plymouth Plantation*, 79–80.

19 Opechankanow, a brother of Powhatan, succeed him as paramount chief and led a confederated attack on the colonists in 1622. He was still hostile in the 1640s. Following the treaty of 1646 and lax controls imposed in the colony during the English Civil War period, the colonists gradually displaced the Indians and developed an Indian Reserve policy in the Chesapeake Bay area. See R. L. Morton, *Colonial Virginia*, vol. 1, 177, 228–30, and Rountree, *Pocahontas's People*, chap. 4.

20 Rountree has discussed the economic and land use changes that were rapidly altering the areas around Jamestown in the years between 1619 and 1622. Opechancanough's "ambition" needs now to be seen in this context. See Rountree, *Pocahontas's People*, 66–67.

21 Baraga here repeats the conventional account of his day, as received largely from Smith's *Generall Historie of Virginia* of 1624. Rountree has placed this account into a broader context based on the Records of the Virginia Company. There were undoubtedly many others aware of the conspiracy. See Rountree, *Pocahontas's People*, 73–75.

22 The reference is to the Pequot sachem, Sassacus, who, according to John Winthrop in his *History of New England* (1630–1649), had jurisdiction over 26 lesser sachems, in the

early 1630s, in the southern Connecticut region. See *John Winthrop's Journal*; and see *Handbook of the North American Indians*, vol. 15, *Northeast*, 168, 172.

23   The reference is to Captain John Mason. In addition to Mason's account published in 1736, another important source is that of John Underhill, one of Mason's military associates, in his *News from America* (1638). The latter contained an illustration of the English attack on the Pequot fort at Mystic. See Mason, *Brief History of the Pequot War*; Underhill, *News from America*. See also *Handbook of the North American Indians*, vol. 15, 90–91.

24   The Pequot war had involved English troops supplemented by Narragansetts, allied through the interventions of Roger Williams. Of the few Pequots who survived, many were sold, at English insistence, into slavery in the West Indies. See Woodhead, *Algonquians of the East Coast*, 81–82; and *Handbook of the North American Indians*, vol. 15, 90.

25   Details of the treaty were provided by Bradford in 1650. See Bradford, *Of Plymouth Plantation*, 330f., and Appendix XII, Document 5, 430f.

26   The general thrust of this paragraph is given scholarly precision in such recent works as Morrison, *Embattled Northeast*, and Cronon, *Changes in the Land*.

27   King Philip, one of the sons of Massasoit, was known as Metacomet.

28   In his carefully researched study, Leach raises the strong possibility that on the 23rd of June a young Wampanoeg "looter" was murdered by a young colonist, thus setting the condition desired by King Philip, that the English initiate hostilities. See Leach, *Flintlock and Tomahawk*, 42–43.

29   While Captain Edward Hutchinson was clearly involved in ongoing military protection of the Plymouth Colony, there is more evidence to suggest command was exercised by Captain James Cudworth, Captain Daniel Henchman, or perhaps another. See Leach, *Flintlock and Tomahawk*, 40–41, 45–46, 50–51.

30   Captain Thomas Lathrop of Beverly. The account is derived from Church. See Leach, *Flintlock and Tomahawk*, 87–88, and see note 28.

31   Probably familiar to Baraga was Benjamin Church's account, first published in 1716 and available in an 1829 edition compiled by Thomas Church. See Church, *History of King Philip's War*. See also *Handbook of the North American Indians*, vol. 15, 92f. and Burke, *Puritans at Bay*.

32   See Church, *History of the Great Indian War*, 309–10.

33   Josiah Winslow (1629–81), Governor of Plymouth Colony from 1673 to 1681.

34   The reference is to Captain Michael Pierce. The battle took place on the banks of the Pawtucket River some five miles north of Providence. See Leach, *Flintlock and Tomahawk*, 167.

35   Captain Samuel Wadsworth, in charge of a Massachusetts company of regulars at Marlborough. The altercation has become known as the Battle of Sudbury. See Leach, *Flintlock and Tomahawk*, 155–75.

36   Sources that would have been available to Baraga for his account of King Philip's War would have included: Penhallow, *Wars of New England*; Hubbard, *Narrative of Indian Wars*; Church, *History of King Philip's War, 1675–76*. See also Speck, *Territorial Subdivisions and Boundaries*, 12–16. For a recent review, see Steele, *Warpaths*, 96–109.

37   It would be another fifteen years before Francis Parkman published his *Conspiracy of Pontiac* (1851). Baraga's statement tends to be accurate with respect to the writings of his time. Later historians have continued to reveal the much greater coherence and persistence of Native life and culture associated with resistance movements. See Sugden, "Early Pan-Indianism," and *Tecumseh*.

38   In Baraga's lifetime, but after publication of his *History*, some of the first commentaries on Native history prepared by Native writers started to appear, presenting a somewhat different picture of warfare between the eastern tribes. In the work of Jones, Warren and Copway, for example, there is much to suggest that intertribal warfare

of a well-organized nature remained a significant factor in the eighteenth century. In particular, the extent of Ojibway–Iroquois warfare was taken up by these writers. See Eid, "The Ojibwa–Iroquois War." In addition, the onset of the American Revolution altered the circumstances of the Iroquois after the defeat of the British under Bourgoyne at Saratoga in 1779. American forces began the long conquest of tribes to the west, which would not end until the 1890s. A standing Iroquois army was the first to be defeated by George Washington and his troops. See Mintz, *Seeds of Empire*.

39 Hickerson reviewed the dynamics of this process thoroughly on a number of occasions. His main point was that under conditions of the fur trade, migration and Indian removal, a large territory of transition forest zone in Wisconsin and Minnesota, previously a shared resource area, became subject to settlement pressure by diverse peoples. The general westward movement of Ojibwa peoples suggests it would be more accurate to say that traditional Dakota territories were being encroached *upon*. See Hickerson, *Southwestern Chippewa*, 12–29.

40 Dobyns has suggested Pre-Columbian North American populations may have been as high as 18 million. Dobyns, *Their Number Become Thinned*, 343.

41 Baraga's figures actually add up to 315,900. All estimates of Aboriginal populations prior to the 1890 U.S. Census were impressionistic. Baraga's figures rather closely approximate figures tabled in Washington by Secretary of War H.B. Porter in 1829 and Schoolcraft's figures reported in 1837. See Eaton, *Are the Indians Dying Out?*, 5–6.

42 See note 54 below.

43 John Long provided a description of drinking and violence that extended over three days. Long, *Voyages and Travels of Indian Interpreter and Trader*, 49.

44 Baraga is presumably referring to the great epidemic of 1781–82. The question of disease effects has been the focus of much scholarship since W. H. McNeill published *Plagues and Peoples*. On the dynamics of smallpox and other disease losses among North American aboriginal populations, see Dobyns, *Their Number Become Thinned*, 11–16.

45 A league was about three miles or about 4.8 kilometres.

46 The term "guêtre" (spat) used by Baraga, presumably refers to a larger protective and decorative item, more in the style of an apron, leggings or gaiter, customarily giving added protection to the legs below the knee.

47 John G. Heckewelder (1743–1823). Born in England in 1754, he went to Bethlehem, Pennsylvania with his Moravian parents. After 1762, he became involved in the mission activity of the Moravians of Pennsylvania, associated with David Zeisberger. His work took him among several tribes, particularly the Muskingum and the Delawares. His studies on Algonkian (Lenape) language were significant, as was his *History*, published in 1819 for the American Philosophical Society, of which body he was a member. See his *History, Manners and Customs of the Indian Nations*; and see also Gray, *Wilderness Christians*.

48 On traditional tattooing among the Cree and other Algonkians, see Light, *Tattooing Practices of the Cree Indians*.

49 For a traditional analysis of personal totem symbols, see Warren, *History of the Ojibway People* (1885), chap. 2.

50 Baraga was probably correct in this observation. See Densmore, *Chippewa Customs*, 22f. Baraga employs the French *cabane* in his discussion. In his later dictionary he defines "wigiwâm" as "cabin" or "house."

51 As early as Fr. Paul Le Jeune's time in New France, there have been comments and policies favourable to a town planning separation of the converted from the traditionalists, with implications for social control. See Le Jeune, "Annual Relation of Events in New France, 1634," 145–53. See also Jaenen, *Friend and Foe*, chap. 5.

52 Densmore documented a number of variations of this dwelling type along with the seating and living arrangements. See Densmore, *Chippewa Customs*, 23f.

53   The concept of the "seasonal round" has become important in twentieth-century anthropology and archaeology of Amerindian cultures. While there has been lively debate over the concept of family hunting territories since Speck first raised the issue in 1915, there still remained room to incorporate varying degrees of fur trapping activity into a larger seasonal-round matrix. The fundamental economic opportunities open to a given group on a yearly basis naturally determined the features of the seasonal round. Alexander Henry the Elder gave a typical reference to the seasonal character of Native economy when he referred to the "gens de terre" moving inland from the north shores of Lakes Superior and Huron during the winter and spreading out in small family units in order to survive the winter. See Alexander Henry, *Travels and Adventures in the Indian Territories*, 6, 209.

54   Baraga underestimated the systematic nature and distribution of Native agriculture. Geographer Carl Sauer has described the "Maize-Beans-Squash Complex" in North America, embracing areas as far north as the St. Lawrence River and the Mandan country on the Missouri. These crops were planted in a "symbiotic relationship." See Sauer, *Seeds, Spades, Hearth and Herds*, 64f.

55   Densmore affirmed that "salt was unknown in the old days." Densmore, *Chippewa Customs*, 40.

56   See ibid., 128.

57   This is a clear reference to the great fishery at Sault Ste. Marie. See MacDonald, "The Ancient fishery at Sault Ste. Marie," and *Saulteur-Ojibwa Fishery at Sault Ste. Marie*.

58   See Densmore, *Chippewa Customs*, 123–24.

59   See ibid., 123, and relevant sections in Densmore, *Uses of Plants by the Chippewa Indians*, 275–397.

60   There is a considerable literature on this topic. F. G. Roe summarized many of the primary references in Appendix EE of *North American Buffalo*.

61   John Fullartine, at Albany Fort on Hudson Bay, reported the following about his local traders on Aug. 2, 1703: "... they eat me at least 16,000 fish besides peas, oatmeal and geese that I gave them every now and then. It was a very hard winter (for provision) all over the Country, for abundance of the poor Indians perished and were so hard put to it that whole families of them were killed eaten by one another." *Letters from Hudson Bay, 1702–1749*, 8–9. There is a notable account of this type recorded by Alexander Henry the Elder during an episode on the east shore of Lake Superior. Henry, *Travels and Adventures in the Indian Territories*, 198–200. Other accounts continue to show up in the record. See, for example, Baudry "Cannibalism in Early Days" regarding the country north of Lake Huron. Sault Ste. Marie (Ont.) Public Library. Local History Collections. History Binder No.2. Roe has summarized the literature in Roe, *North American Buffalo*, Appendix EE.

62   Clearly, the Windigo was in many instances a personification of starvation. See Henry, *Travels and Adventures in the Indian Territories*, 207–209. See also Teicher, *Windigo Psychosis*.

63   This account is drawn from Alexander Henry the Elder's experiences on the north shore of Lake Superior. See Henry, *Travels and Adventures in the Indian Territories*, 198–200.

64   One quintal = 100 kilograms = 112 pounds.

65   See Adney, *Bark Canoes and Skin Boats*, 220.

66   An extraordinary number of snowshoe types were in use among northern Native peoples. See Drummond, "The Canadian Snowshoe."

67   Since American introductions of reindeer into Alaska after 1892 and V. Stefansson's efforts to introduce caribou domestication into the Canadian arctic, much has been learned about the unique ecological circumstances of Lapp domestication practices

and the limitations of the idea in the North American context. See Canada, *Reindeer and Musk-Ox*. See also Ruong, *Lapps in Sweden*, chaps. 1–4.

68 See Heckewelder, *History, Manners and Customs of the Indian Nations*, 255–56.

69 Observations on bear ceremonialism have come down through first-hand accounts and anthropological field work. See Skinner, "Bear Customs of the Cree."

70 Baraga's contemporary, Canadian artist Paul Kane, executed a remarkable painting of a comparable situation in which Natives in the Pacific Northwest are fishing by torchlight.

71 There is a large literature on the caribou and its relationship with Native peoples. The range of the species used to lie much further to the south during the last glaciation. It gradually moved north and subdivided into the ranges of the standard subspecies recognized today. See Banfield, *Revision of the Reindeer and Caribou*.

72 For a review of traditional native garments and skins of choice, see Thompson, *Pride of the Indian Wardrobe*; and Densmore, *Chippewa Customs*, 30f.

73 Teit, writing in the first decade of the twentieth century, noted the parallel between this surround-mode of deer hunting and caribou hunting in the southern Selkirks and Monashee Mountains according to the practices of the Okanagan. Teit, *Coeur D'Alene, Flathead and Okanagan Indians*, 210; Roe has included a report on "Caribou" in his authoritative historical study of bison. Roe reviewed the notion of predictability of caribou migration based on the historical record. Appendix D in Roe, *North American Buffalo*.

74 See Peterson, *North American Moose*.

75 Much has been learned about the mechanics of bison jumps since Baraga's day. An important focal point for social and archaeological research has been the Head-Smashed-In Buffalo Jump site in southern Alberta. See Brink et al., *Final Report of the 1983 Season at Head-Smashed-In*; and Reeves, "Head-Smashed-In: 5500 Years of Bison Jumping in the Alberta Plains," 151–78.

76 Baraga's observation needs to be considered in light of the fairly recent acquisition of horses by northern plains Indians. The bison as the "staff of life" was much more effectively consumed and utilized over the long centuries when pounding and jumps were used as techniques by migratory peoples moving on foot and with the aid of dog travois. The literature is large and informative on this topic. For a review of the archaeological connection of bison with Native peoples over time, see Davis and Wilson, *Bison Procurement and Utilization*.

77 This is an unclear reference, as the term "wild bull" is not in use in the wildlife literature. Possibly this is a confused reference to "wild boar."

78 Densmore reported this as "Nettle-stalk fibre" *(Urticatru divaricatum)*. Densmore, *Chippewa Customs*, 153–54.

79 This is an elusive and perhaps garbled reference. Baraga has partially taken this passage from Adair, where there is described a method of taking catfish in the southwest (see Adair, *History of the American Indians* [1775], 432). Baraga is clearly speaking here, however, of a large ocean creature of the Pacific Northwest. It may be a reference to a practice of the Southern Nootkan tribe, the Makah, a proficient coastal fishing culture centred on the Olympic Peninsula of Washington State. They captured the Basking Shark *(Cetorhinus maximus)* for its oil value, in demand from the Europeans. But the method of capture would not be as related in this passage, for the Makah were experienced whalers, and the shark in question, while not carnivorous, was much too large to take in the way Baraga describes. See Suttles, "Environment," 25.

80 Baraga is probably describing the fishery at the Sault Ste. Marie rapids. See MacDonald, *Saulteur–Ojibwa Fishery at Sault Ste. Marie* and "The Ancient Fishery at Sault Ste. Marie."

81 This procedure is somewhat akin to the one described by Densmore, except that in her description, the mother (once again), plays a stronger role. See Densmore, *Chippewa Customs*, 72–73.

82 Variations on many of the observations given by Baraga may be found in Ruth Landes, *Ojibwa Woman*, part 2, "Marriage."

83 This observation accords with Densmore, *Chippewa Customs*, 73.

84 One "Wawanosh," possibly connected in some way to the figure described by Baraga, received the attention of Schoolcraft. In his "The Philosopher of Algoma" the letters of an "Indian Sachem" (apparently of Northern Algonkian stock) are recounted following his travels in the United States. See Schoolcraft, *Oneota*, 436–43; 461–66.

85 See Densmore, *Chippewa Customs*, 52–55; and Landes, *Ojibwa Religion and the Midéwiwin*, 227–28.

86 Among the Algonkians, and others, the actual significance and meaning of the term "Master of Life," or of a supreme being, has become more problematic since Baraga's time, when it was certainly widely accepted as an interpretation. See Cooper, *Northern Algonkian Supreme Being*; and Vecsey, *Traditional Ojibwa Religion*, 80–83.

87 Such was reported in Alexander Henry the Elder's account of his journey along the east coast of Lake Superior. Henry, *Travels and Adventures in the Indian Territories*, 198–200.

88 C. W. Penny left an account of a similar offering of tobacco undertaken by the Saulteur fisherman about to escort him through the rapids at Sault Ste. Marie. Penny, *North to Lake Superior*, 7–8.

89 Baraga's source may be George Catlin, active with his artwork on the plains and on the Lake Superior frontier in these years and allowed to paint the ceremony among the Mandans. Catlin had published some of his letters on this topic in the 1830s, in the popular press. See McCracken, *George Catlin and the Old Frontier*, 101–108; and Dippie, *Catlin and His Contemporaries*, 322–30.

90 This extended passage is clearly a description of the Sun (or Thirst) Dance, which was normally drawn out over several days and coincided with the spring revival of plant life. Ewers gave a description of the ceremonies among the Blackfoot. See Ewers, *Horse in Blackfoot Indian Culture*, 127–28. European observers tended to be preoccupied with those elements in which an individual underwent ordeals, as in the version rendered by Baraga. It was eventually prohibited by Government officials both in the U.S. and Canada. See Pettipas, *Severing the Ties that Bind*, 54–61; 107f.

91 References to ceremonial and ritualistic cannibalism are very rare in the literature. Jenness cites two instances only, one of a military nature among the Mohawks, and a ritualistic form of cannibalism among the Tsimshian and Kwakiutl. See Jenness, *Indians of Canada*, 305, 338.

92 This may be a reference to the Algonkian "White Dog" ceremony described by Norval Morrisseau and others, and for which the place name White Dog in northwestern Ontario may be a recollection. See Dewdney, *Sacred Scrolls of the Southern Ojibway*, 145–46; 157. Tooker has summarized the literature pertaining to a White Dog ceremony among the Iroquois; see Tooker, "The Iroquois White Dog Sacrifice in the Latter Part of the Eighteenth Century."

93 See Densmore, *Chippewa Customs*; for a discussion of the non-idolatrous nature of Native religion and outlook, see Hallowell, "The Ojibwa Self and Its Behavioural Environment," 172–82; and the results of the interviews undertaken in the early 1970s by Johnson concerning the significance of the "Manitokan" in Johnson, "Bits of Dough, Twigs of Fire."

94 As may be noticed in the discussion below, this reverence for the rattlesnake still did not prevent Indians from developing a good series of antidotes for snakebite. There are traditions of referring to other animals, particularly the bear, as "grandfather." See

Dewdney, "Ecological Notes on the Ojibwa Shaman-Artist," 17, and Skinner, "Bear Customs of the Cree." For a comprehensive bibliography on traditional Native medical practice, see Vogel, *American Indian Medicine*.

95 Vecsey suggests that the Ojibwa distinguished four types: common dreams, meaningful dreams, children's dreams and visions. The dreams were journeys of the free soul, while visions were visitations from manitous. Vecsey, *Traditional Ojibwa Religion*, 122–23. See also Radin, "Ojibwa and Ottawa Puberty Dreams."

96 See Densmore, *Chippewa Customs*, 78f.

97 Landes has left a thorough discussion of the vision quest among youth in her *Ojibwa Woman*, part 1. Dewdney has drawn attention to prospects for use of the so-called "Pukasaw Pits" on the northern Lake Superior shore as possible vision-quest sites. See Dewdney, "Insights on Vision Sites: A Matter of Relevance."

98 For a stimulating account of the importance of the dream in traditional Algonkian culture, see Brown and Brightman, *"Orders of the Dreamed"*.

99 This notion of the "imposter" or "charlatan" was widespread among nineteenth-century frontier clergymen. The term "juggler" was given currency in early commentary by Quebec writers such as Antoine Raudot in his *Memoir* of 1710. See Kinietz, *Indians of the Western Great Lakes*, Appendix, Letter 31 (1709). Hoffman noted the use of the term "sorcerer" as early as 1613 in the literature of French Canada. Hoffman, *The Midéwiwin*, 276–78. For a review of Amerindian medicine, see Vogel, *American Indian Medicine*, 13–27.

100 The reference is to the party of Michigan Territory Governor Lewis H. Cass and Thomas L. McKenney, federal negotiator of the Treaty of Fond du Lac. See McKenney, *Tour to the Lakes, 1826*. Of Quaker background, McKenney was an important figure in guiding much Indian affairs legislation between 1816 and 1830 and in the founding of American ethnology. See Viola, *Thomas L. McKenney*.

101 For a review of the variants of the so-called "Shaking-Tent" ceremony and the role of conjuring in Algonkian society, see Hallowell, *Role of Conjuring in Saulteaux Society* (1942). Publications of the Philadelphia Anthropological Society, vol. 2, 9f.

102 The reference is to the Quaker trader, John Anderson and the incident, about 1776, is adapted from Heckewelder, *History, Manners and Customs of the Indian Nations*, 241f.

103 A dramatic reconstruction of a shamanistic duel on the east shore of Lake Superior – "The Manitou of Wabasoons" – may be found in Read, *Four Way Lodge*, 33f. See also Landes, *Ojibwa Religion and the Midéwiwin*, 61–76.

104 Baraga is presumably referring to the Apostle Islands at La Pointe, where he composed his *History* in 1836–37.

105 The anecdote regarding "Old Scrany" appeared first in Adair's *History of the American Indians* and Long's *Voyages and Travels*. In his discussion of torture, Lafitau contended that "this heroism is real and the result of a great and noble courage" and that "the Indians … seem to prepare for this event from the tenderest age." Lafitau, *Customs of the American Indians*, vol. 2, 158. A common theme in the literature is pride in the ability to endure pain before one's enemies, thus avoiding a dishonourable death.

106 General Edward Braddock (1695–1755). The son of Major General Edward Braddock, he entered the British Army in 1710 as an ensign. In 1754 he was appointed Commander in Chief of the British forces in North America. During the campaign against Fort Duquesne in 1755, he was mortally wounded in the battle of the Monongahela. See Ian K. Steele, *Warpaths*, 188–89.

107 Concerning this battle, see Stanley M. Pargellis, "Braddock's Defeat"; the commentary in Eccles, *France in America*, 182–85; and Kopperman, *Braddock at the Monongahela*.

108 This is a reference to the "running of the gauntlet." See Driver, *Indians of North America*, 375.

109 See Heckewelder, *History, Manners and Customs of the Indian Nations*, 219.

110 Baraga is probably referring to Simon Kenton (1755–1836), who adopted the name Simon Butler in the aftermath of a manslaughter incident when he was sixteen. Baraga may have obtained his information from direct or indirect contact with John McDonald, who in 1838 published in Cincinnati his *Biographical Sketches … of Early Settlers in the Western Country*. See also Kenton, *Simon Kenton: His Life and Period, 1755–1836*, and Cochran, *Simon Kenton*.

111 Baraga's account is adapted from Carver, *Travels through the Interior Parts of North America*, 332f.

112 The observations on this point owe much to Carver, *Travels through the Interior Parts of North America*, 255–59.

113 In Quebec, there are early records of acknowledgement by the Indians of the force of European Law. In 1664, for example, following upon a council meeting with Quebec officials, Native leaders agreed to abide by the terms of the French Code with respect to murder and rape. See D. G. Smith, *Canadian Indians and the Law*, 27–28.

114 For this account, Baraga may have had access to McKenney, *Tour to the Lakes*.

115 Swanton noted that the technique was widespread among tribes of the Pacific Northwest and some of the southeast. The Salishan group which goes by the name today in western Montana, did not actually flatten the head according to early reports, although slaves "with deformed heads" taken from tribes further west, were noted among them, according to traders. See Swanton, "Flathead," in *Handbook of Indians of Canada*, 169.

116 Smallpox epidemics swept New England Native communities as early as 1634. See Vogel, *American Indian Medicine*, 40–41. Baraga's reference to the Cherokees comes from Adair's *History of the American Indians*, who attributed it initially to slave imports at Charleston in 1738. See Vogel, *American Indian Medicine*, 155. There is a considerable literature on the epidemic of 1781–82, with many primary-source references in the fur-trade literature. The general dynamics of disease effects in North American Native peoples' history have been given an important formulation in Dobyns, "Estimating American Aboriginal Populations," and his more recent, *Their Numbers Become Thinned*.

117 For summaries of traditional Native medical practices, see Vogel, *American Indian Medicine*; and Hutchens, *Indian Herbology of North America*.

118 See the comments of Boutwell in 1832: "The Journal and Letters of the Reverend William Thurston Boutwell," Appendix E of Mason, *Schoolcraft's Expedition*, 311–12.

119 See Hickerson, "The Feast of the Dead among the Seventeenth Century Algonkians of the Upper Great Lakes."

120 The "eyewitness" for this account was John Carver. See Pozar, "Frederick Baraga and his Book," 64.

Bibliography

ARCHIVE AND SPECIAL COLLECTIONS

BBC Bishop Baraga Collection. Marquette Michigan
BPL Bayliss Public Library. Sault Ste. Marie, Michigan
MHS Minnesota Historical Society
NA-OIA National Archives, Washington, Office of Indian Affairs
PFAP Propagation de la Foi, Paris
RCCA Roman Catholic Church Archives. Archdiocese of Detroit
SSMHS Sault Ste. Marie Historical Society (Ontario)
UNDA University of Notre Dame Archives, Notre Dame, Indiana: Bishop Baraga Papers
WHSA Wisconsin Historical Society: History Centre and Archives, Ashland, Wis.

BIBLIOGRAPHY

Abel, Annie E. "The History of Events Resulting in Indian Consolidation West of the Mississippi River." *Annual Report. American Historical Association, 1906*, vol. 1 (1908), 235–450.

Acosta, Fr. Joseph de. *The Natural and Moral History of the Indies* (1590). The Hakluyt Society. Reprinted from the English edition of 1604. New York: Burt Franklin, n.d.

Adair, James. *History of the American Indians* (1775). New York: Promontory Press, 1973.

Adney, Edwin Tappen. *The Bark Canoes and Skin Boats of North America*. Washington, DC: Smithsonian Institution, 1964.

Agassiz, Louis. *Lake Superior*. Boston: Gould, Kendall and Lincoln, 1850.

Allan, Robert S. *The British Indian Department and the Frontier in North America, 1755–1830*. Canadian Historic Sites. Occasional Papers in Archaeology and History, No. 14. Ottawa: Department of Indian and Northern Affairs, 1975.

Andrews, K. R. "Christopher Newport of Limehouse, Mariner." *William and Mary Quarterly* 3rd ser., 11 (1954): 28–41.

Andrews, K. R., N. P. Canny, and P.E.H. Hair, eds. *The Westward Enterprise: English Activities in Ireland, the Atlantic and America, 1480–1650*. Liverpool: University of Liverpool Press, 1978.

Armstrong, Benjamin G. "Reminiscences of Life among the Chippewa," *Wisconsin Magazine of History* 55 (Spring, Summer, 1972): 175–196, 287–309; 56 (Autumn, 1972; Winter, 1972–73): 37–58, 140–161. The above is an abridged verson of *Early Life among the Indians: Reminiscences of Life among the Chippewa*. Dictated to and written by Thos. P. Wentworth. Ashland: A. W. Bowron, 1892.

Arthur, Elizabeth. "Frémiot." *Dictionary of Canadian Biography*, vol. 8, 308–309. Toronto: University of Toronto Press, 1985.

———, ed. *Thunder Bay District: 1821–1892*. Toronto: Champlain Society, 1973.

Artz, Thomas. "St.Clement Hofbaur – a man of vision." *Baraga Bulletin* 52, no. 4 (1998): 12.

Attwater, Donald. *The Penguin Dictionary of Saints*. Harmondsworth: Penguin, 1982.

Axtell, James. *Beyond 1492: Encounters in Colonial North America*. New York: Oxford University Press, 1992.

Axtell, James, and Ronda, James P. *Indian Missions: A Critical Bibliography*. Newberry Library. Bloomington: Indiana University Press, 1978.

Banfield, A.W.F. *A Revision of the Reindeer and Caribou, Genus Rangifer*. National Museum of Canada. Bull. No. 177. Ottawa: Northern Affairs and National Resources, 1961.

Baraga, Frederic. *Abrégé de l'histoire des indiens de l'Amérique septentrionale*. Paris: Société des Bons Livres, E. J. Bailly, 1837.

———. *Chippewa Indians as recorded by Rev. Frederic Baraga in 1847*. New York: *Studia Slovenica*, 1976. (Digest of Report to H. R. Schoolcraft: Library of Congress, Washington.)

———. *The Diary of Bishop Frederic Baraga*, ed. Regis M. Walling, and N. Daniel Rupp; trans. Joseph Gregorich and Paul Prud'homme. Detroit: Wayne State University Press, 1990.

———. *A Dictionary of the Ojibway Language*. Introduction by John D. Nichols. Minneapolis: Minnesota Historical Society Press, 1992.

———. *A Dictionary of the Otchipwe Language, Explained in English*. Cincinnati: Jos. A. Hemann, 1853.

———. *A Dictionary of the Otchipwe Language, Explained in English*. Revised and enlarged by Fr. Albert Lacombe and Rev. G. Belcourt. Montreal: Beauchemin and Valois, 1878. (Reprint edition: Minneapolis: Ross and Haines, 1957.)

———. *Geschichte, Character, Sitten und Gebräuche der nord-amerikanischen Indier*. Laibach: J. Klemens 1837.

———. "A Lecture Delivered by Bishop Baraga" (1863). *Acta et Dicta* 5 (1917), 99–110. Trans. from the German by J. L. Zaplotnik. Originally published in *Wahrheitsfreund* 27 (1863).

———. *Theoretical and Practical Grammar of the Otchipewe Language*: Detroit: Jabez Fox, 1850.

Barbeau, Peter B. *Papers*. (BPL).

Bardon, John A. *Papers* (MHS).

Bardon, Thomas. *Papers*. (WHSA).

Baudry, Pierre. "Cannibalism in Early Days." Sault Ste. Marie (Ont.) Public Library. Local History Collections. History Binder No. 2.

Beales, Derek. "Christians and Philosophes: The Case of the Austrian Enlightenment," in *History, Society and the Churches: Essays in Honour of Owen Chadwick*, ed. Derek Beales and Geoffrey Best, 169–94. Cambridge: Cambridge University Press, 1985.

———. "The False Joseph II." *The Historical Journal* 18, no. 3 (1975): 467–95.

———. *Joseph II – In the Shadow of Maria Theresa: 1741–1780*. Cambridge: Cambridge University Press, 1987.

Berg, Carol J. "Agents of Cultural Change: The Benedictines of White Earth." *Minnesota History* 48 (Winter, 1982): 158–70.

Bibliography

Berkhofer, Robert F., Jr. *Salvation and the Savage: An Analysis of Protestant Missions and American Indian Responses, 1787–1862.* Lexington: University of Kentucky Press, 1965.

———. *The White Man's Indian: Images of the American Indian from Columbus to the Present.* New York: Alfred A. Knopf, 1978.

Bernard, Paul B. *Jesuits and Jacobins.* Urbana: University of Illinois Press, 1971.

———. *Joseph II.* New York: Twayne Publishers, 1968.

———. "The Origins of Josephism: Two Studies." *Colorado College Studies* VII (1964).

Biggar, H. P. *The Early Fur Trading Companies of New France.* Toronto: University of Toronto Library, 1901.

Bigglestone, William E. "Oberlin College and the Beginning of the Red Lake Mission." *Minnesota History* 45 (Spring, 1976): 21–31.

Biography of Major Irwin, The Fur Trade and Factory System at Green Bay, 1811–1821. Madison: Wisconsin Historical Society, 1908.

Blackbird, Andrew J. (Mack-A-De-Pe-Nessy). *Complete History of Ottawa and Chippewa Indians of Michigan.* Harbor Springs, MI: Babcock and Darling, 1897.

Blanning, T.C.W. *Joseph II.* London: Longman, 1994.

Blied, Benjamin J. *Austrian Aid to American Catholics: 1830–1860.* Milwaukee, 1944

———. "Leopoldine Stiftung (Leopoldine Society)." *New Catholic Encyclopedia*, vol. 8, 664. New York: McGraw-Hill, 1967.

Bokenkotter, Thomas. *A Concise History of the Catholic Church.* Revised and expanded edition. New York: Doubleday, 1990.

Bradford, William. *Of Plymouth Plantation: 1620–1647*, ed. Samuel E. Morison. New York: Modern Library, 1967.

Brink, Jack, Milt Wright, Bob Dawe, and Doug Glaum. *Final Report of the 1983 Season at Head-Smashed-In Buffalo Jump, Alberta.* Archaeological Survey of Alberta. Manuscript Series. No. 1. Edmonton: Alberta Culture, 1985.

Brown, Jennifer S. H. *Strangers in Blood: Fur Trade Company Families in Indian Country* Vancouver: University of British Columbia Press, 1980.

Brown, Jennifer S. H. and Brightman, Robert. *"The Orders of the Dreamed": George Nelson on Cree and Northern Ojibwa Religion and Myth, 1823.* Winnipeg: University of Manitoba Press, 1988.

Brown, Jennifer S. H., and Vibert, Elizabeth, eds. *Reading Beyond Words: Contexts for Native History.* Peterborough, ON: Broadview Press, 1996.

Brown, Ralph H. *Historical Geography of the United States.* New York: Harcourt, Brace, 1948.

Buley, R. C. *The Old Northwest: Pioneer Period, 1815–1840.* Bloomington: Indiana University Press, 1964.

Burke, Charles T. *Puritans at Bay: The War Against King Philip and the Squaw Sachems.* New York: Exposition Press, 1967.

"Cabinet of Curiosities." *Baraga Bulletin* 52, no. 3 (1998): 10–11.

Cadieux, Lorenzo. *Un Héros du Lac Superior: Frederic Baraga.* Documents Historique 27. Sudbury: La Société Historique du Nouvel-Ontario, 1954.

———, ed. *Lettres des Nouvelles Missions du Canada.* Sudbury: La Société historique du Nouvel-Ontario, 1973.

Caesar, Julius. *The Gallic War.* Trans. Carol Hammond. Oxford: Oxford University Press, 1996.

Canada. *Reindeer and Musk-Ox: Report of the Royal Commission upon the possibilities of the Reindeer and Musk-Ox Industries in the Arctic and Sub-Arctic Regions.* Ottawa: Department of the Interior, 1922.

Canada. Public Archives of Canada, *Report.* Ottawa: 1939.

Carver, Jonathan. *Travels through the Interior Parts of North America* (1778). Toronto: Coles, 1974.

Cass, Lewis. *Considerations on the Present State of the Indians and Their Removal to the West of the Mississippi*. Boston: Gray and Bowen, 1828.

———. "Indians of North America." *North American Review* 22 (Jan. 1826): 53–119.

Ceglar, Charles A., ed. *The Works of Bishop Frederic Baraga*. Baragiana Collection, vols. 1 and 2. Hamilton, ON: Baragiana Publishing, 1991.

Ceglar, Charles A., and France Baraga, eds. *Frederic Baraga: Letters and Documents (1797–1830)*. Baragiana Collection, vol. 3. Ljubljana: Druzina, 2001. (Original documents with English and Slovenian translations.)

Chadwick, Owen. *The Popes and European Revolution*. Oxford: The Clarendon Press, 1981.

Church, Thomas. *History of King Philip's War, 1675–76*. 2d ed. With notes and an appendix by S. G. Drake. Exeter: 1834.

———. *The History of the Great Indian War of 1675 and 1676, Commonly Called King Philip's War. Also the Old French and Indian Wars from 1689 to 1704*, ed. S. G. Drake. New York: Dayton, 1860.

Chute, Janet E. *The Legacy of Shingwaukonse: A Century of Native Leadership*. Toronto: University of Toronto Press, 1998.

Cochran, Samuel J. *Simon Kenton*. Strasbourg, VA: Shenandoah Publishing, 1932.

Colden, Cadwallader. *The History of the Five Nations of Canada* (1750). Toronto: Coles, 1971.

Collins, Aileen. "Chronicle of the Roussains and Mamainse," manuscript. (SSMHS).

Conkling, Robert. "Legitimacy and Conversion in Social Change: The Case of French Missionaries and the Northeastern Algonkian." *Ethnohistory* 21 (1974): 1–24.

Cooper, John M. *The Northern Algonkian Supreme Being*. Washington, DC: Catholic University of America, 1934.

———. *Notes on the Ethnology of the Otchipwe of Lake of the Woods and Rainy Lake*. Washington, DC: Catholic University of America, 1936.

Coues, Elliott, ed. *The Manuscript Journals of Alexander Henry and David Thompson, 1799–1814* (1897). Minneapolis: Ross and Haines, 1965. 2 vols.

Cronon, William. *Changes in the Land: Indians, Colonists and the Ecology of New England*. New York: Hill and Wang, 1983.

Cross, Whitney R. *The Burned-Over District: The Social and Intellectual History of Enthusiastical Religion in Western New York, 1800–1850*. Ithaca, 1950.

Cruikshank, E. A. "The 'Chesapeake Crisis' as It Affected Upper Canada." *Ontario Historical Society: Papers and Records* 24 (1927): 281–322.

Cujes, Rudolph, P. *Ninidjanissidog Saiagiinagog: Contributions of the Slovenes to the Socio-cultural Development of the Canadian Indians*. Publication No. 2. Research Centre for Slovenian Culture. Antigonish, NS: St. Francis Xavier University Press, 1968.

Danziger, Edmond J., Jr. *The Chippewas of Lake Superior*. Norman: University of Oklahoma Press, 1978.

———. "They Would Not Be Moved: The Chippewa Treaty of 1854." *Minnesota History* 43 (Spring, 1973): 175–85.

Davis, Leslie B., and Michael C. Wilson, eds. *Bison Procurement and Utilization: A Symposium*. Plains Anthropologist Memoir No. 14 (1978).

Densmore, Frances. *Chippewa Customs*. Bureau of American Ethnology, Bulletin No. 86. Washington, DC: Smithsonian Institution, 1929.

———. *Uses of Plants by the Chippewa Indians*, Bureau of American Ethnology, Forty-fourth Annual Report. Washington, DC: Smithsonian Institution, 1928.

Dewdney, Selwyn. "Ecological Notes on the Ojibwa Shaman-Artist." *Arts Canada* 27 (1970): 19–21.

Bibliography

———. "Insights on Vision Sites: A Matter of Relevance." *Archaeological Newsletter*, New Series, No. 69 Toronto: Royal Ontario Museum, 1971.

———. *The Sacred Scrolls of the Southern Ojibway*. Toronto: Glenbow Alberta Institute and University of Toronto Press, 1975.

Dickason, Olive Patricia. *The Myth of the Savage and the Beginnings of French Colonialism in the Americas*. Edmonton: University of Alberta Press, 1984.

Dippie, Brian, W. *Catlin and His Contemporaries: The Politics of Patronage*. Lincoln: University of Nebraska Press, 1990.

Dixon, E. James. *Quest for the Origins of the First Americans*. Albuquerque: University of New Mexico Press, 1993.

Dobyns, Henry F. "Estimating American Aboriginal Populations." *Current Anthropology* 7 (1966): 395–416.

———. *Their Number Become Thinned*. Knoxville: University of Tennessee Press, 1983.

Driver, Harold E. *Indians of North America*, 2d ed. Chicago: University of Chicago Press, 1969.

Drummond,Thomas. "The Canadian Snowshoe." *Transactions of the Royal Society of Canada*, series 3, sec. II, vol. 10 (1916): 305–26.

Dudley, Edward, and Maximillian E. Novak, eds. *The Wild Man Within: An Image in Western Thought from the Renaissance to Romanticism*. London: University of Pittsburgh Press, 1972.

Eaton, John. *Are the Indians Dying Out?: Preliminary Observations Relating to Indian Civilization and Education*. Washington: Department of the Interior, 1877.

Eccles, W. J. "The Role of the Church in New France," in his *Essays on New France*. Toronto: Oxford University Press, 1987.

———. *France in America*. Vancouver: Fitzhenry and Whiteside, 1972.

Edmunds, R. David. *The Potawatomis: Keepers of the Fire*. Norman: University of Oklahoma Press, 1978.

———. "Tecumseh's Native Allies: Warriors Who Fought for the Crown," in *War on the Great Lakes: Essays Commemorating the 175th Anniversary of the Battle of Lake Erie*, ed. W. J. Welsh and D. C. Skaggs, 56–67. Kent, OH: Kent State University Press, 1991.

Eid, Leroy V. "The Ojibwa-Iroquois War: The War the Five Nations Did Not Win." *Ethnohistory* 26 (1979): 295–324.

Eiseley, Loren. *Darwin's Century: Evolution and the Men Who Discovered It*. Garden City, NJ: Doubleday, 1961.

Elliott, J. H. *The Old World and the New: 1492–1650*. Cambridge: Cambridge University Press, 1992.

Elliott, Richard R. "The Apostolate of Father Baraga among the Chippewas and Whites of Lake Superior." *American Catholic Quarterly Review* 21 (July, 1896): 596–617.

———. "Father Baraga Among the Ottawas." *American Catholic Quarterly Review* 21 (July, 1896): 106–129.

Emerson, J. Norman. "The Mystery of the Pits." *Sylva* 14, no. 6 (1958): 15–19.

———. "The Puckasaw Pits and the Religious Alternative." *Ontario History* 52 (1960): 72–73.

Ewers, John C. *The Horse in Blackfoot Indian Culture*. Washington, DC: Smithsonian Institution Press, 1985.

Feest, Johanna E. and Christian A. Feest. "Ottawa," in *Handbook of the North American Indians*, vol. 15: *Northeast*, 772–86. Washington, DC: Smithsonian Institution, 1978.

Ferguson, Wallace K. *Europe in Transition*. Boston: Houghton Mifflin, 1962.

Field, Thomas W. *An Essay on Indian Bibliography* (1873). New Haven, CT: William Reese, 1991.

Forbis, Richard. "Flathead Apostasy: An Interpretation." *Montana Magazine of History* 1 (Oct. 1951): 35–40.

Foster, Frank Hugh. "The Oberlin Ojibway Mission." *Ohio Church History Society, Papers* 2 (1892): 1–25.

Freeman, John E., comp. *A Guide to Manuscripts Relating to the American Indian in the Library of the American Philosophical Society.* Philadelphia: American Philosophical Society, 1966.

Freeman, John F. "The Indian Convert: Theme and Variation." *Ethnohistory* 12 (1965): 113–27.

Frémiot, Fr. Nicholas. "Father Frémiot's Report to His Superior in New York, Fort William, Oct. 18, 1849," in *Thunder Bay District: 1821–1892*, ed. Elizabeth Arthur, 13–16. Toronto: Champlain Society, 1973.

Fullartine, John. "Letter One, Aug. 2, 1703," in *Letters from Hudson Bay, 1702–1749*, ed. K. G. Davies, 5–14. London: Hudson's Bay Company Record Society, 1965.

Furlan, William P. *In Charity Unfeigned: The Life of Father Francis Pierz.* St. Cloud, MN: 1952.

Getty Ian A. L., and Antoine S. Lussier, eds. *As Long as the Sun Shines and Water Flows: A Reader in Canadian Native Studies.* Vancouver: University of British Columbia Press, 1983.

Giraud, Marcel. *The Métis in the Canadian West.* Trans. George Woodcock. Edmonton: University of Alberta Press, 1986. 2 vols.

Gleach, Frank W. "Controlled Speculation: Interpreting the Saga of Pocahontas and Captain John Smith," in *Reading Beyond Words: Contexts for Native History*, ed. Jennifer S. H. Brown and Elizabeth Vibert, 21–42. Peterborough, ON: Broadview Press, 1996.

Goddard, Ives. "The Classification of the Native Languages of North America," in *Handbook of the North American Indians*, vol. 17: *Languages*, 290–323. Washington, DC: Smithsonian Institution, 1996.

———. "The Description of the Native Languages of North America before Boas," in *Handbook of the North American Indians*, vol. 17: *Languages*, 17–42. Washington, DC: Smithsonian Institution, 1996.

Golob, France. *Misijonarji Darovalci Indijanskih Predmetov.* Ljubljana: Zbirka Slovenskega etnografskega muzeja, 1997.

Grant, John Webster. *Moon of Wintertime: Missionaries and the Indians of Canada in Encounter Since 1534.* Toronto: University of Toronto Press, 1984.

Gray, Elma E. *Wilderness Christians: The Moravian Mission to the Delaware Indians.* Toronto: MacMillan, 1956.

Gray, Leslie R., ed. "From Bethlehem to Fairfield, 1789: Diary of the Brethren John Heckewelder and Benjamin Mortimer." *Ontario History* 46, nos. 1–2 (1954): 37–61; 107–132.

Gregorich, Joseph. *The Apostle of the Chippewas: The Life Story of the Most Rev. Frederick Baraga.* Lamont, IL: Bishop Baraga Association, 1932.

———. "Baraga," in *New Catholic Encyclopedia*, vol. 2, 84. New York: McGraw-Hill, 1967.

———. "Contributions of the Slovenes to the Chippewa and Ottawa Indian Missions." *Michigan History Magazine* 25 (1941): 168–87.

———. *Manuscript Biography* (1951). (BBC).

Haeger, John Dennis. *John Jacob Astor: Business and Finance in the Early Republic.* Detroit: Wayne State University Press, 1991.

Hallowell, A. Irving. "The Beginnings of Anthropology in America," in *Selected Papers from the American Anthropologist, 1888–1920*, ed. Frederica De Laguna. Evanston, IL: Row, Peterson and Co., 1960.

———. "The Ojibwa Self and its Behavioural Environment," in his *Culture and Experience*. Philadelphia: University of Pennsylvania Press, 1955.

———. *The Role of Conjuring in Saulteux Society*. Publications of the Philadelphia Anthropological Society (1942). New York: Octagon, 1971.

Harmon, G. D. *Sixty Years of Indian Affairs, Political, Economic and Diplomatic, 1789–1850*. Chapel Hill: University of North Carolina Press, 1941.

Heckewelder, John. *History, Manners and Customs of the Indian Nations Who Once Inhabited Pennsylvania and the Neighboring States* (1818). New and rev. Edited with an Introduction and Notes by W. C. Reichel. Philadelphia: Historical Society of Pennsylvania (1876). New York: Arno Press; New York Times facsimile reprint, 1971.

Henry, Alexander. *Travels and Adventures in the Indian Territories Between the Years 1760 and 1776*, ed. James Bain. Edmonton: Hurtig, 1971.

Hickerson, Harold. *The Chippewa and their Neighbours: A Study in Ethnohistory*. Rev. and expanded edition. Introduction by Jeniffer S. H. Brown and Laura Peers. Prospect Heights: Waveland Press, 1988.

———. "The Feast of the Dead among the Seventeenth Century Algonkians of the Upper Great Lakes." *American Anthropologist* 62 (1960): 81–107.

———. "The Genesis of a Trading Post Band: The Pembina Chippewa." *Ethnohistory* 3 (1956): 289–345.

———, ed. "Journal of Charles Jean Baptiste Chaboillez: 1797–1798." *Ethnohistory* 6 (1959): 265–316; 363–427.

———. *The Southwestern Chippewa: An Ethnological Study*. American Anthropological Association, Memoir 92. *American Anthropologist* 64 (1962).

———. "The Virginia Deer and Intertribal Buffer Zones in the Upper Mississippi Valley," in *Man, Culture and Animals*, ed. A. Leeds and A. P. Veyda, 43–65. Washington, DC: American Association for the Advancement of Science, 1965.

———. "William Boutwell of the American Board and the Pillager Chippewa: The History of a Failure." *Ethnohistory* 12 (1965): 1–29.

Higham, C. L. *Noble, Wretched and Redeemable: Protestant Missionaries to the Indians in Canada and the United States, 1820–1900*. Calgary: University of Calgary Press, 2000.

Hilger, M. Agnes, ed. "Letters and Documents of Bishop Baraga Extant in the Chippewa Country." *Records of the American Catholic Historical Society of Philadelphia* 47 (1936): 292–302.

Hodge, F. W. *Handbook of American Indians North of Mexico*. Washington, DC: U.S. Government Printing Office, 1907–1910.

Hoffman, W. J. *The Midéwiwin or "Grand Medicine Society" of the Ojibwa*. Bureau of American Ethnology, 7th Annual Report. Washington, DC: 1891.

Hollis, Christopher. *A History of the Jesuits*. London: Weidenfeld and Nicolson, 1968.

Hoover, Roy. "'To Stand Alone in the Wilderness': Edmund F. Ely, Missionary." *Minnesota History* 49 (Fall, 1985): 265–280.

Horan, James D. *The McKenney-Hall Portrait Gallery of American Indians*. New York: Crown, 1972.

Horr, David Agee, ed. *American Indian Ethnohistory: North Central and Northeastern Indians. Chippewa Indians*, vol. 5 New York: Garland, 1974.

Horsman, Reginald. "The British Indian Department and the Resistance to General Anthony Wayne, 1793–1795." *Mississippi Valley Historical Review* 44 (1962–63): 269–284.

Hubbard, William. *Narrative of Indian Wars.* Brattleboro, VT: 1814.

Huddleston, Lee E. *Origins of the American Indian: European Concepts, 1492–1729.* Austin: University of Texas, 1967.

Hutchens, Alma R. *Indian Herbology of North America.* 12th ed. Windsor, ON: Merco, 1986.

Jablonski, Nina G., ed. *The First Americans: The Pleistocene Colonization of the New World.* San Francisco: California Academy of Sciences, 2002.

Jackson, John C. *Children of the Fur Trade: Forgotten Metis of the Pacific Northwest.* Missoula, MT: Mountain Press, 1995.

Jacobs, Wilbur R. "Cadawallander Colden's Noble Iroquois Savages," in *The Colonial Legacy,* ed. Lawrence H. Leder, vols. 3–4, 34–58. New York: Harper and Row, 1973.

Jaenen, Cornelius. *Friend and Foe: Aspects of French–Amerindian Cultural Contact in the Sixteenth and Seventeenth Centuries.* New York: Columbia University Press, 1976.

Jaklic, Franc. *Irenej Frederik Baraga.* Celje: 1931.

Jamison, James K. *By Cross and Anchor: The Story of Frederic Baraga on Lake Superior.* Paterson, NJ: St. Anthony Guild Press, 1946.

Jenness, Diamond. *The Indians of Canada.* 5th ed. Ottawa: National Museum of Canada, 1960.

Johnson, Nick. "Bits of Dough, Twigs of Fire," in *Stones, Bones and Skin: Ritual and Shamanic Art.* Special issue of *Arts Canada* 30, nos. 5/6 (1973–74): 61–69.

Jones, Howard. *To the Webster-Ashburton Treaty: A Study in Anglo-American Relations, 1783–1843.* Chapel Hill: University of North Carolina Press, 1977.

Jones, William. *Ojibwa Texts,* ed. Trueman Michelson. *Publications of the American Ethnological Society,* vol. 7, parts 1 and 2 (1917). New York: AMS, 1974.

Kabinet Cudes? Baragova Zbirka Predmetov Iz Severne Amerike. Ljubljana: Slovenski Etnografski Muzej, 1997.

Kenton, Edna. *Simon Kenton: His Life and Period, 1755–1836.* Garden City, NJ: Doubleday, Doran and Co., 1930.

Kidd, Ian J. "Posidonius." *Oxford Classical Dictionary.* 3d ed. London: Oxford University Press, 1996, 1231–1233.

Kidder, Homer H. *Ojibwa Narratives of Charles and Charlotte Kawbawgam and Jacques LePique, 1893–1895,* ed. A. P. Bourgeois. Detroit: Wayne State University Press, 1994.

Kinietz, Vernon. *Chippewa Village: The Story of Katikitegon.* Bloomfield Hills, MI: Cranbrook Institute of Science, Bulletin No. 25, 1947.

———. *The Indians of the Western Great Lakes, 1615–1760.* Ann Arbor: University of Michigan Press, 1940.

Knopf, Richard C., ed. *Anthony Wayne: A Name in Arms: The Wayne–Knox–Pickering–McHenry Correspondence.* Pittsburgh: University of Pittsburgh Press, 1960.

Knott, Betty I. "Introduction" to Thomas à Kempis, *The Imitation of Christ,* 1–29. London: Collins, 1963.

Kohl, J. G. *Kitchi-Gami* (1860). Minneapolis: Ross and Haines, 1956.

Kopperman, Paul K. *Braddock at the Monongahela.* Pittsburgh: University of Pittsburgh Press, 1977.

Kotnik, Bertrand. "Bp. Baraga's Copy of Butler's Lives of the Saints." *Ava Maria Koledar* 61 (1974): 2–34.

Lafitau, Fr. Joesph Francois. *Customs of the American Indians Compared with the Customs of Primitive Times,* ed. and trans. William N. Fenton and Elizabeth Moore. Toronto: Champlain Society, 1974. 2 vols.

Lamb, W. Kaye, ed. *The Letters and Journals of Sir Alexander Mackenzie*. Cambridge: Cambridge University Press, 1970.

Lambert, Bernard J. *Shepherd of the Wilderness: A Biography of Bishop Frederic Baraga*. L'Anse, MI, 1967.

Landes, Ruth. *Ojibwa Religion and the Midéwiwin*. Madison: University of Wisconsin Press, 1968.

———. *The Ojibwa Woman*. New York: Columbia University Press, 1938.

LaRocque, Emma. "The Métis in English Canadian Literature." *Canadian Journal of Native Studies* 31, no. 1 (1983): 85–94.

Le Jeune, Paul. "Annual Relation of Events in New France, 1634." *The Jesuit Relations*, ed. R. G. Thwaites. New York: 1896–1901, vol. 6.

Leach, Douglas Edward. *Flintlock and Tomahawk: New England in King Philip's War*. New York: Norton, 1966.

Lefebvre, Georges. *Napoleon*. 5th ed. New York: Columbia University Press, 1969. 2 vols.

Leighton, Douglas. "Assiginack." *Dictionary of Canadian Biography*, vol. 9, 9–10. Toronto: University of Toronto Press, 1976.

Lemieux, Lucien. "Le Jeune." *Dictionary of Canadian Biography*, vol. 2, 453–58. Toronto: University of Toronto Press, 1969.

———. "Provencher." *Dictionary of Canadian Biography*, vol. 8, 718–23. Toronto: University of Toronto Press, 1985.

"Letters on the Fur Trade." *Michigan Pioneer and Historical Collections* 37 (1909–10): 132–41.

Light, Douglas W. *Tattooing Practices of the Cree Indians*, Glenbow Occasional Paper No. 6. Calgary: Glenbow-Alberta Institute, 1972.

Long, John. *Voyages and Travels of an Indian Interpreter and Trader*. London: 1791; Toronto: Coles [facsimile reprint], 1971.

Lowie, Robert, ed. *Essays in Anthropology Presented to A. L. Kroeber*. Berkeley: University of California Press, 1936.

Lyell, Charles. *The Antiquity of Man* (1863). Introduction by R. H. Rastall. London: J. M. Dent, 1914.

———. *Principles of Geology*. London: John Murray, 1830–33. 3 vols.

MacDonald, Graham A. "The Ancient Fishery at Sault Ste. Marie." *Canadian Geographical Journal* 94, no. 2 (1977): 54–58.

———. "Baraga: A Habsburg Prelate in the New World." *The Beaver: Exploring Canada's History* 74, no. 5 (1994): 4–11.

———. "The Sacred Shore." *Ontario Naturalist* 14, no. 4 (1974): 15–19.

———. *The Saulteur–Ojibwa Fishery at Sault Ste. Marie: 1640–1920* (M.A. thesis). Waterloo, Ontario: University of Waterloo, 1978.

Mackenzie, Sir Alexander. "A General History of the Fur Trade," in *The Letters and Journals of Sir Alexander Mackenzie*, ed. W. Kaye Lamb, 63–159. Cambridge: Cambridge University Press, 1970.

MacLeod, D. Peter. "The Anishinabeg Point of View: The History of the Great Lakes Region to 1800 in Nineteenth-Century Mississauga, Odawa and Ojibwa Historiography." *Canadian Historical Review* 73, no. 2 (1992): 194–210.

Mail, Patricia D., and David R. McDonald. "Native Americans and Alcohol: A Preliminary Annotated Bibliography." *Behaviour Science Research* 3 (1977): 169–81.

Mason, J. *A Brief History of the Pequot War*. Boston: 1736.

Mason, Philip P., ed. *Schoolcraft's Expedition to Lake Itasca*. East Lansing: Michigan State University Press, 1958.

McCracken, Harold. *George Catlin and the Old Frontier*. New York: Bonanza Books, 1959.

McGivern, J. S. "Baraga." *Dictionary of Canadian Biography*, vol. 9, 31–32. Toronto: University of Toronto Press, 1970.

McKenney, T. L. *A Tour to the Lakes, 1826*. Baltimore: 1827.

McNeill, W. H. *Plagues and Peoples*. Chicago: University of Chicago Press, 1976.

Michigan Superintendent of Indian Affairs, U.S. Department of the Interior. *Correspondence, 1825–1850*. (UNDA).

Mintz, Max M. *Seeds of Empire: The American Revolutionary Conquest of the Iroquois*. New York: New York University Press, 1999.

Mochon, Marion Johnson. "Stockbridge-Munsee Cultural Adaptations: 'Assimilated Indians'." *Proceedings of the American Philosophical Society* 112, no. 3 (1968): 182–219.

Morison, Samuel Eliot. *Admiral of the Ocean Sea: A Life of Christopher Columbus*. Boston: Little Brown, 1942.

———. *The Great Explorers: The European Discovery of America*. New York: Oxford University Press, 1978.

Morner, Magnus, ed. *The Expulsion of the Jesuits from Latin America*. New York: Alfred A. Knopf, 1965.

Morrison, Kenneth M. *The Embattled Northeast: The Elusive Ideal of Alliance in Abenaki-Euramerican Relations*. Berkeley: University of California Press, 1984.

Morse, Jedidiah. *Report to the Secretary of War on Indian Affairs*. Washington, DC: 1822.

Morton, R. L. *Colonial Virginia*. Chapel Hill: University of North Carolina Press, 1960.

Morton, W. L. "Bellecourt." *Dictionary of Canadian Biography*, vol. 10, 46–47. Toronto: University of Toronto Press, 1972.

Musulin, Stella. *Vienna in the Age of Metternich*. London: Faber and Faber, 1975.

Nichols, John D., ed. *Statement Made by the Indians: A Bilingual Petition of the Chippewas of Lake Superior, 1864*. London: Centre for Research and Teaching of Canadian Native Languages, 1988.

Norton, Sr. Mary Aquinas. *Catholic Missionary Activities in the Northwest, 1818–1864*. Washington, DC: Catholic University of America 1930.

Nute, Grace Lee, ed. *Documents Relating to Northwest Missions: 1815–1827*. St. Paul: Minnesota Historical Society, 1942.

———. "Father Scolla's Report on his Indian Missions," trans. Thomas J. Shanahan. *Acta et Dicta* 7, no. 2 (1936): 217–268.

———. *Lake Superior*. New York: Bobbs-Merrill, 1944.

O'Brien, Charles H. *Ideas of Religious Toleration at the Time of Joseph II. Transactions of the American Philosophical Society*. N.S. vol. 59, part 7, 1969. Philadelphia: American Philosophical Society, 1969.

O'Brien, F. A. "Father Frank Pierz." *Michigan Historical Collections* 39 (1915): 225–30.

———. "Lady Antoinette Von Hoeffern." *Michigan Historical Collections* 39 (1915): 221–24.

Oleson, Triggvi J. *Early Voyages and Northern Approaches*. 2d ed. Toronto: McClelland and Stewart, 1967.

Padover, Saul, K. *The Revolutionary Emperor: Joseph II of Austria*. 2d ed. London: Eyre and Spottiswoode, 1967.

Pagden, Anthony. *European Encounters with the New World*. New Haven, CT: Yale University Press, 1993.

———. *The Fall of Natural Man: The American Indian and the Origins of Comparative Ethnology*. Cambridge: Cambridge University Press, 1982.

———. "Foreword" to Carl Sauer, *The Early Spanish Main–*. Berkeley: University of California Press, 1992.

————, ed. *The Languages of Political Theory in Early-Modern Europe*. Cambridge: Cambridge University Press, 1986.

————. "The Savage Critic: Some European Images of the Primitive." *Yearbook of English Studies* 13 (1983): 32–45.

Pagès, George. *The Thirty Years War: 1618–1648*. New York: Harper and Row, 1971.

Pargellis, Stanley M. "Braddock's Defeat." *American Historical Review* 41 (1936): 253–69.

Parkman, Francis. *History of the Conspiracy of Pontiac*. London: Bentley, 1851. 2 vols.

Peers, Laura. *The Ojibwa of Western Canada: 1780 to 1870*. Winnipeg: University of Manitoba Press, 1994.

Penhallow, S. *Wars of New England*. Boston: 1726.

Penny, C. W. *North to Lake Superior: The Journal of Charles W. Penny, 1840*. Marquette, MI: John M. Longyear Research Library, 1970.

Peterson, R. L. *North American Moose*. Toronto: University of Toronto Press, 1955.

Pettipas, Katherine. *Severing the Ties that Bind: Government Repression of Indigenous Religious Ceremonies on the Prairies*. Winnipeg: University of Manitoba Press, 1994.

Pilling, J. C. *Bibliography of the Algonquian Languages*. Washington, DC: Smithsonian Institution, 1891.

Pitezel, John H. *Lights and Shades of Missionary Life*. Cincinnati: Western Book Concern, 1860.

Plut-Pregelj, Leopoldina, and Rogel, Carole. *Historical Dictionary of Slovenia*. European Historical Dictionaries No. 13. Lanham, MD: Scarecrow Press, 1996.

Pozar, Breda. "Frederick Baraga and his Book on the Manners of American Indians." *Acta Neophilologica* 6 (1973): 29–71.

"Procession Day at Goulais Bay." *Sault Daily Star* (Ont.), June 6, 1958.

Prucha, Francis Paul. *American Indian Policy in the Formative Years: The Indian Trade and Intercourse Acts, 1790–1934*. Lincoln: University of Nebraska Press, 1962.

————. *American Indian Treaties: The History of a Political Anomaly*. Berkeley: University of California Press, 1994.

————. "Army Sutlers and the American Fur Company." *Minnesota History* 40 (Spring, 1966): 22–31.

————, ed. *Documents on United States Indian Policy*. 2d ed. Lincoln: University of Nebraska Press, 1990.

Prud'homme, Paul. "Our Lady of Dolours," *Baraga Bulletin* 25 (Winter, 1972): 1–4.

Quaife, Milo M, ed. *The John Askin Papers*. Detroit: Detroit Public Library, 1928. 2 vols.

————. *The Kingdom of St. James*. New Haven, CT: Yale University Press, 1930.

Quinn, David B. *North America from Earliest Discovery to First Settlements*. New York: Harper and Row, 1977.

Quinn, David B. *The Roanoke Voyages, 1584–1590*. Cambridge: Hakluyt Society, 1955. 2 vols.

Radin, Paul. "Ojibwa and Ottawa Puberty Dreams," in *Essays in Anthropology Presented to A. L. Kroeber*, ed. Robert Lowie, 233–64. Berkeley: University of California Press, 1936.

Ray, Arthur J. *The Indians and the Fur Trade*. Toronto: University of Toronto Press, 1974.

Read, C. B. *Four Way Lodge*. Chicago: Pascal Covici, 1924.

Reardon, James M. *George Anthony Belcourt: Pioneer Catholic Missionary of the Northwest, 1803–1874*. St. Paul, MN: North Central Publishing, 1955.

Reeves, B.O.K. "Head-Smashed-In: 5500 Years of Bison Jumping in the Alberta Plains," in *Bison Procurement and Utilization: A Symposium*, ed. Leslie B. Davis and Michael C. Wilson, 151–78. Plains Anthropologist Memoir No. 14, 1978.

Reinerman, Alan J. *Austria and the Papacy in the Age of Metternich*, Vol. 1. *Between Conflict and Cooperation, 1809–1830.* Washington, DC: Catholic University of America Press, 1979.

Résé, Bishop Frederic. *Correspondence.* (RCCA).

Rezek, Antoine Ivan. *History of the Diocese of Sault Ste. Marie and Marquette.* Chicago: 1906. 2 vols.

Rickett, Richard. *A Brief Survey of Austrian History.* Vienna: George Prachner, 1966.

Roe, F. G. *The North American Buffalo.* 2d ed. Toronto: University of Toronto Press, 1970.

Ronda, James P. *Astoria and Empire.* Lincoln: University of Nebraska Press, 1990.

Roufs, Timothy G. *The Anishinabe of the Minnesota Chippewa Tribe.* Phoenix: Indian Tribal Series. Minnesota Chippewa Tribe, 1975.

Rountree, Helen C. *Pocahontas's People: The Powhatan Indians of Virginia through Four Centuries.* Norman: University of Oklahoma Press, 1990.

———. *The Powhatan Indians of Virginia: Their Traditional Culture.* Norman: University of Oklahoma Press, 1989.

Ruong, Israel. *The Lapps in Sweden*, trans. Alan Blair. Stockholm: Swedish Institute, 1967.

Ryan, Michael T. "Assimilating New Worlds in the Sixteenth and Seventeenth Centuries." *Comparative Studies in Society and History* 23 (1981): 519–38.

Sapir, Edward. *Culture, Language and Personality: Selected Essays.* Edited by David G. Mendelbaum. Berkeley: University of California Press, 1970.

Sauer, Carl Ortwin. *The Early Spanish Main.* With a new foreword by Anthony Pagden. Berkeley: University of California Press, 1991.

Sauer, Carl. *Seeds, Spades, Hearth and Herds: The Domestication of Animals and Foodstuffs.* 2d ed. Cambridge, MA: MIT Press, 1969.

Saunders, R. M. "The Emergence of the Coureur de bois as a Social Type." *Canadian Historical Association Reports* (1939): 22–33.

Schoolcraft, Henry R. *History, Conditions and Prospects of the Indian Tribes of the United States.* Washington, DC: Library of Congress, 1847–1853. 6 vols.

———. *Oneota.* New York: Burgess, Stringer and Co., 1845.

Schultz, George A. *An Indian Canaan: Isaac McCoy and the Vision of an Indian State.* Norman: University of Oklahoma Press, 1972.

Sharrock, D.J. "Hofbauer," in *New Catholic Encyclopedia*, vol. 7, 45 and vol. 12, 161–62. New York: McGraw-Hill, 1967.

Shea, John G. *Catholic Missions Among the Indian Tribes of the United States.* New York: Edward Dunigan, 1855 (reprint ed., New York Times: Arno Press, 1969).

———. *A History of the Catholic Church with the Limits of the United States.* New York: J. G. Shea, 1892.

Skinner, Alanson. "Bear Customs of the Cree and Other Algonkian Indians of Northern Ontario." *Ontario Historical Society: Papers and Records* 12 (1914): 203–209.

Smitek, Zmago. "Baraga, Schoolcraft and the Beginnings of American Ethnology." *European Review of Native American Studies* 7, no. 2 (1993): 39–41.

Smith, Derek G., ed. *Canadian Indians and the Law: Selected Documents, 1663–1972.* Toronto: McClelland and Stewart, 1975.

Smith, Donald B. *Sacred Feathers: The Reverend Peter Jones (Kahkewaquonaby) and the Mississauga Indians.* Toronto: University of Toronto Press, 1987.

———. *Le Sauvage: The Native People in QuebecHistorical Writing on the Heroic Period (1534–1663) of New France.* National Museum of Man, Mercury Series. History Division Paper, No. 6. Ottawa: National Museums of Canada, 1974.

Bibliography

Speck, Frank G. "The Family Hunting Band as the Basis of Algonkian Social Organization." *American Anthropologist* 17 (1915): 289–305.

———. *Territorial Subdivisions and Boundaries of the Wampanoag, Massachusett, and Nauset Indians.* Indian Notes and Monographs, No. 44. New York: Heye Foundation, 1928.

Steele, Ian K. *Warpaths: Invasions of North America.* New York: Oxford University Press, 1994.

Stevens, Michael E. "Catholic and Protestant Missionaries Among Wisconsin Indians: The Territorial Period." *Wisconsin Magazine of History* 58, no. 2 (1974–75): 140–48.

Sugden, John. "Early Pan-Indianism: Tecumseh's Tour of the Indian Country, 1811–1812." *American Indian Quarterly* 10 (Fall, 1986): 273–304.

———. *Tecumseh: A Life.* New York: Henry Holt, 1997.

Suttles, Wayne. "Environment," in *Handbook of the North American Indians,* vol. 7, *Northwest Coast–.* Washington, DC: Smithsonian Institution, 1990.

Swanton, J. R. "Flathead," in *Handbook of Indians of Canada,* ed. J. R. Swanton. Ottawa: Geographic Board of Canada, 1913.

Talman, James J., ed. *Loyalist Narratives from Upper Canada.* Toronto: Champlain Society, 1946.

Tanner, John. *A Narrative of the Captivity and Adventures of John Tanner During Thirty Years Residence Among the Indians,* ed. Edwin James (1830). Minneapolis: Ross and Haines, 1956.

Teicher, Morton I. *The Windigo Psychosis: A Study of a Relationship between Belief and Behaviour among the Indians of Northeastern Canada.* Seattle: American Ethnological Society, 1960.

Teit, James. *Coeur D'Alene, Flathead and Okanagan Indians.* Bureau of American Ethnology. Forty-Fifth Annual Report. Washington, DC: Smithsonian Institution, 1930. Fairfield, WA: Ye Galleon Press, n.d.

Thatcher, B. B. *Indian Biography.* New York: J. and J. Harper, 1832. 2 vols.

Thomas, N. Gordon. *The Millennial Impulse in Michigan, 1830–1860: The Second Coming in the Third New England.* Studies in American Religion, No. 44. Lewiston, NY: Edwin Mellon Press, 1989.

Thompson, Judy. *Pride of the Indian Wardrobe.* Toronto: Bata Shoe Museum and University of Toronto Press, 1990.

Treuer, Anton, ed. *Living Our Language: Ojibwe Tales and Oral Histories.* St. Paul: Minnesota Historical Society Press, 1998.

Tobias, John L. "Protection, Civilization, Assimilation: An Outline of Canada's Indian Policy," in Getty Ian A. L., and Antoine S. Lussier, eds. *As Long as the Sun Shines and Water Flows: A Reader in Canadian Native Studies.* Vancouver: University of British Columbia Press, 1983.

Tooker, Elizabeth. "The Iroquois White Dog Sacrifice in the Latter Part of the Eighteenth Century." *Ethnohistory* 12 (1965): 129–140.

Underhill, John. *News from America.* London: 1638.

Van Kirk, Sylvia. *Many Tender Ties: Women in Fur-Trade Society, 1670–1870.* Winnipeg: Watson and Dwyer, 1980.

Vecsey, Christopher. *Traditional Ojibwa Religion and its Historical Changes.* Philadelphia: American Philosophical Society, 1983.

Verwyst, P. Chrysostomus. *Life and Labours of Rt. Rev. Frederic Baraga.* Milwaukee: M. H. Wiltzius, 1900.

———. *Missionary Labours: Fathers Marquette, Menard and Allouez in the Lake Superior Region.* Milwaukee: Hoffmann Brothers, 1886.

Viola, Herman J. *Thomas L. McKenney: Architect of America's Early Indian Policy, 1816–1830*. Chicago: Swallow Press, 1974.

Viola, Herman J., and Caroline Margolis, eds. *Seeds of Change: Five Hundred Years Since Columbus*. Washington, DC: Smithsonian Institution, 1991.

Vizenor, Gerald. *The People Named the Chippewa: Narrative Histories*. Minneapolis: University of Minnesota Press, 1984.

Vogel, Virgil J. *American Indian Medicine*. Norman: University of Oklahoma Press, 1970.

Voncina, L. *Baraga*. Celovec: n.p., 1869.

Wallace, W. S., ed. *Documents Relating to the North West Company*. Toronto: Champlain Society, 1934.

Warren, William W. *History of the Ojibway People* (1885). Introduction by W. Roger Buffalohead. St. Paul: Minneapolis Historical Society, 1984.

Washburn, Wilcomb E. "James Adair's 'Noble Savages,'" in *The Colonial Legacy*, ed. Lawrence H. Leder, vols. 3–4, 91–120. New York: Harper and Row, 1973

————, ed. *The American Indian and the United States: A Documentary History*. New York: Random House, 1973. 4 vols.

Weeks, Robert P. "A Utopian Kingdom in the American Grain." *Wisconsin Magazine of History* 61 (Autumn 1977): 3–30.

Welsh, W. J. and D. C. Skaggs, eds. *War on the Great Lakes: Essays Commemorating the 175th Anniversary of the Battle of Lake Erie*. Kent, OH: Kent State University Press, 1991.

Wheeler-Voegelin, Erminie, ed. "John Heckewelder to Peter S. DuPonceau, Bethlehem, 12th Aug. 1818." *Ethnohistory* 6 (1959): 70–81.

Williams, Roger. *A Key into the Language of America, or An Help to the Languages of the Natives in that Part of America called New England*. London: Gregory Dexter, 1643. Bedford: Applewood Books, 1997.

Williams, Steven. *Fantastic Archaeology: The Wild Side of North American Prehistory*. Philadelphia: University of Pennsylvania Press, 1991.

Winthrop, John. *John Winthrop's Journal, 'History of New England,'* ed. James K. Hosmer. New York: C. Scribner, 1908. 2 vols.

Wissler, Clark. "The American Indian and the American Philosophical Society." *Proceedings of the American Philosophical Society*, 86, no. 1 (1942): 189–204.

Wood, William, ed. *Select British Documents of the Canadian War of 1812*. Toronto: Champlain Society, 1926. 3 vols.

Woodhead, Henry, ed. *Algonquians of the East Coast*. Alexandria: Time-Life, 1995.

Woodward, Grace Steel. *Pocahontas*. Norman: University of Oklahoma Press, 1969.

Wroth, Lawrence C. *The Voyages of Giovanni da Verrazzano, 1524–1528*. New Haven, CT: Yale University Press, 1970.

Index

Acosta, Joseph, 39–40, 175
Adair, John, 32, 40
Adams, John Quincy, 174
Agriculture, 35, 50, 67, 88–90, 127, 147
Alcohol, 5–6, 30, 36, 68
American Board of Commissioners
    (Protestant), 6
American Philosophical Society, 40
Anderson, 151–52
Andowish, 22
Arbre Croche, (Crooked Tree; Harbor
    Springs; Little Traverse), 6, 18–19,
    20–21, 69, 91
Architecture. 87–88
Armstrong, Benjamin, 38
Assiginack, Jean-Baptiste, 19, 21–22
Astor, John J., 4–5
Ayer, Frederick, 29
Axtell, James, xi

Baptist Board of Missions, 6
Baraga, Ignatius, 8
Baraga, John Nepomucene, 8
Baraga, Katherine (Jencic), 8
Beaver Island, 20
Belcourt, (Bellcourt) George, 27–28
Bering Strait, 50
Bison. See Wildlife: buffalo
boats/canoes, 100–101
Braddock, General Edward, 161
Brethren of the Common Life, 10
Bruce Mines, 18
Butler, Simon, 163

Cabot, John, 50
Caesar, Julius, x, 43

Calumets (pipes), 170
Campeau, Louis, 18
Campeau, Sophie de Marsac, 18
Cannibalism, 67, 93–95
Carniola (Slovenia), 8, 13, 35
Carver, John, 32
Cass, Lewis, 19–21, 42
Ceremonies, 64, 141–43, 148–50, 156, 170
Charleston (S.C.), 179
Chateaubriand, 43
Chesapeake Crisis, 4
Childrearing, 132
Choné, 24
Cincinnati, 5, 17–18, 21, 30–32
Clautier, Benjamin, 19
Columbus, Barthélemy, 48
Columbus, Christopher, xi, 47–50
Connecticut, 57, 59, 62
Cotté, Pierre, 19
Cottreville (Marine City), 22
Crebassa, Pierre, 19, 22, 24
Crime, 172–73
Crooked Tree. See Arbre Croche.
Crooks, Ramsay, 5, 32–33

Detroit, 16, 171
Diplomacy, 174–75
Disease, 68–69, 179–84
Dobrnic (Slovenia) 43
Dogs, 57, 90, 102, 106–7, 112, 137, 142, 175,
    189
Dogsleds, 102
Dolinar, Anna, 10
Dolinar, George, 8, 10
Douglas, Fifth Earl (Lord Selkirk), 19
Dreams, 143–44
Dushna Pasha (Souls Pasture), 15, 17

Dvorák, Jan. *See* Hofbauer, Clement.

Edict of Toleration, 1781 (Habsburg), 11
Education, 132
England, 48
Everts, Jeremiah, 6

Fallen Timbers (Battle of), 3–4
Famine/hunger, 67, 90, 93–95
Fasting, 144
Feast of the Dead, 38
Fenwick, (Bp.) Edward, 17, 21, 32
Ferdinand V (Spain), 48
Fisheries, 90–91, 95, 121–23
Fond du Lac, 19, 144, 150, 173
Fort William, 19, 24
Francis I (Franz) (Habsburg Emperor), 17
Francis I (France), 50
Frederic II (Prussia), 11
Frémiot, (Fr) Nicholas, 24
Fur/Fur trade. 4–6, 52, 65, 68, 88, 101–2,
    151

Gauls, x
Georgia Compact, 5
Gifts, 128
Glassakos, Chief, 57
Goulais Bay (Ont.) (Baie de Goulée), 24–25,
    30
Government, 169–75
Grand Medicine Society. *See* Midéwiwin.
Grand River (Mich.), 5–6, 18, 22

Hamlin, Augustus, 21
Hanipaux, M.S.V., 24
Harbor Springs. *See* Arbre Croche
Heckewelder, John, 34, 42, 82, 108, 162
Henry VIII (England), 48
Hofbauer, (St.) Clement, 9–10, 14–15, 31
Horses, 115–17
Hunting, 90–91, 105–17, 181
Hutchinson, Captain Edward, 59

Indians (Tribes)
    Algonkians, 7, 32, 75
    By census groupings: (c. 1826), 66
    Cherokee, 5, 179–80
    Chippewa (Pillager), 7. *See also* Ojibwa.
    Choctaw, 28

Creek, 28
Delaware, 135
Hurons, 38
Illinois, 159–60
Iowa, 28
Mennomini, 75
Ojibwa, 7, 9, 18, 22, 26, 28, 33, 38, 65,
    91, 144, 171–74, 188, 190
Osage, 75,
Oto, 28
Ottawas, 67, 91, 75, 108
Potawatomi, 28
Shawnees, 28
Sioux, 7, 65, 75, 101, 173, 188, 191
South American, 50
Virginia, 50–52, 55–56
Wea, 28
Indians, origins of, 32, 38–41, 49–50
Isabella (Queen of Spain), 48–49

Jackson, Andrew, 5, 39
James I (England), 51
James River (Va.) 51
Jamestown (Va.) 51, 53, 55–56, 65
Jansenism (Jansenists), 14, 17
Jefferson, Thomas, 5,
Jencic, Barnard, 8
Jesuits, xii, 6, 9, 11, 19, 24, 31, 39
Johnson, General, 148
Johnson, John (fur trader), 6
Joseph II (Hapsburg Emperor), 9, 11–13, 17
Josephism, 14, 17

Kalan, George, 15
Kaunitz, Wenzel Anton (Prince) 11, 13
Kawbawgam, Charles, 38
Keewenaw Reserve, 23
King Philip (Indian chief), 34, 59, 61,
    63–64
Kingsborough, Viscount, 40
Knox, Henry, 3
Kohler, August, 24

Laibach (Ljubljana), 30–31
Lafitau, Joseph, 40, 42
Lahontan, Baron; (Louis-Armand Le
    Fascheaux de Couttes), 43
L'Anse, 18–19, 21–22,
La Pointe, 18, 21–24, 38

Lapplanders, 102, 114
Lathrop, Captain Thomas, 60
Leech Lake (Minnesota), 7
Leopoldine Society (Leopoldine Stiftung), 1, 17, 30
Liguori (St.) Alphonsus, 9
Little Traverse. *See* Arbre Croche.
Long, John, 32
Lost Tribes of Israel, 39
Ludwig Mission Central of Bavaria, 1, 17
Lyell, Charles, 39

McCoy, Isaac, 6, 28
Mackenzie (Sir) Alexander, 44
McKenney, Thomas L., 5
Maine, 183
Makatebinessi, William, 21
Mamainse, 24
Maple sugar. *See* Sugar, wild.
Marine City. *See* Cottreville.
Marquette (Michigan), 30, 38–39,
Marriage, 127–31
Mason, Captain, 57
Massachusetts, 53, 60
Massasoit, Chief, 54–55, 59
Medicine, 179–84
Meeker, Jotham, 28
Metlika (Slovenia), 15
Metternich, Count, 14
Mexico, 55
Michigan, Lake, 21, 101
Michigan Territory, 2, 4–6, 18–20, 23–24, 26, 30, 143
Michilimackinac, 20–21
Midéwiwin (Rites), 37–38
Mississippi River, 6
Montreal, 4, 19, 22, 149
Moraviantown (Ont.), 4
Mormons, 20
Morse, Jedidiah, 6
Mortuary customs, 187–91
Mosely, Captain, 60

Napoleon, 4, 8–9, 11, 13
Nelson, George, 38
Newfoundland, 50
Newport, Christopher, 51
Niagara Falls, 149
Northwest Ordinance, 2

Oberlin Mission, 28
Ontonagon, 30
Opechanacouw, Chief, 55, 169
Oral tradition, 172

Pagden, Anthony, xi
Payrère, Isaac, de la, 40
Piercy, Captain, 63
Pierz, (Fr.) Francis, 24
Pitizel, (Rev.) John, 23
Plant use, 67, 88, 93, 181
Plymouth, Mass. 54, 59, 61, 65
Pocahontas, 52–53
Pokasset Forest, 59
Population, 58, 65–69
Posidonius, x
Powhatan, Chief, 51–53, 55, 169
Prairie du Chien (Wisconsin), 4

Raleigh, Walter, 50
Rautenstrauch, Franz Stephen, 12–13
Redemptorists, 9
Reindeer. *See* Wildlife: Caribou.
Religion, 135–52
Removal (Indian), 4–7, 20–23
Résé, (Fr.) Frederic, 17
Rice, wild, 90–91
Richard, Gabriel, 19
Rolfe, John, 53
Roman Empire, x
Rousseau, Jean Jacques, xii, 43

Salt, 90, 152
Samoset, 54
Sassacus, Chief. *See* Gassakos.
Sasussosoit, Chief. *See* Massisoit.
Sault Ste. Marie, 6, 16, 18, 24, 38, 182,
Scalping, 157–58
Schoolcraft, Henry Rowe, 20–21, 29, 41–42
Shamanism, 147–52, 181
Shawanibinessi, Chief, 23
Slovenia, 5, 8, 13,15, 24, 30, 43
Smartno (Slovenia), 15
Smith, Captain John, 51–2
Snowshoes, 101–2
Society for the Propagation of the Faith (Societé pour la propagation de la foi), 17

South Carolina, 179
Strang, James J., 20
Sugar, wild, 91–93
Sugar Island, 23
Suicide, 180
Sun Dance (Thirst Dance), 37, 139–41
Superior, Lake, 91, 94–95, 101, 105, 114, 138, 182, 187

tattooing, 36, 82–83
technology, 88–89, 99–102, 105–7, 121–23, 155
Tecumseh, 4
Thatcher, B.B., 32
Theresa, Empress Maria, 11–12
Thomas à Kempis, 10, 15, 17
Torture, 159–64
Totems, 83
Tracking, 74, 106–7
Treaties
    Colonial (1621), 54
    Colonial (1643), 58
    Detroit (1807), 4
    Ghent (1814), 4
    Greenville (1795), 3–4
    La Pointe (1842), 194n19
    Paris (1783), 2
    Robinson-Superior (1850), 24

Ussher, Bishop, 39

Verrazzano, 50
Vienna, 1, 8–9, 11–14, 17, 30, 40
Vienna, Congress of, 11
Virginia, 51, 53, 55–56, 62

Wadsworth, Captain, 63
Walking (Indian), 73–74
Warfare (Indian), 64–65, 155–65
Wars
    1812, 4, 20
    American Revolutionary, 3–4, 64
    Austrian Succession, 11
    King Philip's, 34
    Napoleonic, 4, 14
Wawanosh, 130–32
Wayne, Anthony (General), 3–4
Weapons, 89, 155
Weintridt, Vincint, 9

Whales, 122
Wild rice. See Rice, wild.
Wildlife
    bears, 107–8
    beaver, 111
    buffalo, 87, 115–17
    caribou, 102, 111, 114
    deer, 7, 79, 111–13
    elk, 111–13
    moose, 115
    otter, 111–12
    porcupine, 111–12
    snakes, 143, 182
    wild bull, 117
    wildcat, 112
    wolves, 90, 94, 112, 189
Williams, Roger, 42
Winslow, Governor, 61
Wolfart, H.C., xx